Visions of Whiteness in
Selected Works of Asian
American Literature

ALSO BY KLARA SZMAŃKO

*Invisibility in African American
and Asian American Literature:
A Comparative Study* (McFarland, 2008)

Visions of Whiteness in Selected Works of Asian American Literature

KLARA SZMAŃKO

McFarland & Company, Inc., Publishers
Jefferson, North Carolina

Excerpt(s) from *The Woman Warrior: Memoirs of a Girlhood Among Ghosts* by Maxine Hong Kingston, copyright © 1975, 1976 by Maxine Hong Kingston. Used by permission of Alfred A. Knopf, an imprint of the Knopf Doubleday Publishing Group, a division of Random House LLC. All rights reserved. Excerpt(s) from *China Men* by Maxine Hong Kingston, copyright © 1977, 1978, 1979, 1980 by Maxine Hong Kingston. Used by permission of Alfred A. Knopf, an imprint of the Knopf Doubleday Publishing Group, a division of Random House LLC. All rights reserved. Excerpt(s) from *The Fifth Book of Peace* by Maxine Hong Kingston, copyright © 2003 by Maxine Hong Kingston. Used by permission of Alfred A. Knopf, an imprint of the Knopf Doubleday Publishing Group, a division of Random House LLC. All rights reserved.

LIBRARY OF CONGRESS CATALOGUING-IN-PUBLICATION DATA

Szmańko, Klara.
    Visions of whiteness in selected works of Asian American literature / Klara Szmańko.
        p.   cm.
    Includes bibliographical references and index.

    ISBN 978-0-7864-9701-0 (softcover : acid free paper) ∞
    ISBN 978-1-4766-2043-5 (ebook)

    1. American literature—Asian American authors—History and criticism.   2. Whites in literature.   I. Title.

PS153.A84S96 2015
810.9′895—dc23   2015002133

BRITISH LIBRARY CATALOGUING DATA ARE AVAILABLE

© 2015 Klara Szmańko. All rights reserved

No part of this book may be reproduced or transmitted in any form or by any means, electronic or mechanical, including photocopying or recording, or by any information storage and retrieval system, without permission in writing from the publisher.

Cover image © iStock/Thinkstock

Printed in the United States of America

McFarland & Company, Inc., Publishers
  Box 611, Jefferson, North Carolina 28640
    www.mcfarlandpub.com

To my parents, Bożena Szmańko, Tadeusz Szmańko,
and my grandmother, Helena Golec

Contents

Acknowledgments	ix
Introduction	1
1. Drawing in the White: Defamiliarizing Whiteness in Maxine Hong Kingston's *The Woman Warrior*	13
2. Demonic and Oxymoronic Whiteness in Maxine Hong Kingston's *China Men*	67
3. Dreaming and Living White Terror in Leonard Chang's *The Fruit 'N Food*	122
4. Representation of Whiteness in Joy Kogawa's *Obasan*	137
5. Towards Transformation of Whiteness in Maxine Hong Kingston's *The Fifth Book of Peace*	149
Conclusion	166
Chapter Notes	171
Bibliography	187
Index	197

Acknowledgments

I am grateful to John F. Kennedy Institute in Berlin and Deutscher Akademischer Austausch Dienst for scholarships which enabled me to compile most of the literature essential for this study.

I would like to express my gratitude to the reviewers of the book, Professor Dominika Ferens and Professor Sebnem Toplu, for their thorough reading of the manuscript, for all their comments and suggestions.

My thanks go to the Main University of Wrocław Library and cooperating Karlsruhe Library, Tübingen University Library and State Library in Berlin for loaning the books which contributed to this study. I also thank Urszula Sasimowicz-Andrzejewska of Gale Cengage in Poland for helping me to obtain trial access to the Gale databases in 2011, particularly to the Modern Language Association's catalogue.

I am grateful to Professor Werner Sollors and Professor Traise Yamamoto for their kindness and advice over the years.

I also deeply value the time that I spent at the University of North Carolina, Greensboro, as a graduate student.

My debt of gratitude goes to my parents, Bożena and Tadeusz Szmańko, for all their love, help and support.

I express my warm thanks to Joy Kogawa for the gracious permission to quote from her novel, *Obasan*.

I thank Maxine Hong Kingston, Allison Jakobovic of Random House and Naomi Perry of Abner Stein for a speedy execution of my permission request to cite Maxine Hong Kingston's works.

Selected sections of the book were published in an altered form in the following journals and collections: *Studies in Culture and Literature*. *PASE Papers* 2008. Ed. Anna Cichoń and Ewa Kębłowska Ławniczak. Wrocław: Oficyna Wydawnicza ATUT, 2009; *Peer English: The Journal of New Critical Thinking* (University of Leicester Journal) 6 (2011) Ed. Ben Parsons; *Interactions* 20.1–2 (2011) (MLA indexed Ege Journal of British and American Studies); *The Dream. Readings in English and American*

Literature and Culture 3. Ed. Ilona Dobosiewicz and Jacek Gutorow. Opole: University of Opole Press, 2011; *Comparative Studies in Anglophone Literatures: (Trans) National, (Post) Colonial, and (Auto)Thematic (Re) Considerations and (Re)Visions* Ed. Grzegorz Koneczniak. Toruń: Nicolas Copernicus Press, 2012; *Interactions* 23.1–2 (Spring-Fall 2014). I would like to emphasize that the book has always been envisioned as one, coherent whole. The publication of selected sections at the consecutive stages of writing provided extra feedback for which I am grateful. I am also grateful to the editors and publishing houses for permission to use, in an expanded, revised form, my articles.

"A manifest truth disappear[s] ... when one begins to detect the very conditions that made it seem manifest: the familiarities that served as its support, the darknesses that brought about its clarity and all those far-away things that secretly sustained it and made it 'go without saying.'"—*Michel Foucault,* Power *447*

"You're not just a writer in an ivory tower. You are a citizen of this country and of this world, and so what are your responsibilities? As Norman Mailer puts it, are you a participant or are you an observer? ... How distant are you going to be from the material, from the readers, from the doings of your time?"—*Maxine Hong Kingston in Lim's Interview "Reading Back, Looking Forward: A Retrospective Interview with Maxine Hong Kingston" 168*

Introduction

This book is a study of the representation of whiteness in selected works of Asian American literature. Initiating contemporary whiteness studies with her seminal work, *Playing in the Dark* (1989), Toni Morrison emphasized the need to analyze the construction of racial categories in canonical and non-canonical works of American literature by white authors, claiming that her "project is an effort to avert the critical gaze from the racial object to the racial subject, from the describers and imagined to the describers and imaginers, from the serving to the served" (Morrison 90). There is a similar need to critically examine both canonized and non-canonized works of so-called ethnic literature, in this case Asian American literature. The purpose of the book is to show what happens when the positions of "the described" and "the describers" are switched, when visual dynamics is reversed and the people who were traditionally cast as objects of the gaze are endowed with the power to look, evaluate and formulate critical judgements, subjecting to their critical gaze those who usually had the power to study, describe and draw conclusions about representatives of racial minorities. Participating in a dialogue on the definition of whiteness and its impact on the life of Asian Americans and other people of color, all works discussed here make whiteness visible and defamiliarize it, contributing a heterogeneous definition of whiteness, whiteness revealing its many faces, whiteness stripped of its self-assumed esoteric, mystique and indeterminacy. The exposure of whiteness allows the authors analyzed in this project to at least partly reverse power dynamics and undermine the white privilege to define and categorize racial minorities. Exercising the power to look back and to name, they empower themselves and other minorities. It is whiteness and white people featured in the works scrutinized here that find themselves in the position of the "other." The overarching metaphor of the book is the metaphor of sight, of seeing and not seeing, of looking in order to see and of merely sweeping the surface of racialized subjects' body with an ethnographic gaze. Privileged insight of Asian American subjects and visual exchanges between people from different racial groups occupy a central place in all works examined in this study: Maxine Hong Kingston's *The Woman Warrior* (1976) and *China Men* (1980), Leonard Chang's *The Fruit 'N Food* (1996), Joy Kogawa's *Obasan* (1981) as well as Maxine Hong Kingston's *The Fifth Book of Peace* (2003).

Whiteness studies scholars to whom I am particularly indebted in my research are Ruth Frankenberg, Cheryl Harris, Robyn Wiegman, David Roediger, George Lipsitz, Linda Frost, Valerie Babb and Gary Taylor. All of them underscore the socio-historical construction of whiteness, exposing white people's attachment to the privileges accruing to their whiteness. Of particular importance for this interdisciplinary investigation of whiteness in Asian American literature is the research of Ruth Frankenberg, who speaks of the invisibility of whiteness. The invisibility of whiteness is two-fold. White people often construct themselves as invisible by marking others, the process on which hinges the invisibility of whiteness: "whiteness makes itself invisible precisely by asserting its normalcy, its transparency, in contrast with the marking of others on which its transparency depends" ("Introduction: Local Whitenesses, Localizing Whiteness" 6). This mode of invisibility rests on the paradox created by whiteness, which casts itself as an "'empty' but simultaneously normative space" ("Whiteness and Americanness" 64). I devote a special place to the oxymoronic construction of whiteness in the discussion of Maxine Hong Kingston's *China Men*. The other type of white invisibility consists in white people's erasure of their white privilege and the making of the system of racism "structurally invisible" ("Whiteness and Americanness" 70).

The invisibility of whiteness is also a recurring trope in other whiteness studies scholars' research and it is essential to acknowledge at least some of those researchers who consciously reflect on the invisibility of whiteness, emphasizing the need to undermine it. Frances Maher and Mary Kay Thompson note that whiteness "is the often silent and invisible basis against which other racial and cultural identities are named as 'Other,' measured and marginalized" (139). Annalee Newitz claims that whites "imagine themselves as racially invisible" and that "their self-image as whites is thus both underdeveloped and yet extremely presumptuous" (132). In a similar vein, Valerie Babb presents whiteness as a matter of fact thing, a non-marker, almost a non-race in the 1970s and 1980s (1). According to Babb, white people were unmarked by their race because it was never mentioned in relation to them. Race was mentioned only in relation to non-white people. Babb's observations dovetail with the color-blind rhetoric of the 1980s as well as the attempts to obfuscate the history of discrimination against non-white people, closely linked with whiteness. Michael Vannoy Adams observes that "the category 'people of color' excludes whites on the dubious basis that whiteness is colorless—while blackness, redness, brownness and yellowness are colorful" (14). Ironically, the optic definition of color provided by Naomi Zack and cited by Adams undermines the definition of whiteness as colorless because "white" is the "perceptual experience of the presence of all colors" (14).

Acknowledging the scholars who ponder on the self-constructed invisibility of whiteness, I would also like to stress the continuity of my own research and note that the present work is the first book-length study of the representation of whiteness in Asian American literature. In my first book, my field of investigation was invisibility in African American and Asian American literature as well as African Americans and Asian Americans striving for visibility, the present work shows how Asian American authors undo the invisibility of whiteness and white people. Both types of invisibility are diametrically different. Racial and ethnic minorities in the United States were metaphorically invisible because of the negative marking attributed to them by whites. As illustrated above, whites rendered themselves invisible by unmarking themselves and marking others. Both types of invisibility depend on each other. The other type of white invisibility consisted in the masking of its own privilege and practices of oppression. All of the authors analyzed here make whiteness visible, but whiteness features in each of these works in a slightly different way, affecting the lives of Asian American narrators and characters in a different manner. White people are present in all of these works to a different extent without always coming in direct contact with their protagonists. Still, even if whiteness does not directly materialize itself in the presence of white figures, it nonetheless features prominently in the larger power structure exposed by the authors belonging to this study.

It is not without significance that all of the works under scrutiny here represent postmodernism. Mike Hill points to postmodernism as crucial for the emergence of whiteness studies as a discipline and "essential to the critique of whiteness" because "it denies even the most stubborn forms of unremarkability" (158). Each work performs the marking of whiteness in its own unique way.[1] Maxine Hong Kingston's *The Woman Warrior* (1976) defamiliarizes whiteness in a three-fold manner. The novel presents whiteness through the eyes of the immature Chinese American female narrator, who estranges it in the figures of "ghosts" that in her portrayal gain the semblance of aliens. From the perspective of the immature narrator growing up in the 1940s and 1950s, ghosts are undesirable, unattractive, intrusive, scary and overwhelming through their sheer numbers. The second vision of whiteness emerging from the narrative is constructed by the mature narrator, who in the 1960s and 1970s no longer looks at whiteness through the prism of first impressions, but offers a sober-eyed view of whiteness implicated in the structures of oppression. The narrative also presents the first generation of Chinese Americans' vision of whiteness; in their eyes the critique of whiteness often fuses with the critique of American lifestyle and the critique of their own children—second-generation immigrants. Finally, much of the defamiliarization of whiteness in *The Woman Warrior* takes place through the imagery of the narrative.

Kingston's *China Men* (1980) highlights the contradictions underlying the socio-historical and legal construction of whiteness: its simultaneous particularization and universalization. The implication of whiteness in oppression and exploitation of Chinese Americans and other minorities is much more tangible in *China Men* than in *The Woman Warrior*. Chinese American immigrant subjects depicted by the narrator of *China Men* come face to face with their white exploiters in the nineteenth-century United States. In *China Men*, Kingston presents an incisive analysis of white power, taking under a magnifying glass both its executive mechanisms and its legislative underpinnings.

Unlike in *The Woman Warrior* and *China Men*, in Leonard Chang's *The Fruit 'N Food* (1996) whiteness is seemingly invisible. The Korean American protagonist of the novel, Tom Pak, barely ever comes into direct contact with white people. Still, the racial upheaval of the 1990s, into which Tom as well as the Korean Americans and African Americans of the inner city neighborhood of New York are drawn, is the direct result of the urban restructuring of the 1960s, the restructuring in which the white apparatus of power played a crucial role.[2] Seemingly invisible, whiteness operates from a safe distance, placing African Americans and Korean Americans in particular positions in relation to each other and imparting an impression that these are two minorities confronting each other without any role of white people in the conflict. Patterning the events of the novel on the Rodney King–related riots of 1992 and the shooting death of Latasha Harlins in 1991, Leonard Chang points to larger systemic problems as responsible for the conflict between African Americans and Korean Americans unfolding in the inner city, which he terms as a "larger problem of inner city discontent" (219). Never naming whiteness directly as responsible for the "inner city discontent," Chang articulates its role through Tom's dreams, in which whiteness has a blinding quality, being the source of pain and terror.

Joy Kogawa's *Obasan* (1981) offers a much more explicit critique of whiteness and its entwinement in the oppression and dispossession of

Japanese Canadians during the internment of World War II and in the postwar years. Through the first-person participant narrator Naomi and her aunt, Emily, the novel levels very direct charges at the Canadian apparatus of power and white Canadians for treating Japanese Canadians like pariahs, potential spies rather than the rightful citizens. Formulating an express critique of whiteness, Kogawa still does not limit herself exclusively to overt pronouncements on whiteness, encoding a significant portion of the representation of whiteness in the imagery of the work, as it is also the case in other works analyzed here. Apart from being the color of death, betrayal, domination, repression, separation and distance, whiteness invites positive associations in *Obasan*, being also the color of light, brightness, liberation and salvation, albeit liberation and salvation at a price.

The last work belonging to this study, Maxine Hong Kingston's *The Fifth Book of Peace* (2003), does not confine the analysis of whiteness to the perimeter of one nation, but places it in a broader, transnational context, exposing the implication of whiteness in the imperial and colonial ventures outside the United States embodied in the narrative by the colonization of Hawaii, the wars in Vietnam and Iraq. *The Fifth Book* documents the narrator's quest for peace, transcending ethnic or racial barriers as well as national borders, incorporating individuals across the racial, ethnic and national divide in the narrator's transnational venture that, ideally, is to bring definitive peace to all mankind. As in Joy Kogawa's *Obasan*, apart from featuring explicitly in the narrative, whiteness reveals itself to the reader in *The Fifth Book of Peace* through a whole gamut of images, bringing up positive and negative associations. On the one hand, it signifies death, mourning, loss, destruction, expansive nationalism and colonization. On the other hand, it stands for opulence, plenitude, luxury, comfort, empowerment, light, brightness and visibility.

None of the authors belonging to this study forecloses the possibility of the transformation of whiteness. In Kingston's *The Woman Warrior* and Kogawa's *Obasan* the potential of whiteness for transformation becomes visible through the imagery of the work. In his explicit commentary on racial relations in the United States, the narrator of Chang's *The Fruit 'N Food* speaks not so much about the possibility of the transformation of whiteness itself but about the systemic changes that would solve the problem of the "inner city discontent" (219). The potential of whiteness for transformation is the most conspicuous in Kingston's *The Fifth Book of Peace*. The narrator of the work speaks extensively about the need to change the national narrative of the United States from that dominated in the second half of the twentieth century by participation in what she perceives as various colonial and imperial enterprises into that of peaceful cooperation. This need for the transformation of whiteness is best expressed in the narrative through the portrayal of two flags: that of the United States and that of the United Nations. In the depiction of the narrator, the "Red, White and Blue stands for competition and nationalism" (12). She would like to resignify the red, white and blue of the Star Spangled Banner in such a way as to make them "stand for peace and cooperation" (12) embodied by the white dove of peace on the United Nations flag.

Each of the works analyzed here subscribes to transformational identity politics. Proponents of conventional identity politics set themselves apart from other oppressed groups, prioritizing their own interests over those with whom they might strike potential alliances. Supporters of transformational identity politics treasure their cultural distinctness, but at the same time they search for points of convergence with other marginalized groups, often pursuing broader coalitions. It is not unusual for oppressed groups or individuals espousing conventional identity politics to attack other marginalized people. Transformational identity politics, on the other hand, underscores the very experience of oppression that unites all oppressed. It acknowledges the differences, but it does not see these differences as hurdles on the way to potential alliances. Throughout this study the term transformational identity politics recurs consistently. Scholars who propagated the term are Analouise Keating, Liz Bondi and Manning Marable, the latter reaching for "transformationism" (Marable 227). Still, it needs to be noted that other terms are also employed by scholars who reach similar conclusions: for instance, Judith Butler employs the metaphor of translation, coining the term "politics of translation" (169). Butler speaks about a "language between languages" that has to be found (178). According to Butler, translation is successful only if it allows "foreign vocabulary into its lexicon" (168). Kimberlè Crenshaw and other black feminist critics, including Nira Yuval-Davis, Michelle Fine, Gloria I. Joseph, and Elizabeth Higginbotham, employ the term "intersectionality" to speak about the intersecting lines of oppression involving race, gender, class, sexuality, pointing out that these lines of oppression often intersect in one individual or certain oppressed groups of people, the group of special attention to them being black women.

Solidarity with other oppressed or vulnerable groups as well as intersecting lines of oppression are at least to some extent a part of each work examined here. In Maxine Hong Kingston's *The Woman Warrior*, the criticism of the marginalization suffered by the narrator's Chinese American family interweaves with the charges leveled against the chauvinism of the Chinese and Chinese Americans. The nationalist critics of *The Woman*

Warrior claimed that Kingston targeted first of all the Chinese and Chinese American community in her work. Through close textual analysis juxtaposed with the socio-historical reading I undermine these claims, observing that she is no less critical of the white world. Still, it needs to be observed that the narrator of *The Woman Warrior* is as sensitive to gender oppression as she is to racial oppression. Both in *The Woman Warrior* and *China Men*, one can also find solidarity with other racial groups marginalized in the United States and overtones of class sensitivity. Besides exposing the wrongs suffered by Japanese Canadians, the narrator of Joy Kogawa's *Obasan* sheds light on other types of oppression and trauma associated with it, such as sexual exploitation, the ravages of the war, war-incurred orphanhood, the aftermath of the Nagasaki nuclear explosion and the plight of the elderly, especially those of a minority racial group. Leonard Chang's *The Fruit 'N Food* shows the Korean American protagonist of the novel, Tom Pak, sympathizing with African Americans of the inner city, bodily defending one of them and shuddering from racial bigotry displayed by his Korean American employee, Mrs. Rhee. His already mentioned concern with the "larger problem of inner city discontent" (219) suggests that he understands the need for broader systemic solutions and cooperation between various racial groups rather than solutions involving only one side of the conflict between Korean Americans and African Americans. *The Fruit 'N Food* also brings to light exploitation within the same racial group: in this case of Korean Americans by other Korean Americans. Tom's remuneration for his work in a Korean American grocery store is below the minimum wage and his working time does not match the standards of employment either. The Chinese American narrator of *The Fifth Book of Peace*, identified as Maxine Hong Kingston herself,[3] forms an alliance including survivors of different traumas, people of diverse racial and ethnic heritage. Most of them suffer or suffered from the postwar stress syndrome. Many, if not most of the survivors belonging to the narrator's veteran creative writing workshops, are white, serving as an example of whites working together with representatives of other racial and ethnic groups suffering from similar traumas and collaborating for the same cause—the cause of peace, both in a broader international sense and peace signifying mental equilibrium. The presence of white people in the veteran workshops exposes the impact of what the narrator identifies as imperial ideology of consecutive American governments on the lives of other white people who find themselves in the roles of the executors of the policies in many ways underlain by the rhetoric of the white national narrative, also undermined by Kingston in *China Men*.

Traditionally, racial and ethnic minorities have been represented as objects of the gaze, not its subjects, as is the case in the works analyzed in the book. The visual objectification of racial "others" attracted particular attention from African American authors, some of them pioneers of whiteness studies before the discipline earned the status of a field of research. In *Black Looks: Race and Representation* (1992), bell hooks claims that black slaves and servants were not allowed to observe whites or look at them (166). Looking at whites was an act of visual trespassing for which they could be severely punished. An illustration of the situation depicted by hooks comes in Sterling A. Brown's poem "Old Lem" (1937) in which the African American I–speaker observes resignedly that in the face of visibly overpowering whiteness, "our eyes must fall" (333). In "Leaves from the Mental Portfolio" (1909), the pioneer of Asian American literature, Sui Sin Far (Edith Eaton), employs a whole gamut of visual expressions to render the hostility and the ethnographic interest of white subjects of the gaze, approaching her as an object. White people around the narrator "scan [her] curiously from head to foot," "survey [her] critically," "call [her] from play for the purpose of inspection" (886). They "gaze" upon her, "very much in the same way that [she has seen] people gaze upon strange animals in a menagerie" (887).

While direct visual exchanges in the works examined here are fairly limited, all of the authors in question metaphorically reverse the gaze, taking whiteness under the magnifying glass and turning the white subjects of the gaze into its objects. Vision plays a crucial role both in the major story lines and in the imagery of the works under scrutiny in this study. Their first person narrators or protagonists are usually endowed with extraordinary prescience allowing them to see more than the people around them and sometimes making them similar to "ethnic"[4] visionaries. All of them display what an African American sociologist, activist and fiction writer, W.E.B. Du Bois, termed as "second-sight" (*The Souls of Black Folk* 5). Du Bois used the term in reference to African Americans in his double consciousness formula first expounded in his 1897 essay "Strivings of the Negro People," republished in 1903 in *The Souls of Black Folk* in order to describe black people's incisive sight counterbalancing the alienating power of the "veil" standing primarily for the color line: "the Negro is a sort of seventh son, born with a veil, and gifted with second-sight in this American world" (Du Bois 5).[5] African Americans are not the only minority endowed with second sight. Grappling often with multiple marginalization, Asian American subjects of this study are equally predisposed to the gift of second sight. It is their second sight that allows them to see their own position in a broader perspective as well as to draw conclusions on racial relations in American and Canadian society.

Du Bois's reflections on second sight highlight the socio-historical grounding of vision. In *The Visual Nature of Color* (1989), Patricia Sloane explicitly ponders on the cultural nature of vision, noting that seeing cannot be reduced to a purely physiological function since these are people, not eyes alone, that do the seeing (33–34). People look through diverse socio-historical layers of meaning. Therefore the socio-historical context is crucial for the understanding of the visions of whiteness emerging from the narratives analyzed here. Like the rest of my research, this study is grounded in the New Historicist method of literary criticism, which refuses to "observe strict and fixed boundaries between 'literary' and other texts," perceiving "writing, reading and teaching as modes of *action*" (Montrose 26). Hence I draw not only on literary criticism, but also on already discussed whiteness studies, race studies, sociology and history. New Historicist literary critics like Stephen Greenblatt, Dominick La Capra, Louis Montrose and H. Aram Veeser are not the only ones to note the connection between fiction and other types of literature. Sociologists make a similar link. In her 1997 study of haunting and the sociological imagination, sociologist Avery F. Gordon observes that "Literary fictions … enable other kinds of sociological information to emerge" (25). Sixty years before Gordon, famed Chinese anthropologist and sociologist Fei Xiaotong recounted his professor Robert E. Park's advice on conducting sociological research: "The founding father of the Chicago school of sociology, he maintained that sociology should take as its subject understanding human nature. Perhaps I liked him because he wanted me to read novels and not sociology textbooks. More than reading novels, he urged going and personally experiencing different kinds of life" (176). In his 1876 study of folklore in China, N.B. Dennys identifies himself as an ethnologist and philologist, indicating that he perceives the study of literature and language as intertwined with the study of culture of particular people (1).

A substantial portion of the analysis of whiteness in the aforementioned works is devoted to the imagery of whiteness. Yet I do not view aesthetics as severed from the socio-historical sphere, but as firmly connected to it. As Toni Morrison notes, it is important to analyze how authors "transform aspects of their social grounding into aspects of language" (*Playing in the Dark* 4). In the above citation, Morrison is interested in the works by white authors writing about racial minorities, specifically African Americans. This study is devoted to Asian American authors' representation of whiteness. Power dynamics are different in the two cases. While through their linguistic choices Asian American authors reversed the gaze and changed power dynamics in the works examined here, they still did not speak from the position of power if one takes into account the broader American literary community. There were written and unwritten constraints on Asian American authors from both the white reading public and their own Asian American communities. White readers expected at least a certain amount of difference and "exoticism," whereas Asian American communities, especially their nationalist sections expected an unequivocally positive portrayal of Asian American ethnic minorities, perceiving any criticism aimed at Asian Americans as an act of betrayal and selling out. In this often cramped atmosphere, the aesthetic sphere of the work offered extra space to speak about certain issues.

This book is written in the spirit of particularism and critical multiculturalism, emphasizing the impact of diversified access to privilege and power on the experience of different racial and ethnic groups. Still, professing at the very outset commitment to transformational identity politics, I need to stress that the cornerstone of all my literary explorations is looking for bridges and points of intersection between people from different socio-cultural contexts. The motto of my research can be encapsulated in Catherine Clement's words: "To become an analyst, one must have had the ideal at least once: the will to heal" (quoted in Avery Gordon 44). The picture of interracial relations drawn in contemporary American literature shows that the process of healing is complicated by persisting social exclusion and by different socio-historical experience. While this research will not cure anyone's physical heart or eyes, it does concern the "inner eyes" of which Ralph Ellison's Invisible Man speaks, explicating his invisibility: "That invisibility to which I refer occurs because of a peculiar disposition of the eyes of those with whom I come in contact. A matter of the construction of their *inner* eyes, those eyes with which they look through their physical eyes upon reality" (3, emphasis original). The inner eyes that made the Invisible Man invisible are also responsible for the invisibility of white people. However, while the Invisible Man's invisibility is thrust upon him by whites, white invisibility is self-constructed. I hope that this study in some measure fulfills the task that Michel Foucault sets before intellectuals, claiming that they ought "to bring assumptions and things taken for granted again into question, to shake habits, ways of acting and thinking, to dispel the familiarity of the accepted, to take the measure of rules and institutions" (quoted in Colin Gordon xxxiv). All of the authors analyzed here shatter the familiarity of whiteness, undoing its invisibility, showing it in a raw light without any varnish, stripping it of its mystique, undermining its self-assumed normativity and exposing its contradictory construction.

Having at the very outset acknowledged contemporary whiteness studies scholars to whom I am most indebted in the book, I would like to wrap up by giving credit to those who originated the discipline before it was still an established field of study. What follows below is a selected list of works by some of the very first writers who consciously reflected on the construction of whiteness:

- Charles Waddell Chesnutt's "What Is a White Man" (1889);
- W.E.B. Du Bois's "The Souls of White Folk" (1920) in which he declares himself "singularly clairvoyant" of white souls: "I see in and through them. I view them from unusual points of vantage.... I see these souls undressed and from the back and side.... I see them ever stripped—ugly, human" (923);
- Du Bois's "The White World" (1940);
- Richard Wright's Introduction to *Black Metropolis* (1945);
- James Baldwin's *Notes of a Native Son* (1955);
- Ralph Ellison's essays collected in *Shadow and Act* (1964);
- Black nationalists' writings, for example those by Sam Greenlee, George Jackson, Amiri Baraka, Eldridge Cleaver, Malcolm X and Stokely Carmichael.

All of the authors named above look at a whole myriad of issues involving whiteness, such as the hypocrisy of white people, the financial motives behind the persisting color line, the fear of miscegenation, the absurdity of anti-miscegenation laws, double consciousness of white people,[6] to mention only some of the issues recurring in the works cited above.

The Asian American authors analyzed here figuratively mark whiteness, undermining its self-constructed normativity and consistently defamiliarizing whiteness on different levels. The portrayal of whiteness emerging from the narratives explored in the book shows that depending on who does the looking and judgment formation, whiteness does not necessarily need to enjoy the status of the desired quality valorized unreservedly. Seen through the eyes of racial minorities, whiteness was often an emblem of terror, death, oppression, otherness and alienness. Kingston, Chang and Kogawa expose the implication of whiteness in the structures of oppression, shedding light on the mechanisms employed by white people in order to exclusively create meanings, pass laws and assign definitions. Some of the works examined here perform the act of exposure directly, whereas others do it in a much more nuanced way. All of them chip away at the hegemony of whiteness, switching the subject-object positions, claiming the power to look back, name and define those who, on the one hand, assiduously cherished their all too visible privileges, while on the other, rendered themselves invisible.

1

Drawing in the White: Defamiliarizing Whiteness in Maxine Hong Kingston's *The Woman Warrior*

> How do we know that ghosts are the continuance of dead people? Couldn't ghosts be an entirely different species of creature?—*Kingston 77*
>
> Once upon a time the world was so thick with ghosts, I could hardly breathe; I could hardly walk, limping my way around the White Ghosts and their cars. There were Black Ghosts too, but they were open eyed and full of laughter, more distinct than White Ghosts.—*Kingston 113*
>
> "Hair color doesn't measure age, Mother. White is just another pigment, like black and brown. You're always listening to teacher Ghosts, the Scientist Ghosts, Doctor Ghosts."—*Kingston 120*

Introduction

Whiteness is much more than just another pigment in Maxine Hong Kingston's *The Woman Warrior* (1976). The novel offers a dynamic definition of whiteness, conditioning the semiotics of racial categories on location,[1] the speaking subject, and the historical moment. The narrative reveals whiteness through the eyes of:

- the immature narrator
- first-generation immigrants represented mostly by the narrator's mother Brave Orchid
- the mature narrator.

Kingston makes a significant contribution to defamiliarizing whiteness, undermining its self-proclaimed normative status and placing white people in the position of the "other." It is not accidental that the term "ghosts" recurs in each of the epigraphs opening the chapter. "Ghosts" are an overarching metaphor representing whiteness in Kingston's narrative. The term "ghosts" becomes a vehicle for conveying major qualities of whiteness delineated by the immature narrator: alienness and the ability to haunt as well as intrude when unexpected. Looking at whiteness through the eyes of the immature narrator, Kingston shifts the status of the alien intruder from Chinese Americans to white people.

Whiteness, as presented in *The Woman Warrior*, is not only alien to the immature narrator, but it also has an alienating quality. Like Joy Kogawa in *Obasan* and Leonard Chang in *The Fruit 'N Food*, Kingston reaches for the white color in her imagery in order to illustrate the alienation and isolation of particular characters. Alienating whiteness is often juxtaposed in the narrative imagery with iciness and coldness. Additionally, whiteness inscribes itself into the broader alienness around the immature narrator who is estranged in her strange native land of the United States and in her immediate community of Chinatown. Avoiding totalizing or essentialist definitions, Kingston does not locate the source of oppression in whiteness alone. Throughout the narrative, she also links oppression and exploitation with the narrator's Chinese and Chinese American relatives and ancestors. In the narrator's portrayal, her own house is full of ghosts, of unrevealed secrets, and of chauvinism. Kingston was consistently accused by Chinese American cultural nationalists like Frank Chin and Ben Tong[2] of tilting excessively towards "white" American "culture" and denigrating Chinese American heritage as chauvinistic and inferior to that of white Americans. I hope to show in this study that the narrator of *The Woman Warrior* strikes a middle ground, neither unconditionally embracing one nor categorically rejecting the other.

Kingston contrasts the child's perception of whiteness with the perception of the mature narrator. The immature narrator's seeing bears the traces of fearful first encounters with people who look and behave differently than her family and community. The immature narrator essentializes and pluralizes whiteness, treating it en-masse. The pluralization and homogenization of whiteness inverts the practices employed by white people towards racial minorities. In "The Unexamined" Ross Chambers reflects on white people's practice of individualizing themselves while pluralizing and homogenizing non-white racial and ethnic groups (190). The narrator[3] of *The Woman Warrior* changes power dynamics, individualizing herself and select female members of her community while essentializing white people. The literary form of the first person narrative helps the narrator in the act of self-individualization. When the narrator reaches maturity, white people lose their ghost-like transparency and indistinctness. The mature narrator's vision of whiteness is marked by the recognition of oppressive faces of whiteness. She can easily "recognize" the modern guise of oppression and discrimination, identifying whiteness as implicated in the dispossession and domination of other people. Undermining the normative status of whiteness, the narrator does not underestimate its power to exert control over the lives of non-whites.

Many of the critical comments on whiteness in *The Woman Warrior* also extend to Americanness, both of which are largely interlinked in the narrative, illustrating Ruth Frankenberg's statement that "whiteness and Americanness on the one side and non-whiteness/non–Americanness on the other" are "discursively dependent on one another" ("Whiteness and Americanness" 70). Kingston's first major three works *The Woman Warrior* (1976), *China Men* (1980) and *Tripmaster Monkey* (1989) expose a discursive link between whiteness and Americanness. However, the latter two make a more concerted effort to anchor Chinese Americans within the domain of Americanness.[4]

Since *The Woman Warrior* is the first of Kingston's three selected works analyzed in the book, I find it essential to put the analysis of whiteness in *The Woman Warrior* into the broader framework of Kingston's philosophy undergirding all of her works. Like all other authors examined in this study, Kingston subscribes to transformational identity politics. Transformationism underwrites the philosophy of the mature narrator of *The Woman Warrior*. Supporters of transformational identity politics accentuate the common ground between representatives of diverse marginalized groups. Acknowledging their different socio-historical experience of oppression, they search for commonalities, assuming that only by joining forces, the oppressed can withstand those responsible for their oppression. The narrator of *The Woman Warrior* strikes out not only against racism, but also against other forms of discrimination such as class and gender oppression. In *The Woman Warrior* all of them are interwoven with each other, affecting the narrator herself, her relatives and utter strangers whose stories find their way into the narrator's text. As mentioned earlier, whiteness is not the only source of oppression in the narrative. The narrator enumerates the wrongs suffered by her Chinese family at the hands of communists. Envisioning her alternative life story in the "White Tigers" chapter, the narrator imagines herself as an embodiment of Fa Mu Lan, the Woman Warrior, who fights against the oppressors of the poor and women, against rich Chinese barons. The rebellion launched by the narrator's Fa Mu Lan alterego inaugurates a peasant as a new emperor. The following passage is one of the best illustrations of transformational identity politics in the narrative, exposing the intersection of racism and class oppression as well as identifying the task before the narrator: "It's not just the stupid racists that I have to do something about, but the tyrants who for whatever reason can deny my family food and work. My job is my own only land" (58). The job in question is withstanding oppressors in a similar way to that in which her imaginary Chinese avatar battles forces of oppression. This should come as no surprise that the narrator defines the purpose of her life in spatial terms. Only through her work can she finally define herself and map out her place in the universe. The narrator finds it difficult, if not impossible to confine herself to a particular geographical location. By leaving Chinatown, she manifests her determination to transcend the bounded space circumscribing minorities.[5] She also runs away from the marginalization within and without. A sense of living apart from the rest of society accounts for external marginalization. The chauvinism of the Chinese American community constitutes internal ostracism. At the moment of writing the narrative, the narrator claims to live among the Chinese Americans and Japanese Americans, "but no emigrants from [her] own village looking at [her] as if [she] had failed them" (62). The narrator dreams of a bigger Chinatown than the one of her childhood. The narrator of *The Woman Warrior* notices the importance of race and ethnicity in the process of subjectivity construction, but at the same time underscores that it is impossible to build one's identity solely on one's race and ethnicity. She manages to construct a satisfactory self-portrait only after distancing herself from exclusively ethnic and spatial identifications. She defines herself first of all through action and through her work.

The philosophy presented in *The Woman Warrior* reaches its apogee in *The Fifth Book of Peace* also analyzed in this study. Kingston's *Mother Jones* article "The Novel's Next Step" outlines the goals which she hopes to achieve in *The Fifth Book of Peace*. She imagines *The Fifth Book of Peace* as a global novel figuratively transcending the borders of a particular country and a particular nationality: "The dream of the great American novel is past. We need to write the Global novel" (39). The protagonist of the global novel will need to go beyond exclusively Chinese American consciousness (40). Recreating the atmosphere of the 1960s, Kingston pictures an all-inclusive community of draft dodgers deriving from diverse ethnic, religious and professional backgrounds, but united by their mutual goal—peace. The action of *The Fifth Book of Peace* unfolds outside the mainland United States—in Hawaii. Kingston paraphrases her protagonist's, Wittman Ah Sing's, philosophy in the following words: "Forget territory. Let's make love, mate and mix with exotic peoples and create the new human being" ("The Novel's Next Step" 38). *The Fifth Book of Peace* is an elaboration on the philosophy articulated by the narrator of *The Woman Warrior* in a conversation with her mother: "We belong to the planet now, Mama. Does it make sense to you that if we're no longer attached to one piece of land, we belong to the planet? Wherever we happen to be standing, why, that spot belongs to us as much as any other spot" (125). By proclaiming her figurative belonging to the whole Earth, the narrator no longer has to mentally confine herself to a single place, but can claim a bond with multiple locations. If we connect the excerpt to the passage in which the narrator states that "[her] job is [her] own only land" (58), we can conclude that through her capacious literary imagination spanning diverse lands, the narrator metaphorically claims the bonding with the whole Earth, again anticipating the writing of *The Fifth Book of Peace*, one of whose sections is entitled "Earth."

All-inclusiveness and reaching out to diverse people of the Earth find their way into the imagery of *The Woman Warrior*. In one of her egalitarian multicultural visions, the narrator as Fa Mu Lan's embodiment pictures two dancers radiating light and gold (32). They symbolize multicultural people of the Earth dancing through time and space in the show of multicultural unity. The vision prompts the narrator to proclaim the parity between the peasant and the emperor: "peasant's clothes are golden, as king's clothes are golden" (32). A strong drive towards multiculturalism and integration is also visible in the imagery depicting the immature narrator's entrance into the guru couple's hut. The floor of the hut is carpeted with yellow, green and brown pine needles according to age. Yellow, green and brown appear to the narrator as "earth colors" (26), contrasting with black and white repeatedly identified as bland colors. Unlike the narrator's gurus who tread so lightly as to never upset the design of the needles, the narrator treads "carelessly," creating new myriads of "earth colors" (26). The narrator strategically jostles fixed color categories, blending them into a variegated palette. Mixing earth colors symbolizes her proclivity towards integration and miscegenation among representatives of various human races. The passage corresponds closely to the fragment of the *Mother Jones* article cited before: "Let's make love, mate and mix with exotic peoples, and create the new human being" ("The Novel's Next Step" 38). The fragment also bears correspondence to the excerpt from Kingston's third work, *Tripmaster Monkey*: "My idea for the Civil Rights Movement is that we integrate jobs, schools, buses, housing, lunch counters, yes, and we also integrate theater and parties. The dressing up. The dancing, The loving. The playing" (52). Apart from expressing the narrator's strong inclination towards multicultural integration, the mixing of "earth colors" and unsettling of the fixed designs shed light on her own storytelling. She jounces set designs, for example by mixing various kinds and genres. By her own admission, she is a knot-maker "twist[ing]" her stories "into designs" (189–190). The generic hybridity of *The Woman Warrior* has received critical attention from Joan Lidoff, Khani Begum, Patricia Lin Blinde, Sarah Gilead and Kathleen Brogan. Lidoff argues that "by re-creating and revising generic forms, Kingston constructs a fiction of the self that questions the construction of the self" (118). The "self" constructed by the mature narrator shows a higher degree of inclusiveness and willingness to embrace others and their stories. Weaving her first person narrative, the narrator does not limit herself to telling her own story, but brings to light the stories of other marginalized women: Brave Orchid, the No Name Woman, Moon Orchid, Ts'ai Yen, Pe-a-nah, the crazy village woman. While the narrator's voice reigns supreme over the whole narrative, it also funnels other voices, creating the effect of polyvocality. Brave Orchid's voice features as ancillary to that of the narrator. In line with Lidoff's statements on a collective and relational character of *The Woman Warrior* as a first-person narrative, Begum notes that the text "resists categorization as individual autobiography because it concurrently interweaves myth, fiction, and reality to create its own unique tapestry of form" (143). Lin Blinde speaks about the collage of such genres as a novel, an autobiography, a series of essays and poems, claiming that "while the work capitalizes on the conventions and expectations of various genres, it also evades the limitations of any one genre" (52). It is also worth mentioning that the opening chapter of the narrative, "No Name Woman,"[6] was first published independently as a short story in the January 1975 issue of *Viva*. The fourth chapter, "At the Western Palace," narrated in the third person could also function independently as a short story. Lidoff ponders on the generic permeability of *The Woman Warrior*, wondering whether it is fiction, non-fiction, autobiography or novel (118). Concurring with Lidoff, Brogan reflects on the relation of history and fiction. Brogan cites Michel de Certeau, who observes that history reaches for rhetorical and narrative strategies central to fiction (de Certeau cited in Brogan 17). Brogan also invokes Lynn Hunt whose observations on the definition of history shed further light on the interface between fiction and non-fiction in *The Woman Warrior*. Rather than highlight the differences between history and fiction, Hunt shifts the focus to commonalities. Hunt sees history not so much as a "repository of facts" but as the "telling of stories" (Hunt cited in Brogan 17). The narrator's history as well as the histories of other Chinese and Chinese American women which branch into the narrator's history are not merely a repository of facts either. First of all they are life tales of particular individuals/characters whose lives gain an added significance in the act of the telling. The telling is the postmodern telling.

The postmodern structuring and the postmodern sensibility of *The Woman Warrior* impinge on the vision of whiteness emerging from the narrative. This is also one of the linking features between *The Woman Warrior* and other works analyzed here: Joy Kogawa's *Obasan*, Leonard Chang's *The Fruit 'N Food* and Kingston's *China Men* as well as *The Fifth Book of Peace*. Major hallmarks of postmodernism traceable in *The Woman Warrior* are:

- the valorization of difference, heterogeneity, marginality, diversity
- the emphasis on the instability as well as constructedness of meanings and categories
- the accentuation of the performativity of identities debunking the notion of authenticity
- the stress on the importance of location and positionality
- reaction against structuralist pretensions to scientific objectivity
- the underscoring of partiality
- the rejection of linearity
- circularity
- ambiguity
- open-endedness
- fragmentation
- generic hybridity
- polyvocality
- pastiche[7]
- decentering:
   (a) the decentralized narrator
   (b) decentralized consciousness.

The postmodern, collagic, eccentric[8] structure of *The Woman Warrior* also contributes to the dispersion of whiteness into a multitude of images, some of which are recurring tropes of other works analyzed in this study, for example bones, light, coldness and paper. The imagery of whiteness inscribes itself in the consistent defamiliarization of whiteness in the narrative and the marking of its often camouflaged qualities.

The following analysis of whiteness in *The Woman Warrior* falls into three parts. The first part shows whiteness through the eyes of the immature narrator, marking it mostly as alien, alienating, haunting and intrusive. The second part reveals whiteness through the eyes of the mature narrator, exposing oppressive faces of whiteness. The second part also presents whiteness and Americanness through the eyes of first generation immigrants of the narrative, characterizing whiteness and Americanness as to a great extent dehumanized and dehumanizing. The third and last part centers on the imagery of whiteness. All these parts scrutinize the portrait of whiteness drawn in the narrative, uncovering respective layers of the defamiliarization of whiteness in *The Woman Warrior*. On the one hand, Kingston acknowledges and brings to light the hegemonic status of whiteness in American society, while on the other, she at least partly chips away at this hegemony by questioning its self-proclaimed normativity.

Alien, Alienating and Haunting Whiteness

Kingston focalizes a significant portion of the visions of whiteness through the eyes of the immature narrator, for whom whiteness is first of all alien, alienating and haunting. The immature narrator formulates such a vision of whiteness in her first encounters with white people when she is a child. Inverting the stereotypes of Chinese Americans and Asian Americans as permanent aliens on American soil, the narrator represents whites as aliens approaching the perimeter of her house and often trying to intrude inside. Consecutive Exclusion Acts of 1882, 1884, 1886, 1902, 1907, 1917, and 1924 rendered Chinese Americans as well as other Asian Americans as "aliens ineligible for citizenship" (Lowe 180, Gotanda 136–137). As a result of the 1907 Gentlemen's Agreement, Japan agreed under pressure to decrease the number of emigrants destined for the United States, Hawaii, Mexico and Canada (Gotanda 137). The 1917 Act covered people from South Asia, Southeast Asia and the Islands of the Indian and Pacific Oceans. The 1924 Act barred Japanese Americans and other Asians from immigration to the United States altogether. At that time no people of Asian descent could apply for citizenship. Despite the bans on Asian American immigration, Asian Americans still kept entering the United States illegally, risking their lives during perilous journeys to America, or the "Gold Mountain." Only the 1943 Magnuson Act abolished the ban on Chinese American immigration and the 1952 McCarran-Walter Act on Japanese American immigration (Gotanda 139, 145). The latter act also gave Asian Americans the right to become citizens of the United States. After the passage of the McCarran-Walter Act the label "alien" still kept haunting Asian Americans, exposing them to such questions as: Have you got a green card? Do you speak English? When did you arrive? How do you like this country? In *Orientals: Asian Americans in Popular Culture*,

Robert G. Lee distinguishes between the term "alien" and "foreign" (3). According to Lee, tourists are usually identified as foreigners, whereas immigrants as aliens. While the word "foreign" is rather neutral, "alien" often brings up negative connotations. The presence of aliens in a particular place is unwelcome. Aliens are perceived as unwanted intruders encroaching upon the fabric of a community. The narrator does not explicitly refer to whites hovering in proximity to her house as aliens, but she portrays them in such terms. While there are no exclusion laws against the presence of white people in the vicinity of the narrator's house, they are perceived as *personae non grata*. White customers are a necessary evil in the Chinatown laundry owned by the narrator's family, but they are barely tolerated near and across the threshold of the narrator's house.

One of the most striking first encounters of the immature narrator with whiteness is with the trash collector dubbed the "Garbage Ghost." The encounter registers a visual and verbal exchange between the Garbage Ghost, the narrator and her siblings, who watch the trash collector from inside their house. The trash collector is definitely of ethnographic interest to the narrator's family: "Come see the Garbage Ghost get its food" (115). The pronoun "its" detracts from the capitalization of the term "Garbage Ghost," undermining the trash collector's humanity and reducing him to the ranks of a different species. The next moment of extreme defamiliarization of the trash collector takes place when the narrator reports the trash collector's puzzlement at being called the "Garbage Ghost": "'The … Gar…bage … Ghost,' he said, copying human language. 'Gar…bage … Ghost?'" (115). Suspicions that the trash collector copies the human language may be interpreted as one more example of putting his humanity into doubt. Another interpretation would suggest that "copying human language" implies that he tries to imitate Chinese, designated as the human language. Implicitly, English is reduced at this point to the "ghost language." English is explicitly labeled in the narrative as the "ghost language" by the generation of the narrator's parents. The narrator does not state explicitly whether she and her siblings speak Chinese during the encounter with the Garbage Ghost. Brave Orchid's comment when she comes to close the window: "Now we know … the White Ghosts can hear Chinese" indicates that they speak Chinese (115). Still, Brave Orchid does not witness the encounter proper between the Garbage Ghost and her children, appearing only at the very end.

The verbal exchange between the narrator's family and the trash collector is very limited, recording scraps of words. The visual exchange is much more intense. After being called the "Garbage Ghost," the trash collector "look[s] directly at [them]" (115). The children watch the trash collector approach the window, visually registering the details of his appearance: "cavernous nostrils with yellow and brown hair" and his red mouth (115). In the eyes of the children, the trash collector is a double other: not only white but also visibly standing out because of his disheveled appearance. The encounter with the trash collector marks the moment of the double defamiliarization of whiteness. For the children, the trash collector is different because of his phenotypic features and because of his subservient class status placing him on the margins of whiteness. The trash collector's position is below that of "poor white trash."[9] Closing the window at the sight of the trash collector, the narrator's mother, Brave Orchid, reinforces his status of an alien, unwanted intruder.

The marking of whiteness extends into the space of the family laundry. White people are accepted in the laundry as customers, but they do not escape the marking practices. Ruth Frankenberg notes that whiteness usurped the title of an "unmarked marker," "empty yet taken as normative" ("Whiteness and Americanness" 65). Such a definition of whiteness underscores its oxymoronic character, which Kingston exposes, subverting its self-proclaimed right to stay unmarked while marking others. Through the figure of Brave Orchid and her comments about whiteness, Kingston challenges the prerogative of whiteness to mark non-white people. In response to the white mimicking[10] of Chinese American way of speaking, Brave Orchid marks the rude customer as a "Noisy Red-Mouth Ghost" (123). Commenting on Brave Orchid's practice of labeling customers, the narrator specifically uses the terms "naming" and "marking": "'Noisy Red-Mouth Ghost,' she'd write on its package, naming it, marking its clothes with its name" (123). Like the Garbage Ghost, the Noisy Red-Mouth Ghost is assigned an impersonal "its" pronoun. The Garbage Ghost and the Red-Mouth Ghost are individual representatives of the ghost species, but similar marking practices apply to white people as a separate racial group. A parallel practice is at play when white people are approached en masse. The features attributed to the Noisy Red-Mouth Ghost are traced in other white people as well: "Ghosts are noisy and full of air, they talk during meals. They talk about anything" (214). The pluralization of whiteness goes hand in hand with the marking of its particular features. Kingston's portrayal of white people debunks the theoretical basis on which the sociohistorical construction of whiteness is based. Ruth Frankenberg observes that "To be white within this universe of discourse is thus to *not* be a number of other things" ("Whiteness and Americanness" 70). Kingston builds a "positive" construction of whiteness. For the narrator of *The Woman Warrior* and her fellow members of the Chinese American community, to be white equals being a number of things.

The marking practices taking place in the family laundry illustrate a metonymic approach to whiteness. Apart from judging white customers by their behavior, Brave Orchid evaluates them through the elements of their clothing deposited in the laundry such as socks and white shirts. Describing the steamy, choking air of the laundry, Brave Orchid complains about having to wash "tubercular handkerchiefs" and "lepers' socks" (123). The designation of her white customers as lepers deserves special attention because of the symptoms of leprosy—white spots. Tracing the emergence of white self-consciousness, Gary Taylor, the author of *Buying Whiteness* (2005), argues that Europeans of the twelfth and thirteenth century could not identify as white because of leprosy rampant in Europe of the period (34). By indirectly referring to white customers as lepers, Brave Orchid figuratively adds an extra layer of plague-like whiteness to their white skin. She literally adds an extra layer of whiteness to the clothing of white customers while starching their white shirts. As a Chinese American, Brave Orchid is not only responsible for the immaculate image of white customers and the whiteness of their shirts but is also indispensable for the socio-historical construction of their whiteness based on othering and exclusion of non-white people. Without the presence and marginalization of minorities, whiteness would lose its exclusive status.[11]

The defamiliarization of whiteness through the eyes of the immature narrator reveals its haunting quality, its alienness and its intrusiveness. Whiteness of *The Woman Warrior* shows the ability to haunt and to be omnipresent in a different way than in Leonard Chang's *The Fruit 'N Food*. It is physically hyper visible to the immature narrator. Whiteness of *The Woman Warrior* appears out of nowhere, suffocating and overwhelming the immature narrator:

> But America has been full of machines and ghosts—Taxi Ghosts, Bus Ghosts, Police Ghosts, Fire Ghosts, Meter Reader Ghosts, Tree Trimming Ghosts, Five-and-Dime Ghosts. Once upon a time the world was so thick with ghosts, I could hardly breathe; I could hardly walk, limping my way around the White Ghosts and their cars [113].

Whiteness in the passage terrifies the narrator with its ability to expand, to proliferate and appear unexpectedly. The expansiveness of whiteness leaves the narrator barely any breathing space. Such a portrayal of whiteness can again be perceived as the reversal of the features attributed to Asian Americans[12] as an embodiment of the yellow peril threatening to flood the United States and wreak havoc when it is the least expected. Appearing in overwhelming numbers,[13] white people threaten to inundate the narrator, gaining the semblance of a domineering force. The immature narrator's perception of whiteness as ever-multiplying constitutes an antithesis to the attempts by some white people to minoritize themselves, to present themselves as a "minority identity" (Wiegman 116). Whiteness in the above cited passage also has a synthetic, machine-like quality. White ghosts and their cars are almost inseparable. Like Chungpa Han of Younghill Kang's *East Goes West* (1937), the immature narrator draws parallels between whiteness, artificiality and syntheticity. Yet if Chungpa Han is mesmerized by man-made American technology, the immature narrator is overwhelmed by it. The American synthetic reality, or rather unreality, in this case, elicits a still harsher critique from Brave Orchid. Constantly planning on returning to China,[14] Brave Orchid dismisses the American reality as artificial and unreal. Her skepticism about the American reality is visible, for example, in the statement: "Someday, very soon, we're going home, where there are Han people everywhere. We'll buy furniture then, real tables and chairs. You children will smell flowers for the first time" (115). When Brave Orchid finally accepts the fact of their permanent residence in the United States, the mature narrator is wondering if American flowers will "smell good" for her (125).

Whiteness is inextricably interwoven in the fabric of the immature narrator's life and the life of her family, the life unfolding in the 1940s and the 1950s. An exchange of goods and services takes place between white people and the narrator's Chinese American relatives. While whites depend on Chinese Americans for the cleaning of their clothing, Chinese Americans rely on white people for a variety of services, including food:

> For our very food we had to traffic with the Grocery Ghosts, the supermarket aisles full of ghost customers. The Milk Ghost drove his white truck from house to house every other day. We hid watching until his truck turned the corner, bottles rattling in their frames. Then we unlocked the front door and the screen door and reached for the milk. We were regularly visited by the Mail Ghost, Meter Reader Ghost, Garbage Ghost. Staying off the streets did no good. They came nosing at windows—Social Worker Ghosts; Public Health Nurse Ghosts; Factory Ghosts recruiting workers during the war ... two Jesus Ghosts who had formerly worked in China. We hid directly under the windows, pressed against the baseboard until the ghost, calling us in the ghost language so that we'd almost answer to stop its voice, gave up [114–115].

The narrator again portrays whiteness as intruding into her house through the figures of the above enumerated ghosts: "Staying off the streets did no good" (114). As depicted by the narrator, her house is under constant siege from whiteness. Together with her siblings she hides from whiteness. Hiding from whiteness indicates the fear and uncertainty of whiteness, of the difference entailed by whiteness. The Milk Ghost driving his white truck embodies the greatest accumulation of whiteness, which is why he inspires the narrator and her siblings with greater trepidation. The fact that white people approaching the house speak English magnifies their difference to Chinese American children who cannot speak English in their earliest childhood. As it is the case during the Garbage Ghost incident, English is identified as the "ghost language," of which they are scared and which they would like to silence (115). The white people haunting the narrator's house are socially superior to the Garbage Ghost, but they also belong to the margins of whiteness. There is no sign that they, except for Burglar Ghosts, have any nefarious ends in mind or threaten the well-being of any of the inhabitants, but their very presence produces unease in the youngest members of the household. An air of strangeness and alienness around the white people hovering in the vicinity of the house suffices to make their presence suspicious and unwelcome. What compromises their positioning in the eyes of the children is the very fact that they are white. What also scares the immature narrator is the ability of whiteness to proliferate, to appear in infinite numbers. Whiteness hovering around the immature narrator's house in the 1940s and 1950s is innocuous in comparison with the dispossessing whiteness discussed in the next section of the chapter. It is the dispossessing whiteness revealing itself through the urban restructuring of the 1960s that deprives the narrator's parents of the laundry, which is their primary source of income.

Considering the ability of whiteness to haunt, it should come as no surprise that whiteness is depicted in terms of ghosthood. The narrator introduces the etymology of the term "ghost" after recounting Brave Orchid's story of rope bridge ghosts termed by the narrator's Great Uncle as "Sit Dom Kuei" (103). The narrator explains that "Kuei" means "ghost" (103). Several pages after introducing the etymology of the term "ghost," the narrator elaborates on her explanation, stating that the label "ghost" refers to all non–Chinese except for the Japanese, who are believed to be closely related to the Chinese: "they are not a totally alien species" (109). The translation of "Kuei" as "ghost" sparked an animated debate in the Chinese American community. Chinese American cultural nationalists, Ben Tong and Jeffery Paul Chan,[15] argue that Kingston's term "ghost" is the outcome of mistranslating Cantonese "Kuei" or "Gwai" (Wong 32). It is worth mentioning that Kingston does not use the term "Gwai" in the text. Tong and Chan would translate the term as "demon," "devil" or "asshole." Both claim that Kingston's translation detracts from the criticism of white people (Wong 32). Like Tong and Chan, David Leiwei Li speculates that Kingston chose to translate "Kuei" as "ghost" rather than "devil" or "demon" to offset the negative connotations implied by the term "Kuei" (Li 508–509). Li also traces the use of the term "ghost" to the nineteenth century, when Western empires raided China. Cynthia Sau-ling Wong expresses her skepticism about the significance of the debate on the translation of "Kuei" as "ghost," claiming that "in the case of *The Woman Warrior* debate, correspondence between word and thing is deemed so perfect that a Chinese term, Kuei, is supposed to be translatable by only one English equivalent, with all other overtones outlawed" (Wong 37). Kingston is by no means the first American author to note that foreigners were referred to as "ghosts" by the Chinese. In 1876, precisely one hundred years before the publication of *The Woman Warrior*, N.B. Dennys, ethnologist and philologist, maintained that "the words for 'ghost' and 'devil' are the same, and form a portion of the objectionable epithets applied to foreigners (*Kwei-tsze* in Mandarin or *Fan-kwai* in Cantonese)" (73). Dennys stressed that "ghost" was a pejorative term. The ideograph for ghosts was believed to be so unpropitious as to be very seldom used. Its top presented a human skull. A euphemistic term for the dead, dating back to the time of Confucius, was "bright spirits" or "spiritual intelligences" (Dennys 72). The claim that "ghost" is a pejorative term, superior to devil in English, but not necessarily in Chinese, puts the debate on Kingston's translation of "Kuei" as "ghost" rather than "devil" or "demon" into a broader perspective.

While Kingston reaches for the term "ghost" in *The Woman Warrior*, she opts for "demon" in *China Men*. Gayle K. Fujita Sato accounts for the difference in the translation of the term by invoking gender (199). Since *The Woman Warrior* is woven around the stories of Chinese American and Chinese women, the translation of "Kuei" as "ghost" reflects Chinese American women's vision of reality. *China Men*, woven around the stories of Chinese American men, reflects the male vision: hence the translation reflecting more raw and austere associations. Convincing as Sato's explanation is, I would also like to argue that the term "Kuei" was translated as "demon" in *China Men* because whiteness carries a much more demonic charge in *China Men* than it does in *The Woman Warrior*. The nineteenth century Chinese American workers featuring in *China Men* sample white brutality and exploitation first hand.

The translation of the term "Kuei" as ghost gains further justification if we consider that Chinese Americans depicted by Kingston in her narrative indeed feel haunted by whiteness. Whiteness has the most haunting quality in relation to the narrator. Yet the sense of being haunted and closely watched by white people is visible in the rest of the Chinese American community. Fearing deportation, the narrator's parents keep reminding her: "Don't tell" (213). The admonition not to tell is particularly troubling for the narrator because the community closely guards "immigration secrets," withholding them from the children, whose questions go unanswered. An air of secrecy hovers over the narrator at home and at school. The narrator blames "ghosts" for foisting silence on the Chinese American community. Her resentment is visible in the statement: "I hated the ghosts for not letting us talk" (213). David Leiwei Li links the fear within the Chinese American community to the policies of the McCarthy era (515). The narrator defines herself as the child of war because she was born during World War II, which sets the above discussed period of the narrator's school years in the late 1940s and 1950s (Kingston 113). Although the narrator does not mention the threat of the red scare explicitly, she alludes to it saying: "And, of course, tell them we're against Communism" (215). An injunction "Don't tell" overlaps with an instruction to lie while speaking to white people (215). Lying is a way to avoid deportation and legal consequences. Chinese Americans are to lie about themselves, their own origin and their communities. The purpose of their verbal performance is to create a picture of a near perfect community[16] in order to prevent any interference from outside:

> Lie to Americans. Tell them you were born during the San Francisco earthquake. Tell them your birth certificate and your parents were burned up in the fire. Don't report crimes; tell them we have no crimes and no poverty. Give a new name every time you get arrested; the ghosts won't recognize you. Pay the new immigrants twenty-five cents an hour and say we have no unemployment ... the Han people won't be pinned down [215].

The assurance that "the Han people won't be pinned down" gives Chinese Americans a semblance of African American tricksters excelling in outsmarting white people. An example of such an African American trickster character is Easy Rawlins, the protagonist of Walter Mosley's detective novels unfolding mostly in the 1950s. In *Devil in a Blue Dress*, Rawlins declares that in the presence of white people he habitually "empt[ies] [his] head of everything" because "the less you know the less trouble you find" (13). Like the narrator of *The Woman Warrior*, Rawlins, apart from blaming himself, blames his enforced silence both on white people and his own community: "I hated myself for it but I also hated white people, and colored people too, for making me that way" (13).

Chinese Americans are not isolated in their perception of white people as ghost-like. Trudier Harris reaches for the term "ghostly" to describe the appearance of white men in the South to black people (299). According to Harris, "these white men conveyed to blacks there was always someone watching over their shoulder ready to punish them for the slightest offense or the least deviation from acceptable lines of action" (299). The threat hanging over the heads of African American people for the slightest transgression was lynching. In the "lie to whites" passage of *The Woman Warrior* the threat is deportation.[17]

Scary as "ghosts" (white people) are to the immature narrator, they are preferable to the ghosts that she expects to encounter in China, the ghosts "who took shapes nothing like our own" (116). For the narrator, American ghosts in the end become domesticated, whereas Chinese ghosts remain unknown, never encountered by her except for in her mother's talk stories, which give everyone "good chills up [their] backs" on hot summer afternoons in the family laundry (102). The narrator is aware that unlike American ghosts, who are human beings, Chinese ghosts are believed to be an extension of the dead.

The narrator of *The Woman Warrior* does not reach for the term "ghosts" exclusively in reference to white people. The word also appears in a very specific connotation applied by first generation Chinese Americans to second generation Chinese Americans born in the United States. First generation Chinese Americans addressed the second generation of Chinese Americans as "Ho Chi Kuei" (237–238). Having heard Brave Orchid call her "Ho Chi Kuei," the narrator considers various translations of the term, some of them being: "grub" (an insect in a thick, usually white covering), a "bastard carp," and a "water lily" (238). The translation of Ho Chi Kuei as "water lily" entails whiteness and assimilation into the host society. A "bastard carp" suggests illegitimacy and uncertain birthright on account of being born and raised in the United States rather than China. Apart from implying whiteness, a "grub" suggests a transitional state, a suspension between two different worlds, the world of Chinatown and external broader world of American society. Time and again Chinese American children are reproached by their parents for following white ways. They blame their Americanization and their resemblance to savages and barbarians (white people) on the fact that they grew up "in the wilderness" (154), "away from civilization" (in the United States) (155). Brave Orchid calls the mouth of her children barbarous (140). Pondering on the translation of the term "Ho Chi Kuei," the narrator considers the possibility of having "romanized the spelling wrong" (238) and substituting "Ho Chi Kuei" for "Hao Chi Kuei," which means "Good Foundation Ghosts" (238), the implication being, according to the narrator, that first generation immigrants, on the one hand, scorn their children as the ones who had their way paved for them by an earlier generation of immigrants,[18] while on the other, they are enthusiastic about their children's more auspicious future. "Ho Chi Kuei" is one of the terms which gains the status of the spoken unspeakable, the term which is spoken but whose meaning is assiduously hidden from second generation Chinese Americans.

Beyond rendering the haunting and alien quality of whiteness, the metaphor of ghosthood, with its associations of transparency and the lack of substance, captures the indistinctness attributed by the immature narrator to white people.[19] In the second epigraph to the chapter, the immature narrator contrasts "White Ghosts" with "Black Ghosts" "who were open eyed and full of laughter, more distinct than White Ghosts" (113). Seen through the eyes of the immature narrator, whiteness has relatively few distinct features. The portrayal of whiteness en masse, with limited attempts at individualization dovetails with the pluralization of whiteness. Perceiving whiteness in seemingly infinite numbers, the immature narrator homogenizes whiteness, naming only some of its features. The homogenization of whiteness is partly at odds with the purpose of whiteness studies, the discipline aiming to make whiteness distinct and visible rather than obfuscating its features. Homogenizing whiteness, the immature narrator to a certain extent re-inscribes the self-constructed definition of whiteness as esoteric, mysterious and indeterminate. Whiteness, as seen by many whites, is an "empty signifier" free of any internal heterogeneity (Frankenberg "Introduction" 15). As I argue earlier, the immature narrator marks and defamiliarizes whiteness, undermining the power of whiteness to signify, name and mark others. Yet her portrayal of whiteness lacks the sharpness and distinctness characterizing her mature vision. If the narrator's immature vision of whiteness bears the traces of perceiving for the first time without penetrating beneath, her mature vision of whiteness is informed by critical reflection.

Naming and Resisting Oppressive Faces of Whiteness

The mature narrator of *The Woman Warrior* identifies whiteness as implicated in racial discrimination, dispossession and exploitation of racial minorities. White people ("white ghosts") hovering around the windows of the immature narrator's house are fairly innocuous in comparison with the whiteness examined by the mature narrator. The narrator ensures visibility for the oppressive faces of whiteness by recounting her own brushes with whiteness and the generation of her parents' confrontations with whiteness. Whiteness reveals its close entwinement with oppression in the following ways:

- through racism displayed by the narrator's employers
- through urban restructuring resulting in the dispossession of the narrator's parents

- through exploitation discussed in the narrative by the narrator's mother, Brave Orchid, as a representative of first generation Chinese American immigrants.

The last point, the critique of exploitative practices, interweaves with the critique of Americanness, the American way of living and the United States as a state. Most of the exposure of the oppressive faces of whiteness takes place in the "White Tigers" chapter, in which the narrator confronts her fairy tale inspired dreams with American reality. Both in the fairy tale world and in the American world the narrator fights against various forms of oppression, defying the agents of exploitation. The narrator explicitly critiques whiteness in the sections of the narrative unfolding in the United States. Implicitly, however, the sections unfolding in imperial China also include references to the Western world of the United States and a particular positioning of immigrants in this world. In both worlds the narrator is equipped with different tools. She does not have nearly so many tools at her disposal in the American world as she does in the fairy tale world. Yet the gift belonging to the narrator's arms chest in both worlds is the gift of second sight allowing her to see what may be invisible to other people. Both the narrator and her dream alter ego also have another weapon in their arsenal—the word. Still, if in the case of the narrator's dream alter ego, the word is thrust upon her as a weapon, in the case of the narrator proper, the word is a weapon of her choice.

The narrator's direct confrontations with whiteness occur during verbal and visual exchanges with her white racist employers. These exchanges are never fully complete because representatives of corporate whiteness do not consider the narrator worth looking at or listening to. Invoking her gift of second sight, the narrator declares valiantly: "From the fairy tales, I've learned exactly who the enemy are. I easily recognize them—business-suited in their modern American executive guise, each boss two feet taller than I am and impossible to meet eye to eye" (57). The passage underscores the trope of recognition, the mature narrator's ability to see through the modern face of racism. Her ability to see contrasts with the executives' unwillingness to establish a visual exchange with their subjects. The executives are "impossible to meet eye to eye" (57). Although the narrator does not mention whiteness explicitly in the passage, she enumerates the prerogatives heralded by whiteness in the 1960s virtually exclusively:

- its sway over the corporate world ("executive guise")
- virtual interchangeability of whiteness and Americanness ("modern American executive guise")
- the power to dominate others ("each boss two feet taller")

Whiteness in the passage is assiduously camouflaged by its modern American executive guise. The term "guise" denotes an outer appearance usually designed to deceive. Having spent her childhood in the Chinatown margins of American society, the narrator can see beyond the external polish concealing the racism of her day.[20]

The narrator's first confrontation with a white racist businessman takes place when she works at an art supply house selling paints to artists. Specifying which color he wants the narrator to order, the boss uses the phrase "nigger yellow" (57), later expressing self-satisfaction at coining such a clever phrase: "Bright, isn't it? Nigger yellow" (57). The narrator reacts to the phrase in the following way: "'I don't like that word,' I had to say in my bad, small-person's voice that makes no impact" (57). Exposed to discrimination herself, the narrator feels compelled to protest in whatever small way she can the use of the term "nigger yellow." "Bad, small-person's voice" implies the narrator's awareness of her own insignificance and the inconsequential nature of her stand. Her voice elicits no response. Still, considering the narrator's struggle against her fear of speaking out in public,[21] her articulation of thoughts on this occasion constitutes a personal success. The boss's lack of response reveals his neglect of the narrator's voice and her view on the issue.

The epithet "bad" in "bad, small-person's voice that makes no impact" invites two different interpretations. "Bad" may signify the poor quality of the narrator's voice, a feature brought up repeatedly by Brave Orchid. "Bad" may also allude to the prototype of a "bad Asian," the antithesis of a model minority citizen.[22] In "Model Minority and Bad Subjects" (2002) Viet Thanh Nguyen argues that the model minority discourse and the bad subject discourse are mutually interdependent since "Asian Americans can frequently occupy both situations simultaneously or, at the very least, alternate between them" (144). Receiving "straight A's" (54), graduating from Berkeley (56) and succeeding professionally outside Chinatown, the narrator has more features of the model minority citizen rather than the bad Asian. Kingston and the narrator are also usually represented as model minority citizens catering to the mainstream society by Chinese American nationalists: Frank Chin, Ben Tong and Jeffrey Paul Chan. Growing up in Chinatown, the narrator struggles against similar stereotyping on the part of her most immediate community. Brave Orchid is hardly enthusiastic about the narrator's straight A's because they will not save the village (54). Trying to meet the expectations of her community, some of which she has problems deciphering and some of which she misinterprets, the narrator stops getting straight A's and hopes to turn into a "bad girl" because a "bad girl" is "almost a boy" (56). Boys were highly treasured by the Chinese

American community, whereas girls were looked down upon as not worth bringing up. While I do not equate Kingston with her narrator, it is difficult to overlook the fact that the frictions which the narrator encounters while growing up in her Chinatown community parallel the tensions which Kingston had to face in the broader Chinese American and Asian American literary community.

Protesting against the use of the term "nigger yellow," the narrator may imply that she is offended not only by the use of the word "nigger," but also by its juxtaposition with "yellow." Although "yellow" is not used in this case to signify racial identity, it may conjure up racial connotations for a person of Asian American descent. Originally, the term "yellow," like "oriental" carried negative associations. It could, for example, strike a chord of "yellow peril." Uttered by racists and opponents of immigration, "yellow" essentialized Asian Americans, reducing them to skin color. Apart from pointing to the essentialism of the term, Asian Americans also found it barely exhaustive of various shades of colors within their community. In 1968 Asian American students organized an "Are You Yellow?" conference at UCLA (Espiritu 32). The conference revolved around the construction of their collective identity, the Yellow Power movement and the war in Vietnam. 1970 saw the birth of the new pan Asian organization, which called itself "Yellow Seed." In 1972 Asian American activists gave up the "yellow" label because they concluded that the term was not all embracing enough. Defining themselves as brown, the Filipinos felt excluded (Espiritu 32). Thus "Asian American" emerged as the term including all Americans of Asian descent.

The narrator's second brush with executive whiteness occurs when she works for a land developers' association. The exchange is much more elaborate both on the narrator's and on her employer's part. At the root of the dispute lies the boss's decision to host a banquet for the real estate establishment at the restaurant boycotted by CORE and the NAACP. After hearing from the boss that he chose this particular location intentionally, precisely because it is boycotted by African American organizations on account of its racist policies, the narrator "whisper[s]," her "voice unreliable": "I refuse to type these invitations" (58). The narrator again questions the impact of her own voice,[23] but on this occasion the narrator's voice and her words elicit a response because they stand in opposition to the boss's orders. Responding to the breach of his orders, the boss announces to the narrator that she is fired: "He leaned back in his leather chair, his bossy stomach opulent. He picked up his calendar and slowly circled a date. 'You will be paid up to here,' he said. 'We'll mail you the check'" (58). Introducing the theme of her confrontations with white executives, the narrator speaks of "each boss two feet taller and impossible to meet eye to eye" (57). Repeatedly stressing the size of racist executives, the narrator metaphorically illustrates their power to dominate. The executive who fires her has a "bossy," "opulent" stomach (58), resembling fat barons who oppress the poor in Chinese fairy tales recounted by the narrator.

Rather than limit herself to presenting the factual account of the confrontation with the second racist executive, the narrator imagines an alternative ending of the encounter, the one that does not result in her leaving of the firm and the boss staying at his post. Imagining herself as the swordswoman, the narrator produces the sword out of the air and guts the boss in order to "put color and wrinkles into his shirt" (58). Unlike the previous executive who relishes naming color with the help of racist terminology, this executive is textualized as colorless. The executive's immaculate white shirt constitutes part of a modern American guise which the narrator mentioned several paragraphs earlier in the passage devoted to identifying the enemy. The whiteness of his shirt underscores the boss's white racial identity to which he clings so desperately by disassociating himself from black people. Spilling her employer's blood, the narrator symbolically taints his whiteness and his racial purity, forcing him to see his own color at the moment of death. The spilling of red blood, circulating through the veins of all human beings no matter what their skin color, upon the executive's white shirt also exposes whiteness as performance rather than unadulterable essence.

Both "white executive" episodes illustrate the power of whiteness to exclude and include certain groups of people. Despite nursing prejudice against African Americans, neither of the executives in question objects to hiring a person of Asian American descent.[24] By intervening on behalf of African Americans, the narrator disavows the position of a model minority subject. She also manifests her racial solidarity and pays back a debt going back to her school days, when African American children defended her against Japanese American students, whom the narrator describes as noisy and tough (193). She remembers her admiration for African American children ("Black Ghosts") who, unlike her, spoke out without any inhibition and brimmed over with joy (192).

Taking a retrospective look at her narrative strategies in *The Woman Warrior* and anticipating the publication of *The Fifth Book of Peace*, Maxine Hong Kingston brings up the second employer episode, regarding it as one of the most important in the book. Still, she has second thoughts on her construction of the scene: "it took no more than a paragraph to write that. Can the same scene be done more dramatically? So that when a reader reads it, it stands out more than the story of getting on the horse and riding into battle?" (Schroeder's Interview with Kingston 222). Uttering these words, Kingston re-examines her narrative techniques, expressing an awareness that to some extent combat scenes liken the narrator to her oppressors. Fighting oppression, she uses similar tools to her oppressors. Liberating as the stories of women warriors are for women, they do not give them real power. Liberation through fake or real war is only illusory. Foreshadowing *The Fifth Book of Peace*, Kingston claims that she searches for a more dramatic language of peace, not war: "I'm trying to find the peace language.... I'm trying to find a way to show acts of peace that are as dramatic as acts of war" (Schroeder's 1998 Interview with Kingston 222). Apart from illustrating the mode of peaceful resistance,[25] the executive episodes show the narrator's resistance to white power and racism in the narrator's life rather than her dreams.

The Woman Warrior also exposes the *dispossessing* face of whiteness. Historically, whiteness cautiously guarded access to property. In her article "Whiteness as Property" (1993), Cheryl Harris sees whiteness itself as property and as a property closely protected by its bearers. Hedging privileges attached to their whiteness, white people created an "exclusive club," afraid lest unwanted intruders compromise its exclusivity (Harris 1736). Very much in line with Harris's reasoning, George Lipsitz speaks of whiteness in *The Possessive Investment in Whiteness* (1998) in terms of a "possessive investment" in privileges that accrue to their whiteness (Lipsitz 1). *The Woman Warrior* exposes the implication of whiteness in the dispossession of the narrator's parents through redrafting of urban space. Working at a land developers' association, the narrator finds herself in a very complex position because the real estate business is responsible for the dispossession of her parents. Urban renewal deprives the narrator's parents of the laundry, tearing it down to make room for a parking lot (57). Brave Orchid tersely comments on the loss: "Those Urban Renewal ghosts gave us moving money. It took us seventeen years to get our customers. How could we start all over on moving money, as if we two old people had another seventeen years in us?" (122). The fact that urban renewal gives the narrator's parents relocation money indicates that they are treated like disposable objects that can be moved from one location to another as if they had not developed any bonds to their place of work and residence.

The tearing down of the narrator's family laundry is the direct result of the above mentioned urban renewal, also known as urban restructuring. Urban restructuring diametrically redesigned the urban landscape, deeply affecting various racial and ethnic minorities inhabiting the urban core. The underlying reason behind urban restructuring was the process of suburbanization or, in other words, white people's flight to the suburbs. Reaching mass proportions in the 1950s, suburbanization was spurred by a myriad of factors. After World War II American families were experiencing the baby boom. Seeking more and more space, they turned outside central cities, towards inexpensive land in the suburbs (Massey and Denton 44). Increasing numbers of black people inside the cities were another factor that pushed white inhabitants away from the urban core. The Federal Housing Agency shaped the racial make-up of the cities by directing loans away from inner cities towards white home buyers purchasing houses in the suburbs (Lipsitz 5–6). Suburbanization triggered urban restructuring geared to the needs of the suburbs. Newly constructed highways connected the suburbs to daytime offices of people who worked there during the day and left the city at night. Communities of color found themselves caught in the middle of urban restructuring.[26]

The negative consequences of urban restructuring reverberated across American Chinatowns. Small family businesses as well as low rent apartments inhabited by people of color often had to make place for high-rise projects, financial centres and highways. In an interview with Paul Skenazy, Maxine Hong Kingston reports an even more drastic case of dispossession and neighborhood splintering than that depicted in *The Woman Warrior*. The urban development tore down the block which was the focal point of her hometown Stockton Chinatown, the only easily identifiable landmark of the spread out community. The ostensible purpose was to make room for a freeway, which never saw its completion, but stopped precisely at the Stockton Chinatown. No car ever turned up on the highway, so the demolition of the block served no other purpose than to break up the neighborhood even further. Kingston calls the affair an "insult," also speculating why the freeway was never completed: the lack of funds, "politics," "zoning" or undefinable "something" (Skenazy's 1989 Interview with Kingston, "Coming Home" 115). Leaving possible explanations aside, she says: "Then you get this paranoia" (115). "Paranoia" suggests a more invidious motivation for the rupturing of the Chinatown neighborhood.

In *Longtime Californ': A Documentary Study of an American Chinatown*, Victor and Brett de Bary Nee report a case bearing similarity to that involving the loss of the laundry by the narrator's parents. In both cases Chinatown space is needed for the construction of a new parking lot. The case cited by Victor and Brett de Bary Nee in *Longtime Californ'* does not involve the demolition of a laundry but of a hotel, the two-story International Hotel on San Francisco's Kearney Street, providing housing for one hundred and sixty permanent residents of diverse races and ethnicities, most of them elderly men: Filipinos, Chinese, a few unemployed white people and an unemployed black man (de Bary Nee 389). The initiative to pull down the hotel came in 1968 from the owner of the hotel, Walter J. Shorenstein, chairman and chief stockholder of Milton Meyer, Inc. With the help of community and student organizations, the hotel was temporarily saved. Still, the owner of the hotel introduced unfavourable lease terms, which led to the incurrence of a substantial deficit by 1971 (de Bary Nee 391). In the International Hotel case residents of the Hotel were supported in their struggle against the white corporation by the Chinese American community. Yet in some cases, Chinese Americans were complicit in the dispossession of other Chinese Americans, for example in the New York Chinatown of the 1980s the Chinatown Planning Council, founded in the mid-1960s by second generation Chinese Americans to defend community interests, backed real estate developers rather than promote community interests (Kwong 133). The protest groups resisting the construction of new high-rise projects, which were tearing apart the communities, received no support from the Chinatown Planning Council. Instead of catering to the needs of the community, the Council favoured urban renewal plans forwarded by Mayor Edward Koch (Kwong 133). Critics of the Council argue that its strategy should come as no surprise if one considers its external sources of funding (Kwong 136).

The loss of the laundry suffered by the narrator's parents in California is the second loss of the laundry in the family. The narrator alludes to the prior loss of the laundry suffered by her father when he lives in New York, but the reader never finds out the circumstances under which the loss takes place. Both losses are classified in the narrative as two of the many wrongs committed against the narrator's family both in China and the United States. It is only in *China Men* that the narrator reveals that the father is tricked out of the New York laundry by his Chinese American business partners.

All works analyzed in this book expose the dispossessing face of whiteness and its controlling grip on property relations. The Nakane family of Joy Kogawa's *Obasan* irretrievably loses all property after the internment, including homes and fishing boats that are impounded never to be recovered again. As I argue in Chapter 4, drawing on the historical research of Donald C. Goellnicht and Marie Lo, economic reasons lie behind the very internment itself. While the official explanation was that Japanese Canadians posed a military threat, the most probable cause for the internment was the fear of racial difference and economic competition, mostly from Japanese Canadian fishermen (Goellnicht, "Minority History as Metafiction" 288). The Rhees of Leonard Chang's *The Fruit 'N Food* lose their store in the 1990s riots against Korean Americans. As illustrated in Chapter 3, whiteness is ostensibly absent from the conflict between African Americans and Korean Americans, but it is an instigating force in the dispute.

The critique of whiteness in *The Woman Warrior* interweaves with the critique of the United States as a country whose most severe critics are first generation immigrants. Their vision receives special scrutiny in the "At the Western Palace" chapter. Focalized through the viewpoint of first generation immigrants, "At the Western Palace" provides one more signification of the term "ghost." "Ghosts" of the chapter denote primarily dehumanization traced both in white Americans and in those Chinese Americans who consciously renounce their Chinese relatives and acquaintances. The characterization of the United States as "the land of ghosts" signifies the land of people who significantly compromised, if not totally breached, the ties with other human beings, especially those whom they should particularly treasure on account of preexisting bonds, for instance family ties. An embodiment of such an individual is Moon Orchid's husband, who succeeds in the United States as a neurosurgeon, but disclaims personal contacts with his Chinese wife and daughter, providing for them, yet shunning all personal contact. Commenting on his arrogant, irreverent attitude to the wife and daughter, the narrator reflects: "Her husband looked like one of the ghosts passing the car windows, and she must look like a ghost from China. They had indeed entered the land of ghosts, and they had become ghosts" (178). "At the Western Palace" presents the United States as a country that has the power of estranging people from each other. Unlike all other chapters of *The Woman Warrior*, "At the Western Palace" is narrated from the third person selective omniscient point of view, intensifying a sense of distance between people and indicating the narrator's distance towards the depicted events. The narrator does not participate in all of these events directly, but reports what she has heard.

The harshest criticism of the American reality comes from the chief representative of first generation immigrants—Brave Orchid. It needs to be stressed that Brave Orchid's definitions of the American and Chinese reality are contingent upon each other. The valorization of one usually signifies the disparagement of the other. Brave Orchid portrays the United States as a country of gruelling work for immigrants like herself and for white Americans born in the United States alike:

> This is a terrible ghost country, where a human being works her life away.... Even the ghosts [white people] work, no time for acrobatics (122).... I can't sleep in this country because it doesn't shut down for the night. Factories, canneries, restaurants—always somebody somewhere working through the night. It never gets done all at once here [123–124].

Brave Orchid's indictment of the American labor market comes soon after she complains about the loss of the laundry and the "Urban Renewal Ghosts" giving her relocation money. Criticizing the United States, Brave Orchid ruminates on her life back in pre–Revolutionary China, where time dragged and where she did not need to do any menial work. The reader can infer from the context of the whole work that the specific period of Brave Orchid's Chinese life to which she refers is the time when she practiced medicine after graduating from medical school. It is during her medical practise that she enjoys popular esteem in her own community. Criticism of austere labor conditions in the United States does not make Brave Orchid pause on power relations in pre–Revolutionary China. She does not have any qualms of conscience about having a slave. Brave Orchid's discourse on pre–Revolutionary China is inconsistent if we take into account that on the one hand, she presents her family as basking in opulence, while on the other, she also remembers the lean years of hunger and poverty in the "No Name Woman" chapter. Immigration to the United States degrades Brave Orchid to abject employment in the laundry and to arduous physical labor. Drawing a sharp contrast between her life in pre–Revolutionary China and in the United States, Brave Orchid declares that the passage of time is different in both countries. In the United States she always runs out of time, while in China time drags for her. Lamenting over her life in the United States, Brave Orchid uses the present tense to characterize the Chinese reality, freezing pre–Revolutionary China in time as if it still existed without the ascendance of Communism with its concomitant repressions, of which Brave Orchid reads in letters from her Chinese relatives. Her appraisal of China over the United States takes a sharp turn when Brave Orchid avers that there will be no return to China, recognizing the irrevocability of her family's residence in the United States. Making a virtue of necessity, she also announces that she is not interested in going back because she has "gotten used to eating" (125). After announcing that there will be no return to China, Brave Orchid also makes disparaging statements about the Chinese, accusing them of mischief and stealing. Lumping all Chinese together, in a similar way to her lumping of white people together and labeling them as "ghosts," Brave Orchid labels all Chinese newcomers as Communists. She pays little attention to the narrator's assertions that the Chinese newcomers are not Communists but fugitives from Communism.

Brave Orchid's ruminations on whiteness and Americanness come in the "Shaman" chapter of *The Woman Warrior*. Listening to her mother's complaints, the narrator refuses to cooperate, playing down her criticism, claiming that Brave Orchid's physical exhaustion in the United

States stems from the fact that she gave birth to six children after turning forty five (124). The narrator's stance is strikingly different than her stance in the preceding "White Tigers" chapter, in which she displays the most critical attitude. The recurring trope of the chapter is resistance to oppression, both in imperial China and the United States of the 1950s and 1960s.

The very title "White Tigers" implies potential rapacity. By definition, the tiger is a predatory animal. The tigers encountered by the narrator as the embodiment of Fa Mu Lan in the mountains of the white tigers are very meek. They are "prowling" on the other side of the fire, but they never charge against her (30). If treated symbolically, the white tigers may represent not only the tigers "prowling" in the mountains of the white tigers, but also oppressive forces which the narrator and her family confront in the American world (30). The mountains of the white tigers conjure up associations of the Gold Mountain, signifying the United States in immigrant jargon.[27] The narrator's tests in the mountains of the white tigers may stand for immigrant tests in the United States. Blindfolded in the mountains of the white tigers, the narrator needs to find her way home (29). Similarly, she has to map out her own place in the Chinese American community and the American world outside Chinatown. It is also significant that the narrator opens and closes the "White Tigers" chapter with her American experience, at the end explicitly comparing the performance of her Chinese alter ego with her own performance in the United States.

The connection between the mythic and American section of the chapter is further corroborated by the sources on which Kingston draws in the mythic section. Cheng Lok Chua claims that the Chinese compass includes four beasts and each of them stands for a particular element. The white tiger rules in the West and controls metals—a "useful element for warriors" (Chua 147). Chua cites two different accounts of the compass beasts tale. According to one account, all four beasts are tigers, each of them a different color: red, black, blue and white. Another account of the tale names four different animals of different colors: the vermilion phoenix, the black turtle, the azure dragon and the white tiger. According to Chua, Kingston draws on the latter account. It is significant that in both versions the white tiger reigns in the West. The "white tigers" guarding the riches of the American West are not nearly so benign as those encountered by the narrator as Fa Mu Lan's embodiment in the mountains of the white tigers. The relation between the white tigers and white people is further confirmed by the fact that tigers have a special significance in Chinese folklore. Ethnologist and philologist N.B. Dennys claims that tigers are perceived as demons or ghosts, both phrases also applied to white people and foreigners (91).[28]

The tiger metaphor employed in reference to the United States had circulated in Chinese American and Chinese literature long before Kingston reached for it in *The Woman Warrior*. The metaphor goes back to the poem of an anonymous Chinese immigrant who at the beginning of the twentieth century complains against the austerity of American laws and the treatment which he receives from American officials. The poem was originally published in Chinese in 1911, in *Songs from Gold Mountain* and translated by Marlon Kau Hom in "Some Cantonese Folksongs on the American Experience," *Western Folklore* 42 (1983):132 (Arkush and Lee 58). The imagery of incarceration and visual supervision recurs throughout the poem. A line of the poem reads: "American laws are fierce like tigers" (Arkush and Lee 58). Being thrown into San Francisco prison immediately after arriving in the United States, the anonymous Chinese immigrant declares American liberties false. Prison officials are compared to wolves and tigers, whereas Chinese prisoners to birds "plunged into an open trap" (Arkush and Lee 58). The term "tiger" was also applied to the United States by travelers from the People's Republic of China. Still, the "tiger" no longer signified might, but was applied in such a way as to mock the putative prowess of the United States. Anti-American Communist propaganda essays include such sentences as for example "Look with contempt upon the United States, for she is a paper tiger and can fully be defeated" (Arkush and Lee 246). The repertoire of the Beijing street theatre included a play entitled "Paper Tiger," also maligning the United States and going as far as to compare American soldiers to Nazis.

Immediately after relating her adventures as the avatar of Fa Mu Lan, the narrator expresses disenchantment at falling short of Fa Mu Lan's success: "My American life has been such a disappointment" (54). A moment of sadness is followed by a reflection on the disparity of resources at their disposal. The asset that both the narrator and her fairy-tale alter ego can claim is the gift of second sight, which the narrator overtly attributes to the wisdom derived from fairy tales: "From the fairy tales, I've learned exactly who the enemy are" (57). What follows the passage is the already discussed confrontation with racist executives. Both the narrator's Fa Mu Lan alter ego and the narrator herself are hypersensitive to injustice, be it racism or sexism. Prejudice suffered by the narrator outside Chinatown and verbal denigration of women inside Chinatown sensitize her to various forms of oppression.

The mythic section of "White Tigers" repeatedly underscores the importance of sight and recognition. The narrator as Fa Mu Lan's embodiment "can see behind [her] like a bat" (36). "Seeing behind" symbolizes the completeness of vision, 360° vision. It protects the narrator from any mischief on the part of her enemies. The narrator as Fa Mu Lan evinces outstanding visual powers when, after being taken blindfolded to the mountains of the white tigers, she still manages to find her way home. The blindfold on her eyes does not prevent her from dodging precipices, roots and trees. Before confronting her opponents, she can see them in a magic water gourd. Magic as the water gourd is, it requires cooperation on the part of the seer. Initially, while peering into the gourd, the narrator can see nothing but her own reflection (27). Only after being shaken, does the gourd reveal its magic content, the indication being that to be able to see, one must first learn to look. The water gourd vision can also be deceptive because it misrepresents the properties of reflected images. Once confronted in combat, the narrator's opponents prove to be much more serious than in the water gourd. The common feature of the narrator's fairy-tale and American enemies is their physical size. The general whom she defeats on the battlefield is a man of towering height (45). Invoking her ability to recognize the "enemy" in the American context, she speaks of "each boss two feet taller than [she is]" (57). Like the opulently shaped barons whom she slaughters in the fairy-tale world, the second executive with whom she has a verbal skirmish is a gentleman with a bulging stomach (58). By accentuating particular physical features of oppressive figures, she emphasizes their dominating stance. Still, she also partly becomes embroiled in othering practices herself, essentializing people with certain physical characteristics.

The narrator proper may have no magic water gourd, yet she also possesses exceptional powers of perception. Having lived in two different worlds: Chinatown and American society outside Chinatown, the narrator has the ability to see what may escape the eyesight of other people. Access to both worlds empowers the narrator, broadening her perspective. In Du Bois's double consciousness formula second sight is the reverse side of the veil. The veil symbolizes primarily alienation and marginalization of racial and ethnic minorities in the United States. As mentioned earlier, the narrator suffers double marginalization: as a woman in Chinatown and as a Chinese American in broader American society. Her second sight is the reverse positive side of the "double binds" that "China wraps around [her] feet" (57). The "double binds" are an equivalent of the Duboisian double consciousness. Chinese American prescience is contrasted in *The Woman Warrior* with the dimmed senses of white people: "ghosts could not hear or see very well" (115), "Ghosts have no memory"[29] ... and poor eyesight" (215). Black people, on the other hand, are perceived by the narrator as "open eyed and full of laughter" (113). Speaking of the burden of the "double binds," the narrator also recognizes the power stemming from her Chinese American descent, the power symbolized by eighty invisible ancestral pole fighters who propel her in all actions (58).

Kingston's sensitivity to various forms of oppression finds its way into her adaptation of the Fa Mu Lan tale. The Fa Mu Lan of *The Woman Warrior* identifies and defies diverse manifestations of feudalism and patriarchy. Feudalism manifests itself in the narrative through financial exploitation as well as forced military conscription of poor villagers by oppressive barons. Feudalism and patriarchy intersect in the narrative, complementing each other. The most graphic indictment of feudalism intersecting with patriarchy comes in the following lines: "fat men ate meat; fat men drank wine made from the rice; fat men sat on naked little girls. I watched powerful men count their money, and starving men count theirs" (36). The crowning of the peasant rebellion originated and executed by the narrator as Fa Mu Lan is the enthroning of a peasant as the next emperor of China. Cynthia Sau-ling Wong notes that the Fa Mu Lan of the original ballad[30] is not equally class conscious. Instead of identifying with the underprivileged, she represents the establishment (Sau-ling Wong, "Autobiography as Guided Chinatown Tour" 33). Wong points out that the original Fa Mu Lan embodies the patriarchal spirit (33). The Fa Mu Lan of *The Woman Warrior* revolts against patriarchy at various points of the narrative, for example during the engraving of her back and during the anti-feudal military campaign, especially during the confrontation with one of the barons.

The tale of the woman warrior, Fa Mu Lan, inspires the narrator to action and to resisting oppression which she has to confront on her home turf: "the swordswoman ... drives me" (56). Tracing similarity between the swordswoman and herself, the narrator observes that both have words at their backs. The words which the narrator finds at her back are: "report a crime," "report to five families," "'chink' words" and "'gook' words" (63). Unable to "rage across the United States to take back the laundry in New York and the one in California" as well as to "storm across China to take back [their] farm from the Communists" (58), she can still forge her vengeance through the words out of which she constructs the narrative. Words are her vengeance and her weapon. In the narrative she also figuratively calls back slur words at her offenders.[31] Fighting with her words and drawing inspiration for action from the fairy-tale Chinese character, the narrator resembles Naomi Nakane, the Japanese Canadian first person narrator of Joy Kogawa's *Obasan*. Naomi derives inspiration from the Japanese fairy-tale character, Momotaro, who like Fa Mu Lan, goes to war instead of his elderly father.[32]

The mature narrator of *The Woman Warrior* constructs a comprehensive portrayal of the oppressive faces of whiteness, peeling away a layer after layer of oppression. The facets of oppression implicating whiteness are:

- corporate racism
- institutional racism
- segregation
- dispossessing practices originating in urban restructuring
- the controlling stake of whiteness in property relations
- exploitative labor practices affecting both immigrants and white people as well.

The critique of whiteness overlaps with the critique of Americanness and the United States as a country, both being presented by first generation Chinese American immigrants as potentially transformative in a negative sense. Exposing white oppression, the narrator makes it clear that oppression is by no means a prerogative of whiteness. White oppression inscribes itself in other patterns of oppression discussed in *The Woman Warrior*: Chinese and Chinese American sexism, patriarchy and feudalism. Being a word warrior, the narrator challenges various forms of oppression with words, documenting the trespasses against the Chinese American community, herself and other Chinese and Chinese American women. The narrative constitutes her most powerful weapon in the battle against white and nonwhite manifestations of oppression.

Imagery of Whiteness

After college I thought that I was a painter because I *always see pictures*, and *I see visions before the words come*, and it's always a secondary step to find the words. So at one time I thought that I could go directly from one picture to picture because *when I write I want the readers to see the pictures. So why not forget the words and just paint pictures?*—*Kay Bonetti's "Interview with Maxine Hong Kingston" 33, emphasis added*

words are a medium to get to the seemingly subconscious ... *visions don't just come full-blown and with details* such as chairs and clothes, and where everything is placed—the relationships between bodies in a room. All that becomes more and more accessible as I approach them with words. *Words clarify the vision and memory.... As I paint part of a vision, the next part of it becomes clear.* It's as if I am building the underpinnings of a bridge, and then I can cross it, *and see more and more clearly.*—*Paula Rabinowitz's "Eccentric Memories: A Conversation with Maxine Hong Kingston," emphasis added 68*

THERE'S NO SUCH THING as art for art's sake in non-white North America ... Asian American writers tread deliberately, for every image,

> every phrase, is likely to have lasting reverberations throughout the community.—*Karin Aguilar-San Juan 17, emphasis original*
>
> I mean to give people questions (which I think are very creative things)—and then when people wrestle with them and struggle with them in their own minds and in their own lives, all kinds of exciting things happen to them.—*Maxine Hong Kingston quoted in Silvia Schultermandl, "Writing Against the Grain" 120*

The representation of whiteness in *The Woman Warrior* extends into the imagery of the work. Consistent employment of whiteness in the imagery complements the portrait of whiteness emerging from the narrative, revealing the narrator's attitude to whiteness as well as shedding light on the functioning of whiteness in American society and the process of constructing whiteness as a socio-historical racial category. Whiteness conjures up predominantly negative associations in *The Woman Warrior*, signifying terror, death, insipidity, coldness, alienation and the lack of life and vibrancy. Through her construction of white imagery Kingston inverts associations of whiteness with normativity, the associations "express[ing] the vanity of the Caucasian race" (Birren cited in Adams 36). The imagery of whiteness inscribes itself in the consistent defamiliarization of whiteness in the narrative and the marking of its often camouflaged qualities.

As I argue in the introduction to the chapter, the postmodern, collagic, eccentric structure of *The Woman Warrior* contributes to the dispersion of whiteness into a multitude of images. These are:

- bones
- light
- all engulfing whiteness
- paper
- white masks and white bands
- coldness and iciness
- icicle in the desert
- black and white paintings
- pearls grown in oysters

Paper, bones, light, iciness and coldness are overarching tropes of this study, recurring in other works analyzed here. Whiteness is their explicit or implicit attribute. In some of them whiteness appears in tandem with blackness, exposing the dependence of whiteness for its construction on other racial categories. Aside from the tandemic characteristics of whiteness, the imagery of *The Woman Warrior* also reveals the oxymoronic qualities of the socio-historical construction of whiteness, its capacity to hold untenable contradictions. This capacity is best expressed through such images as the icicle in the desert and white pearls born out of black or grey oysters.

As illustrated in earlier sections of the chapter, at many points of the narrative Kingston overtly critiques whiteness and speaks explicitly about the semiotics of racial categories. The imagery of the narrative allows her to indirectly express her views. While one may not necessarily subscribe to Mieke Bal's statement that "the figural" "is the privileged site of contestation" (1291), it has to be acknowledged that Kingston extends contestation to the figurative language of the narrative. Initiating in 1992 contemporary whiteness studies and in particular the study of whiteness in American literature with her seminal work *Playing in the Dark*, Toni Morrison claims that writers "transform aspects of their social grounding into aspects of language" (4) and that "Knowledge however mundane and egalitarian plays about in linguistic images and forms cultural practice" (49). The second statement corresponds closely to the last opening epigraph by Filipina American sociologist Karin Aguilar-San Juan, who writes in 1994: "Asian American writers tread deliberately, for every image, every phrase is likely to have lasting reverberations throughout the community" (17). Echoing Clifford Geertz's *Local Knowledge*, Morrison focuses to a greater extent on the social sphere providing a stimulus for the creation of particular narrative imagery. Juan shifts the focus to the social ramifications stemming from narrative imagery of a work—the consequences for a particular community. Both note a very close overlap of the social and the aesthetic, an overlap, which is also very conspicuous in *The Woman Warrior*.

Terrorizing and Intrusive Whiteness

On the very first pages of the narrative whiteness features as an avatar of death, terror and fear. Kingston dresses Chinese terror in white. Chinese villagers attacking the No Name Woman's house wear white masks on their faces and white bands around their foreheads, arms and legs (4). The white trimming of their clothing is a clear indication of the intentions with which they arrive at the No Name Woman's house: to unleash death and destruction. This is also how their intentions are received by the inhabitants of the No Name Woman's house. The white color functions as a culturally specific sign employed by the raiding villagers to send a particular culturally specific signal read by the villagers according to a culturally determined code. The accents of their attire amplify what can be deduced from the situational context. Acquainted with the socio-cultural norms of their community, the No Name Woman's relatives know that the raid on the day of the No Name Woman's denouement is a punishment for what is perceived as her violation of aforementioned socio-cultural norms.[33] While the Chinese villagers invest white with a negative cultural signification, it does not invite any inauspicious associations to the immature narrator, who is puzzled at her parents' superstitions about wearing a white ribbon (215).

Apart from signifying death, terror, fear and destruction, whiteness featuring in the raid upon the No Name Woman's house once again appears in the context of unwanted intrusion. It is a different kind of intrusion and a different type of whiteness than in the passages depicting whiteness encroaching upon the perimeter of the immature narrator's house. Yet at this point the textualization of whiteness in the Chinese context of the narrative matches the textualization of whiteness in the American context. While in this study the raid on the No Name Woman's house is important because of its signification of whiteness, the passage attracted critical attention because of its portrayal of the Chinese. Toming Jun Liu compares the Chinese mob to the Ku Klux Klan. Extending the original meaning of the first chapter's title "No Name Woman," Liu speaks of the "no name Chinese" (9). According to Liu, the Chinese also "fit the description of the Yellow Peril: faceless and without individual identification" (9). I would like to argue that the en masse portrayal of the Chinese in the "No Name Woman" chapter can be explained through the overall purpose of the book—the individualization of Kingston's female narrator, particular Chinese and Chinese American women as well as voicing of their stories. The en masse characterization of the Chinese resembles the en masse characterization of white people whom the immature narrator encounters in childhood. Both lack individual features, presenting a mystery to the immature narrator. Kingston herself remains unabashed about her portrayal of Chinese Americans or the Chinese, claiming that those writers who take upon themselves to represent all members of a particular community produce "tourist manuals—chamber of commerce public relations whitewash" (Arturo Islas and Marilyn Yalom's "Interview with Maxine Hong Kingston" 21). She also emphasizes that the Chinese whom she describes belonged to a particular village, which was not necessarily "representative of all of the great, big China" (ibid 21–22).

Bland Whiteness

The imagery of whiteness brings out the qualities of whiteness highlighted by the narrative and discussed in earlier sections of the chapter.

One of the features attributed to whiteness by the immature narrator is its blandness and its lack of substance, life and vitality. As I argue in the first part of the chapter, such a portrayal of whiteness undermines the chief purpose of whiteness studies, which is to mark its qualities rather than present it as an ephemeral, indefinite blank. White people's indistinctness is best captured by the above cited passage contrasting white people ("white ghosts") and black people ("black ghosts"): "There were Black Ghosts too, but they were open eyed and full of laughter, more distinct than White Ghosts" (113). The same line of reasoning continues in the imagery characterizing the speechless Chinese American girl whom the immature narrator holds in contempt because she is her own alter ego, a mirror reflection of diffidence against which the narrator struggles. Introducing the speechless girl, the narrator draws the reader's attention to the white elements of her appearance: her white and pink face (206), "white ears, like white cutworms" (206), paper-like skin of her hands (206), small white teeth. For the immature narrator, all these features represent fragility, weakness and softness, the qualities despised by her. She looks up to Mexican and African American girls because of their toughness. Trying to emulate this toughness and reach the ideal of "tough, hard, brown skin," she roughens her hands and blackens her nails. The immature narrator's valorization of brown skin and denigration of white skin can be perceived as an essentialization and reification of skin, of investing skin with qualities often attributed to representatives of particular races and ethnicities.[34]

The employment of the skin trope is also an example of what Toni Morrison terms as fetishization, of "establishing fixed and major differences where difference does not exist or is minimal" (*Playing in the Dark* 68). Morrison enumerates fetishization as one of the "common linguistic strategies" applied by white authors to establish the presence of black people in their works (*Playing in the Dark* 68). Kingston is not a white author, but she reaches for the same strategy to express the immature narrator's attitude to whiteness and blackness. While white authors often use the strategy to reaffirm the superiority of white people over black people, Kingston employs the strategy to illustrate the immature narrator's admiration for blackness and her aversion to whiteness, the aversion amplified by the narrator's disparagement of the speechless girl's bright colored clothing: pastels and a white blouse (205). The narrator again expresses her predilection for blackness by claiming to always wear black.[35]

In the narrator's portrayal, the silent girl bears a close resemblance to a ghost. She seems to have no bones and muscles. Her perceived softness, fragility and ethereality add to her ghostlike appearance, once again relating her to whiteness, since, as demonstrated above, the term "ghost" signifies, among others, white people. Beyond rendering the girl's physical features, her description as boneless reaffirms an air of indistinctness around her. Bonelessness may stand for the lack of character and clearly articulated views. Such associations originate primarily in the girl's speechlessness. Trying to convince the girl to speak, the narrator tells her that silence implies brainlessness and the lack of personality. The narrator herself is designated a zero intelligence quotient in her kindergarten because of her inability to speak English. Now she assigns a similar categorization to the silent girl, calling her "such a nothing" (207), comparing her to an animal (209) and a plant (210). The silent girl's ambivalent status in the eyes of the immature narrator is underscored through her namelessness. She is another no name figure[36] in *The Woman Warrior*. Considering that the narrator has some knowledge of the silent girl's family, it is much more probable that the she does not reveal the silent girl's name because she chooses not to rather than because she does not know it. The withholding of the silent girl's name is one of the points relating the narrative to nonfiction.[37] Since the silent girl's family presumably also exists in the extratextual reality, the narrator will not reveal their name.

It is significant that the narrator leaves a white thumbprint on the silent girl's forehead (205). Engaging in the persecution of the silent girl, the narrator mimics white oppression, which she so categorically reprehends in the narrative. She may try to emulate other racial and ethnic minorities in their appearance, but through her behavior directed against the silent girl, she reenacts white oppression. Taking a retrospective look at her persecution of the silent Chinese American girl, the mature narrator is aware of reverse power dynamics at play. She describes the voice in which she speaks to the silent girl as the voice in which one speaks "to the familiar, the weak, and the small" (204). Ironically, an attempt to elicit speech from the silent girl is accompanied by a simultaneous injunction not to tell anyone about the bullying incident. An admonition not to tell anyone often goes cheek by jowl with personal oppression. The same admonition also occurs in one of the versions of the No Name Woman story envisioned by the narrator, constituting one more point of intersection between both no name female figures of the narrative.

The No Name Woman's child is portrayed in similar terms as the speechless Chinese American girl. Both lack substance and hence are associated with whiteness and ghostliness. The speechless girl is referred to as "boneless," while the No Name Woman's child is "full of milk": "Full of milk, the little ghost slept" (17). Implying the lack of courage and character, bonelessness corresponds to the liquidity of milk, suggesting the lack of substance and solidity.[38] Born out of wedlock at the time of famine, the No Name Woman's female infant has no right to exist in the Chinese community governed by stringent communal laws. Female children were denigrated in Chinese families. Because of its illegitimate status, the No Name Woman's female child faces additional ostracism. The child is insubstantial for the Chinese community outside whose perimeter she was born. The community denies the child a definition, reducing it to a ghost-like status. Being the child of the No Name Woman, the child is also nameless.

Reflecting on her own writing, Kingston claims that she "want[s] the readers to see the pictures" (Kay Bonetti's "Interview with Maxine Hong Kingston" 33). Whiteness is part of the pictures created by the author and seen by the reader even if it does not appear explicitly as a word. Kingston's construction of the imagery of whiteness exemplifies her postmodern aesthetics. As a postmodern author, Kingston envisions writerly/scriptible works of literature, placing the reader in the position of a co-author rather than a passive consumer. Her readers are to complete her word painted visions with their own imagination. She also takes the concept of a writerly text further, going beyond a strictly textual sphere of production and reception. Apart from filling her works with their own imagination, her readers are also to complete them with their own deeds: "finish up using his or her own words and deeds" (Kingston, "The Novel's Next Step" 41). Allowing the readers to participate in the production of her works and leaving some interpretations open-ended, Kingston still admits that she wants to elicit particular responses from her readers (ibid 41). Her works are a resounding call to action.

Coldness

Whiteness of *The Woman Warrior* is an explicit or implicit attribute of the images related to coldness. As Aristotle points out in 1 BC, "cold is the mother of whiteness" (Aristotle cited in Taylor 394). "Cold" does not signify for Aristotle only a cold climate or cold temperature, but also what he terms as a "cold nature" of certain people (Aristotle cited in Taylor 394).[39] In line with the textualization of whiteness in *The Woman Warrior*, coldness, iciness and frostiness represent desensitization, inhospitality and alienation. Being explicitly linked to whiteness, coldness conjures up these associations in the passages highlighting the alienating power of whiteness:

- the passage in which the immature narrator is stranded alone in the mountains of white tigers

- the passage recounting Brave Orchid's lonely medical call ventures in snowy, frosty conditions creating the landscape of all-encompassing whiteness

Coldness invites parallel connotations in the images entailing whiteness albeit not bringing it up explicitly. An example of such an image is the "icy bone" of the narrator's head (126). The narrator constructs the icy bone metaphor to illustrate the powerful effect of her mother's words. Pleading with the mature narrator to stay in Chinatown, Brave Orchid "is etching spider legs into the icy bone," "pr[ying] open [her] head" (126). Contrasting with sensitive parts of one's body like flesh, skin and internal organs, "bone" is the hard matter difficult to penetrate. The juxtaposition of bone with ice magnifies its desensitized quality. Parallel imagery of coldness, desensitization and whiteness is part of the description of the interior design inside the medical practice of Moon Orchid's husband. While in the image of the "icy bone" whiteness is an implicit, hidden attribute and coldness an explicit one, in the case of the interior design the situation is reverse. Whiteness is its explicit attribute producing the effect of coldness and desensitization: "The wallpaper ... was like aluminum foil, a metallic background for a tall black frame around white paint with dashes of red" (171). Metallic and tinfoil connotations reinforce the vision created by "At the Western Palace," the vision of coldness characterizing interpersonal relations in the United States. The last image bringing together coldness and whiteness is an image of a chill out produced by ghost stories told in the narrator's family laundry on the most torrid summer afternoons. The phrase "a chill" originates from the narrator's mother or father, who, with the ascent of a high temperature, announces that it is time for a ghost story that will send "good chills up [everyone's] backs" (102). The relation of whiteness to coldness is established through "ghosts," a major trope of *The Woman Warrior* and an overarching metaphor of my chapter. White people are one of the chief referents hidden under the term "ghosts." Still, it needs to be pointed out that whiteness is not the referent that the narrator's father conjures up at this point. Therefore, the relation of coldness to whiteness in this instance is fairly remote.

Light

A significant portion of whiteness imagery in *The Woman Warrior* is closely associated with light. The white color in itself has a very specific relation to light, being the only color reflecting all wavelengths (Adams

33). The very etymology of the term "white" links it firmly to light. Ronald W. Casson reconstructs the etymology of the term "white," tracing its derivation from the Indo-European root "kweit," that is, "white, to shine" (227). The Old English reflex of "white" was "hwit," which signified first of all the level of brightness. The hue[40] sense of "hwit" was secondary to brightness, appearing in the following hue denotations:

- "colorless, uncolored" traced back to 888
- hair and complexion color traced back to 900
- snow and milk color traced to 950 (Casson 227).[41]

According to Gary Taylor, the original meaning of "white" as a reference to the racial category also pertains to "light or light sources," signifying primarily brightness (76). Light and the white color have a special connection to each other in *The Woman Warrior* as well. Although light has predominantly positive associations in the narrative, it becomes blinding in conjunction with white. Light has a positive signification when it is tinted with gold or yellow. Kingston's valorization of yellow over white in the construction of the light imagery exemplifies her critical multicultural aesthetics, overlapping with the ideological layer of her work. The aesthetics of *The Woman Warrior* inscribes itself in the questioning of whiteness and valorization of other racial categories.[42] The best illustration of the above discussed situation is the scene in which the narrator as Fa Mu Lan's embodiment has a multicultural, egalitarian vision of two dancers, who first appear as figures of gold and light, representing diverse people of the Earth united in one dance. Towards the end of the vision the dancers are transformed into tall white angels whose brightness blinds the narrator: "I cannot bear their brightness and cover my eyes" (32). The narrator was not blinded by the dancers' brightness when it manifested itself through "gold" (32). It is only after whiteness joins the array of colors that their brightness becomes blinding. The blinding whiteness of the dancers does not match the raw blinding whiteness of a lobotomy machine in Ralph Ellison's *Invisible Man* or the whiteness which blinds Tom Pak in Leonard Chang's *The Fruit 'N Food* in his dreams, but it still hurts the eyes of the narrator. In Joy Kogawa'a *Obasan* light is also often blinding in combination with whiteness, yet it is not the rule.

An appraisal of light in terms of gold rather than white is visible in the passage following the multicultural dance vision. Reminiscing on the vision of multicultural dancers, the narrator claims that protracted hunger always makes her see "light and gold" in other people (33). In a similar vein, the narrator as the embodiment of Fa Mu Lan can see an "orange and warm" face of her mother while looking into the fire (31).[43] The only instance of the valorization of light in terms of white takes place when the narrator declares that in case she was flogged, the "light would shine through [her] like lace" (41). Originating from the words of revenge and resentment inscribed on the narrator's back by her family, the radiance emitting from her body would be a sign of sacrifice, martyrdom and distinction as well as a source of protection, the narrator's shield.[44]

Paper

A significant image implicitly entailing whiteness in *The Woman Warrior* is paper. Paper is also an important trope recurring in other works analyzed here: Kingston's *China Men*, *The Fifth Book of Peace* and Kogawa's *Obasan*. Serving primarily as a vehicle for the word, paper is a vital instrument of *commemoration, communication and legitimization*. Paper features as a tool of commemoration in the No Name Woman's tale. A Chinese custom obliged family members of a deceased person to honor their relative through paper offerings: paper suits, paper dresses, paper spirit money, paper houses and paper cars. In *The Folklore of China*, N.B. Dennys provides detailed accounts of how paper was applied in consecutive stages of commemoration. Paper representations of objects and animals which may be of service to the deceased were burnt during a funeral ceremony (24). Sixty days after the funeral a paper image of a deceased person was hauled by a paper crane to facilitate the passage into the afterlife. The family of the No Name Woman does not honor her after death to mete out punishment for an alleged transgression against community norms. Therefore, according to Chinese beliefs, the No Name Woman does not enjoy the privileges of other spirits because no relatives worship her. Expressing affinity for the forgotten aunt and honoring her courage to transcend borders, the narrator tries to correct the fifty-year neglect of the No Name Woman's spirit and memory:

> My aunt haunts me—her ghost drawn to me because now, after fifty years of neglect, I alone devote pages of paper to her, though not origamied into houses and clothes. I do not think she always means me well. I am telling on her, and she was a spite suicide, drowning herself in the drinking water [19].

The narrator's purpose in telling the No Name Woman's tale is not only to correct the wrongs against the No Name Woman and to recover her lost name, but also to reestablish the ancestral link with the relative whom the narrator perceives as her forerunner, one of the first in the family to transcend boundaries "not delineated in space" (9). Through the figure of the No Name Woman the narrator forges a link between the land of her ancestors and her homeland—the United States. The motif of reconnecting to dead relatives through paper and the written word links the narrator of *The Woman Warrior* to another first person narrator belonging to this study—Naomi Nakane of Joy Kogawa's *Obasan*. Both want to recapture the broken filial link. However, while the rupture of family ties in *Obasan* comes from without, being thrust by external forces, the fissure in the No Name Woman's family comes from within. Unlike Naomi Nakane, who herself suffers graphic oppression, the narrator of *The Woman Warrior* is not herself directly a victim of the wrongs afflicted upon the No Name Woman. For twenty years she herself participates in the conspiracy of silence around her aunt, breaking it only in the narrative.

Apart from serving as a tool of commemoration, paper functions in *The Woman Warrior* as a means of communication between the characters separated by continents and generations. As in Joy Kogawa's *Obasan*, the communicative role of paper is realized primarily through letters. Yet this communication is not always successful or satisfying to both sides. As in *Obasan*, this is partial communication, but partial in a different way. Most of the epistolary exchanges take place between the narrator's Chinatown family and their Chinese family left behind in China. The letters arriving during and after the years of the Revolution of 1949 carry bad news, relating atrocities perpetrated by the Communists on the narrator's Chinese relatives. The narrator's parents are unwilling recipients of the letters. They would like to be spared the gory details of the calamities that befell their relatives. They also feel guilty about being safe, while others fall victim to Communist repressions. Their trauma associated with Chinese correspondence is such that they dread to open it unless it arrives on red festive paper, which cannot convey any bad news. Since many of the letters are pleading letters, carrying requests for money, there is a suspicion that that the relatives at times magnify their suffering to extract money. The context of correspondence between the characters separated by continents is markedly different than in Joy Kogawa's *Obasan*. Unlike the narrator's Chinese relatives, Naomi's Japanese relatives play down their suffering not to add to the problems facing the Nakanes in the United States. Naomi Nakane's grandmother effaces her own pain, focusing on the suffering of others. Drawing parallels between the figurative employment of paper in *The Woman Warrior* and *Obasan*, it is essential to note that both paper and its whiteness feature more explicitly in *Obasan* than they do in *The Woman Warrior*.

The narrator of *The Woman Warrior* envisions a different kind of correspondence between herself and her Chinese grandmother. The narrator's parents are identified mainly as unwilling recipients of letters and dispatchers of money rather than authors of correspondence. The narrator, on the other hand, is eager to recapture a spiritual bond with relatives in China, imagining herself as an author of correspondence. She dreams of a letter air-floating to her grandmother, who must receive it or otherwise they "will lose each other" (60). In the same dream she sees herself as "wire without flesh," which indicates that she is severed from part of her heritage (60). In a similar vein, the narrator of *Obasan* compares her dead mother's letters to "skeletons" and "bones," the only remainder of the mother's bodily presence, the "bone marrow" that remains after the flesh is gone (292). The last example of a letter in *The Woman* Warrior, albeit not written on paper, comes in the form of the word engraving on the narrator's (as Fa Mu Lan's embodiment) back. As mentioned above, the engraving is supposed to be testimony to the sacrifice of her family and her own sacrifice.

Finally, paper appears in *The Woman Warrior* as an instrument of legitimization. Authentication via the means of often fake papers was crucial for so called paper sons, who were able to enter the United States by claiming relation to the men already residing in the country. The only Chinese who were able to bypass exclusion laws and enter the United States were merchants, students and family members of merchants or the Chinese born in the United States and hence American citizens under the auspices of the federal law. Forged birth certificates identified "paper sons" as sons of the above mentioned groups (de Bary Nee 62). Focalizing the Chinese American experience in the United States through the female perspective, Kingston does not limit authentication through paper during the immigration process exclusively to men, to paper sons. The narrator does not specify the gender of Chinese American immigrants when mentioning Chinese American reticence to report at the immigration office to "straighten out" "fake papers" (214). Rather than use the term "paper sons," she employs "wetbacks" and "stowaways" (214), reappropriating[45] the mainstream terminology applied to illegal immigrants.

The question of legitimizing one's presence through "false papers" arises in the dispute between immigrants discussing the rumor that any illegal immigrant who reports at the Immigration Naturalization Service will be awarded citizenship. The reactions of the immigrants are divided. Some sense a trap, while others urge the rest to report because then "we'd have our citizenship for real" (214). The last statement is worth delving into because it presents an altogether different stance on the issue of American citizenship than the one expounded in *China Men*. The narrator of *China Men* asserts that if her great grandfather Ah Goong had not had

American citizenship on paper, he would still have been an American citizen because through his work he made a significant contribution to the country (*China Men* 143). No such assertion is made in *The Woman Warrior*. As I argue earlier, *China Men* makes a more concerted effort to anchor Chinese Americans within the domain of Americanness. While *China Men* shows Chinese men in the act of crossing the border, *The Woman Warrior* shifts the focus to Chinese women: Brave Orchid, Moon Orchid, Moon Orchid's daughter and the No Name Woman crossing the border metaphorically. In line with the masculine discourse of pioneering, the journeys of men are presented as much more perilous. They pave the way for women's future passage into the United States. Brave Orchid does mention a forty-day voyage of starving, taking her into Ellis Island, but in the narrator's portrayal, her journey is free of the dangers which she pictures while imagining her father's passage into the United States in *China Men*. The greatest peril confronting Brave Orchid and the female characters of *The Woman Warrior* is the verification at the border, the verification taking place on the strength of their papers and questions posed by immigration officials. Immigrating into the United States in the early 1940s, Brave Orchid is still questioned at the border, unlike Moon Orchid, entering the country in the 1960s, shortly before or after the 1965 changes in the immigration law,[46] abolishing the quota system based on the national origin of prospective immigrants (Hing 39, Neil Gotanda 147). Contrary to Brave Orchid's expectations, Moon Orchid is not subjected to an interrogation at the airport but simply has her papers stamped by an immigration official.

A different example of authorization through paper is Brave Orchid's medical diploma. It has a gold, red and orange finish (Kingston 67–68), all of which are perceived as auspicious colors in China (Dennys 54). The diploma conjures up connotations of whiteness. When the narrator looks at the several-decade old diploma, she can smell a "thousand-year-old bat," which is "white as dust" (67). For the narrator, whiteness produces associations of old age. Brave Orchid has similar associations of whiteness and old age while looking at the narrator's white hair (120). In the diploma passage the narrator essentializes and ossifies China as an ancient country. Brave Orchid's diploma is several decades old, but it is enough to make the narrator smell a "thousand-year-old bat flying heavy-headed out of the Chinese caverns where bats are as white as dust, a smell that comes from long ago, far back in the brain" (67). A "smell" originating "far back in the brain" reinforces the primeval associations of China, bringing also the echoes of Joseph Conrad's *Heart of Darkness*. The metaphor may evoke a prenatal memory of China, linking the narrator to her ancestral heritage.

Primeval associations of China may also be the result of long-established popular stereotyping of China, to which the narrator herself is not immune.

The last example of legitimization through paper is the narrator's own self-authorization in her first-person narrative. The construction of the narrative is an act of self-definition and individualization, allowing the narrator to constitute herself as an active subject capable of articulation. Since a lot of critical attention has been devoted to the narrator's autobiographic enterprise,[47] I will focus only on the points which directly link the narrative venture to paper. In line with what has been said about paper sons' self-authorization of their presence in the United States through paper, Gayle K. Fujita Sato connects the narrator's autobiographic enterprise to the self-authoring strategies assumed by paper sons, who, according to Sato, "from ... the start were authoring their American lives" (99). While Sato may be slightly overstating the agency of Chinese immigrants, the comparison of both types of self-authorization through the written word deserves attention, especially that both were scrutinized for authenticity: Chinese immigrants' papers by white immigration officials, while *The Woman Warrior* by Chinese American cultural nationalists. Discussing the narrator's self-authorization through the written word on paper, I would like to return to the inscription upon the narrator' back. Paul John Eakin calls the narrator's text "a second skin" that "contain[s] all the words that would not fit on the original body of the self" (*Fictions in Autobiography Studies in the Art of Self-Invention* 263–264). Like Ralph Ellison's Invisible Man, the narrator of *The Woman Warrior* "whips it all up" in the act of telling, funneling at least part of her anger and bitterness into the text (Ellison 433). Eakin's employment of the phrase "second skin" in order to render the narrator's self-negotiation through the text of her narrative becomes all the more relevant if one considers that "skin" itself without any extra qualification often features as a vehicle for contextualizing the self. Sue Golding approaches skin as an "epistemological trope that offers a way to rethink identity and otherness" (Golding cited in Curtin 10). If one thinks of autobiography as an externalization of the subject's interior, then skin is a very apt metaphor. Elspeth Probyn perceives skin as a "process" "by which things become visible and are produced as the outside" (Probyn cited in Curtin 12). Visibility is one of Kingston's main goals which she hopes to achieve through the inscription of the written word on paper. In an interview with Donna Perry, she states "Everything is so invisible and I'm just bringing it into visibility" (181).

Most images of paper in *The Woman Warrior* valorize paper as a vehicle for the word. Yet at least in one instance the narrative exposes a misapplication of paper as a vehicle for the word. This misapplication occurs in the already discussed passage when the narrator's racist white boss orders her to write invitations to the banquet to be hosted by a segregationist restaurant. Refusing to perform the order, the narrator also refuses to participate in the misapplication of paper to nefarious ends. Unlike other applications of paper in the narrative, this one is purely mechanical, featuring outside the context of creation or self-construction through the written word. The words to be transferred onto paper do not emerge from within, but from without, resembling dictation. The source of dictation is directly traceable to a white man. When command over paper and the word is handed over to a white man in the narrative, paper immediately loses its positive signification. The synthetic quality of whiteness discussed in the earlier sections of the chapter is mirrored in this instance by the attempt to apply paper in a mechanical way. The distrust of the purely mechanical application of paper is also evinced by the narrator's parents who never sign "anything unnecessary" (194). Their apprehension about signing papers can be attributed to the fact that they do not understand the English wording on these papers and hence would not relinquish their agency.

Bones

A recurring image implicitly connoting whiteness is the image of bones. Bones of *The Woman Warrior* stand in sharp contrast to the bones of Fae Myenne Ng's *Bone* or Joy Kogawa's *Obasan*. Rather than merely a symbol of death, the bones of *Bone* and *Obasan* are first of all a symbol of remembering, a link between the living and the dead, often the only material remnant of the past. Bones of *The Woman Warrior* produce predominantly negative associations of death, fear and ghostliness. Bones also constitute the border between the outside and the inner private world of the subject. Confronted with the Sitting Ghost, Brave Orchid becomes "sharply herself—bone, wire, antenna" (80). A similar textualization of bones takes place when the mature narrator declares that while pleading with her to stay in Chinatown, Brave Orchid metaphorically cuts through "the icy bone" of the narrator's skull (126). A graphic, literal reenactment of the same scene occurs in Brave Orchid's tale, in which participants of a monkey feast, including Brave Orchid herself, cut through the skull bone of the monkey in order to devour the monkey's brain (107–108). Cutting through the bone into the brain implies not only a violent, cruel invasion of the private sphere, but also quasi brainwashing or spoon feeding of wisdom to which the immature narrator is exposed in childhood through Brave Orchid's storytelling. Both scenes of figurative cutting through one's skull correspond to the scene of Joy Kogawa's *Obasan*, in which Naomi dreams that a hospital nurse violently combs her hair. Bones are valorized in *The Woman Warrior* only when they signify substance, foundation and strength of character. This valorization can be traced in the speechless, boneless girl episode as well as in the passage in which the narrator reflects on the paradoxes of the world, noting that "Pearls are bone marrow" (181).

Oxymoronic Whiteness

The imagery of *The Woman Warrior* reveals oxymoronic whiteness, whiteness holding untenable contradictions. Socio-historically, whiteness is an oxymoron in two different ways:

1. On the one hand, whiteness was legally constructed by white people as a norm, a standard bearer. On the other hand, whiteness dressed itself in a mantle of exclusivity, wielding and reserving exclusive rights. The self-avowed normativity of whiteness clashed with the exclusivity of its rights. Maxine Hong Kingston explicitly reflects on this dichotomy manifested by whiteness in her second work *China Men*.
2. A good illustration of oxymoronic whiteness is Ruth Frankenberg's definition of whiteness as an "unmarked marker or neutral category, in relation to which others are named or marked other" (66). As I argue in earlier sections of the chapter, Kingston challenges this definition of whiteness, portraying it as non-normative and marking its particular features.

The capacity of whiteness as a socio-historical racial category to hold untenable contradictions is best captured through such images as an icicle in the desert and white pearls born out of black or grey oysters.

Kingston constructs the metaphor of an icicle in the desert in the last chapter, "A Song for a Barbarian Reed Pipe," the chapter in which the narrator draws parallels between herself as a Chinese American woman and author and a second-century AD. Chinese female poet, Ts'ai Yen, who lived for twelve years among barbarians, having been kidnapped from her native China. On the most literal level, "an icicle in the desert" refers to the music issuing from barbarian flutes: "a high note, which they found at last and held—an icicle in the desert. The music disturbed Ts'ai Yen; its sharpness and its cold made her ache" (243). The transparent whiteness of the icicle in the desert is reinforced through an already discussed attribute of whiteness—coldness. The synaesthetic association of music with coldness is reminiscent of the "white sound" constructed by the narrator of Joy Kogawa's *Obasan* (Kogawa v). An "icicle in the desert" represents something difficult to reach and to preserve. An "icicle in the desert" will not last long. It will melt soon, sinking into the grains of the sand. Parallelly, white dominance is impossible to maintain. Nor is it possible to build one's identity solely upon whiteness.[48]

The other example of oxymoronic whiteness comes in the form of pearls born out of black or grey oysters. For the narrator as Fa Mu Lan, it is one of the paradoxes to which she learns to open her mind during her apprenticeship with the elderly guru couple: "I learned to make my mind large, as the universe is large, so that there is room for paradoxes" (35). On the most immediate level, the paradox of pearls grown in oysters pertains to the startling origin of pearls. It never occurs to the immature narrator that there is any connection between pearls and oysters. All paradoxes listed by her reveal an integral link between all elements of nature. Every living organism and every desensitized object is a part of a larger organic whole. On the less immediate level of signification, one can also find it paradoxical that white pearls are born out of black or grey oysters. Mixing colors at will without any fixed design, nature observes no color bars. A more sinister interpretation of the passage would imply that blackness is a vehicle or a vessel for whiteness, a means to an end, a coarse protective shield nurturing a precious stone. The term "nurturing" has wide currency in whiteness studies, capturing the representation of blackness and its relation to whiteness. Still, the pioneers of the discipline employ "nurturing" in the context of character construction, not aesthetics. Toni Morrison reaches for the term to discuss the representation of blackness in Twain's and Hemingway's works. Morrison observes that black males feature as nursing figures "enabling" white protagonists while never compromising their illusion of being alone (Morrison, *Playing in the Dark* 82). Morrison portrays the "Africanist character" as "surrogate and enabler" (51), "defin[ing] the goals and enhance[ing] the qualities of white characters" (53). In "Whiteness Studies and the Paradox of Particularity" Robyn Wiegman offers a similar reading of the representation of the black character in *Forrest Gump*. Wiegman does not use the phrase "nurturing" or "nursing," but she portrays the role of the black character Bubba in parallel terms.

Tandemic Whiteness

Finally, many of *The Woman Warrior* images present whiteness side by side with blackness. Rather than perceive the juxtaposition of whiteness and blackness as a mere coincidence, it can be seen as an extension of

Kingston's commentary on racial relations in the United States, a constituent element of a meticulously constructed design, an attempt to "transform aspects of [one's] social grounding into aspects of language" (Morrison, *Playing in the Dark* 4). The juxtaposition of whiteness with blackness reveals what can be termed as the tandemic quality of whiteness, that is, the socio-historical dependence of whiteness for its construction on non-white racial categories. Reflecting on this dependence, Ruth Frankenberg claims that "White/European self-constitution is ... fundamentally tied to the process of discursive production of others" ("Whiteness and Americanness" 63). Whites position themselves in the center, defining themselves in relation to the people, whom they place in the margins.

Beyond rendering the tandemic quality of whiteness, the black-white imagery of *The Woman Warrior* may also be perceived as an illustration of the black-white binary persisting in the United States racial relations at the time when Maxine Hong Kingston wrote and published her work. With the focus on black Americans and white Americans, Asian Americans felt excluded from the political debate of the country. In the black and white American world, the tensions between white Americans and black Americans came to the foreground and other marginalized racial and ethnic groups frequently found themselves left out of the picture. Reducing racial relations in the United States to the black and white binary, white people took Asian Americans out of the equation, banishing them outside the perimeter of the United States. Kingston openly questions the black-white dyad in her third work, a novel, *Tripmaster Monkey* (1989). A sense of being overlooked is the most palpable in a statement by the protagonist of the novel, Wittman Ah Sing:

> I have a nightmare that ... someday Blacks and whites will shake hands over my head. I'm the little yellow man beneath the bridge of their hands and overlooked. Have you been at a demonstration where they sing:
> >Black and white together
> >Black and white together
> >Someday-a-a-ay [308].

Wittman Ah Sing utters these words in the 1960s, the time when the narrator of *The Woman Warrior* "marched to change the world" (56). The lack of any overt reflection in *The Woman Warrior* on the black-white dynamics of American racial relations may stem from the overall character of the book, whose purpose is to find a voice and articulate unique Chinese American experience rather than reclaim America for Chinese Americans. As mentioned earlier, the decisive reclaiming of America takes place in *China Men* and *Tripmaster Monkey*.

While opting for a particularist, socio-historical explanation of black-white imagery in *The Woman Warrior*, I still want to acknowledge an explanation that would be grounded in the archetypal theory of color perception. Cultural critic Tzvetan Todorov looks for the opposition in nature that contributed to the creation of the dichotomy of black versus white across cultures (Todorov cited in Adams 20). White is associated with light and day, while black with darkness and night. Expounding Todorov's theories, Michael Vannoy Adams assures that Todorov withholds from drawing definitive parallels between the polarity of black and white in the world of nature and the world of culture (Adams 21).

Analyzing the juxtaposition of black and white in Kingston's imagery of *The Woman Warrior*, it is also worth noting that traditional color theory identifies both black and white as achromatic colors. What makes both of them achromatic is their relation to light. While white reflects all wavelengths of light, black absorbs all wavelengths of light (Adams 33). It needs to be emphasized that the traditional color theory identifies black and white as non-colors or as achromatic colors because what is of primary importance in the traditional color theory is light, the participation of light waves. While white reflects all wavelengths of light, black absorbs all wavelengths of light (Adams 33). Undermining the traditional color theory, Patricia Sloane shifts the focus from light to sight. Sloane's shift of emphasis to sight and perception in the definition of colors is of particular significance to this study because of the centrality of vision to its subject matter. According to Sloane, both black and white are colors because human beings perceive them as such. Sloane also asserts that the opposition white-black is entirely psychical or symbolic (Sloane cited in Adams 34).

One of the most striking images of blackness in tandem with whiteness can be traced in the narrator's childhood paintings drawn during the three years of her most profound silence (the "thickest"[49] silence) (192). For three years the narrator first draws houses, flowers and suns only to cover them with black paint. The whiteness of paper sheets on which she draws is not explicitly stated, but it is clearly to be deduced from the narrator's assertion that she performs an equivalent operation while drawing on the blackboard, the only difference being that then she covers her paintings with chalk (192). Applying a layer of black paint or white chalk, the narrator has an impression that she constructs a stage curtain, which is momentarily to rise to reveal her private visions. Looking as a child at her black paintings, the narrator sees a world of possibilities: "I spread them out (so black and full of possibilities) and pretended the curtains were swinging open, flying up, one after another, sunlight underneath, mighty operas" (192). Like the stage curtain, the black paint covers the realm of potential. Blackness, like the narrator's silence, entails a multitude of interpretations, carrying the promise of fulfillment.[50] Both are a preparatory stage for a triumph of speech and the narrative language that bursts in a myriad of images.

The black and white paintings passage merits further attention in the context of the opening epigraphs illustrating Kingston's views on the process of composition: "After college I thought that I was a painter because I always see pictures, and I see visions before the words come, and it's always a secondary step to find the words (Kay Bonetti's "Interview with Maxine Hong Kingston" 33). For Kingston, seeing is a crucial step in the process of articulation. Seeing is a prerequisite of writing. Yet words are indispensable as well, helping to bind the visions together and fill the gaps in the visions. As Kingston explains in an interview:

> words are a medium to get to the seemingly subconscious ... *visions don't just come full-blown and with details* such as chairs and clothes, and where everything is placed—the relationships between bodies in a room. All that becomes more and more accessible as I approach them with words. *Words clarify the vision and memory.... As I paint part of a vision, the next part of it becomes clear*. It's as if I am building the underpinnings of a bridge, and then I can cross it, and see more and more clearly [Rabinowitz, "Eccentric Memories: A Conversation with Maxine Hong Kingston" 68, emphasis added].

While Kingston identifies seeing as a prerequisite of word production, she still perceives words as rivets that are essential for the completion of her visions. Words enhance her ability to see and to remember: to "see more and more clearly" (ibid 68).[51] In an interview with Neila C. Seshachari, Kingston speaks of her writing in terms of being at the theater and looking behind the curtain to see "all kinds of gifts and visions" (213). Kingston's outlook on the process of writing matches closely that of Toni Morrison, who also accentuates the importance of the sight of the author: "the author's presence—her or his intentions, blindness and sight—is part of the imaginative activity" (*Playing in the Dark* XII). Sight is also hyper important for both authors when they speak of the reader's reception. Kingston "want[s] her readers to see the pictures" (Bonetti's "Interview with Maxine Hong Kingston 68), whereas Morrison claims that the reader "reads, becomes engaged in and *watches* what is being read all at the same time" (*Playing in the Dark* X, Morrison's emphasis). The term "watches" indicates that Morrison frames reception in theatrical terms, while Kingston perceives production in a parallel way: "When I write, I am at the theater" (Neila C Seshachari, "Reinventing Peace: Conversations with Tripmaster Maxine Hong Kingston" 213).[52]

The black curtain covering the narrator's imaginary visions can also stand for the Duboisian veil separating the narrator and other people of color from the fulfillment of their visions, especially in the context of exclusion and discrimination related by the narrator in the passages immediately following the childhood paintings episode. In *The Souls of Black Folk* Du Bois notes that African Americans are "shut from [the white world] by the vast veil" (4). Life behind the veil entails physical and psychological separation from the world of privilege, the "pale world" (Du Bois, *The Souls* 4). If the black curtain of the narrator's painting visions bears a resemblance to the Duboisian veil, it still has a much more positive signification than Du Bois's original veil. Reaching for the black curtain metaphor, the narrator emphasizes its potential rather than its limiting power. The black curtain recurs as an image when the narrator announces that "the curtain [inside her brain] flaps closed like merciful black wings" (108) whenever she hears Brave Orchid's graphic tale which she resents listening to. In this instance the black curtain functions as a protective device shielding the narrator. Conversely, the black veil features in *The Woman Warrior* in an explicitly negative context of Brave Orchid's medical calls. The "black veil" is said to hang over the face of daughters in law whose relatives are about to die (97).

Through the childhood paintings episode Kingston reverses the representation of black and white as bland colors. While for most of the narrative both white color and black color receive negative signification,[53] the childhood paintings episode explicitly shows up the potential of blackness and implicitly also the potential of whiteness. The narrator's paintings are "so black and full of possibilities" (192). The discussion of blackness continues in the passages immediately following the childhood paintings episode. This accumulation of blackness is hardly accidental. The narrator places her black childhood paintings in the context of the semiotics of racial categories. Looking back to her school days, she compares herself to an African American girl whose mother combs her hair Shanghai style so that they look with the narrator like Shanghai twins, the only difference between them being the skin color: "except that she was covered with black like my paintings" (193). On the one hand, the narrator is very conscious of the semiotics of race, but on the other, she minimizes it, drawing an overt comparison between the blackness of the African American girl's skin and the blackness of her paintings. In both cases blackness is a cover for the world of internal possibilities. The passage underscores the performativity of racial categories and indeterminacy of identity definitions.[54] Finding explicit parallels between herself and the African American girl, the narrator also unsettles the black-white dyad, proposing an alternative racial configuration. A very direct proposal of a cross-racial alliance between Chinese Americans and African Americans comes in the following excerpt, when the narrator remembers how black students walked her home and to school to protect her against rowdy Japanese American children.[55] Black children ("Black Ghosts") impress the immature narrator with their ebullient personalities of "daring talker[s]," who "laugh[ ] the hardest" and treat the narrator as their equal, as if she was "a daring talker too" (193). Explicitly valorizing blackness, the narrator re-centers it, shifting it from the margins of American society to the social center of her childhood world. This re-centering can be traced further in the figurative rendering of the letter "I," startling the narrator with its simple silhouette and riveting her attention to its "black center" (193).

The blankness of the sheets of paper on which the immature narrator unfurls her visions may symbolize the amorphousness of self-definitions embraced by some white people at the time when Kingston wrote the narrative. Ross Chambers speaks about "blank whiteness" parading as an "unexamined 'norm'" and "blank blackness," that is, an "unknowable 'other'" ("The Unexamined" 193). Ruth Frankenberg speaks about the "formlessness of being white" and whiteness presenting itself as "an unmarked or neutral category, in relation to which others are named or marked other" ("Whiteness and Americanness" 66). Covering blank, white sheets of paper with childhood drawings, the narrator figuratively undermines this formlessness and blankness. Before being covered with black paint, the narrator's drawings offer an alternative definition of whiteness—whiteness that defines itself in a positive way instead of reaching for an oppositional, negative self-definition. Rather than define itself against the background of blackness, stating who they are not, white people could define themselves in a beautiful, positive way and state who they are. Their self-definition could be as beautiful and positive as the visions unbridled by the narrator on blank, white sheets of paper. Yet rather than embrace these beautiful, positive self-definitions, they opt for negative, oppositional self-definitions, defining themselves against the background of blackness.

Other examples of tandemic whiteness in *The Woman Warrior* are:

- Black and white photographs of the No Name Woman's long gone husband, so long gone as to make the narrator speculate that the No Name Woman must have forgotten what he looks like. Trying to visualize his face, "she only saw the black and white face in the group photograph the men had taken before leaving" for the United States (7). In Chinese tradition black and white are primarily the colors of death. Staying away from China for years, the No

Name Woman's husband is barely a living presence in her life. He is rather a living absence although he is not physically dead.
- The white dog protecting Brave Orchid on her night medical calls. Brave Orchid ties red yarn to the dog's tail to counterbalance ("neutralize") the "bad luck" connoted by white ("the mourning color") (96). The narrator does not explain why Brave Orchid chooses the white dog if white is so unpropitious in Chinese aesthetics. One can only speculate that the white dog's visibility against the darkness of the night is to scare away any potential attackers.
- The white horse of the narrator as Fa Mu Lan going to battle side by side with a rider on a black horse (43).
- Black and white as the only colors explicitly named in reference to the "remote island of Japan" (109). Black and white are identified as the attributes of some animals inhabiting the island: "black apes" and "white stags" (109). Other, more florid and diverse colors feature only implicitly as the qualities of "magic orchards," "strange trees," "plants of jasper" (109). An explicit naming of only black and white colors in the imagery characterizing Japan may stem from bellicose relations between the Chinese and Japanese as well as Chinese Americans and Japanese Americans, as characterized in *The Woman Warrior*.
- The brightness of the No Name Woman during her labor against the blackness of the surrounding universe: "She was one of the stars, a bright dot in blackness" (16).

The imagery of whiteness in *The Woman Warrior* amplifies the more overt critique of whiteness offered by the narrative, re-inscribing the immature and mature narrator's visions of whiteness. Extending the defamiliarization of whiteness to the imagery of the narrative, Kingston presents whiteness as terrorizing, alienating, intrusive, bland, indistinct, desensitized, related to coldness, shorn of life and vitality. The imagery of whiteness in *The Woman Warrior* further unravels the socio-historical construction of whiteness, the construction based on paradox and othering of non-white American subjects. As in the case of the more direct critique of whiteness, the imagery of whiteness in the narrative does not shut the door to its transformation. Paper imagery as well as black and white paintings touch on the potential of whiteness for transformation. Without at least implicitly acknowledging such potential, the narrator of *The Woman Warrior* would not be able to subscribe to transformational identity politics and claim bonding with people of the whole Earth. Still, the theme is fully developed only in Kingston's fourth major work *The Fifth Book of Peace*.

Conclusion

Maxine Hong Kingston's *The Woman Warrior* significantly contributes to defamiliarizing whiteness by placing whiteness in the position of the "other," marking its particular features and exposing its close entwinement with oppression. Kingston not only sheds light on the hegemonic status of whiteness in American society, but also makes a chink in this hegemony, ousting whiteness from the self-assumed position of the norm. *The Woman Warrior* registers the changing perception of whiteness in the eyes of the narrator, drawing a sharp distinction between the immature and mature narrator's vision of whiteness. While the immature narrator defamiliarizes whiteness, she also essentializes and homogenizes it. Only the mature vision of whiteness reveals the enmeshment of whiteness with oppression. Powerless as the narrator may seem in the face of oppression originating in whiteness, she wields a powerful weapon—the word. Being primarily a word warrior, she challenges white dominance as well as other forms of oppression both directly and indirectly—through the imagery of the narrative. It is also the imagery of the narrative that contains the threads of the representation of whiteness that are further developed in Kingston's other works.

2

Demonic and Oxymoronic Whiteness in Maxine Hong Kingston's *China Men*

Introduction

Maxine Hong Kingston's *China Men* (1980) juxtaposes the vision of normative whiteness enshrined by white Americans in the law and exposed by the author in "The Laws" chapter with the vision of non-normative, strange and alien whiteness captured by fresh Chinese immigrants. The "ghosts" of *The Woman Warrior* make way in the nomenclature of *China Men* for "demons" and "devils." Whiteness delineated by the narrator's Great Grandfather of the Sandalwood Mountains, the Grandfather of the Sierra Nevada Mountains as well as the generation of the narrator's father is a negation of universality to which whiteness aspires in legal and socio-historical terms. The portrayal of whiteness in *China Men* is a further illustration of the epigraph opening this study: "A manifest truth" "disappear[s]" "when one begins to detect the very conditions that made it seem manifest: the familiarities that served as its support, the darknesses that brought about its clarity and all those far-away things that secretly sustained it and made it 'go without saying'" (Foucault, *Power* 444). Unraveling in *China Men* the socio-historical construction of whiteness, Kingston exposes whiteness as built on the exclusion and exploitation of other racial and ethnic groups. She also once again inverts what Michel Foucault termed as dissymmetry of power ("Panopticism" 16). Rather than subordinate Chinese immigrants to the racial gaze as objects, Kingston reverses the gaze and takes a surveying look at whiteness.

China Men exposes the oxymoron underlying the socio-historical construction of whiteness. What was merely signaled in *The Woman Warrior* through the imagery of the work finds its full development in Kingston's second major work. The oxymoronic character of whiteness lies in whiteness, on the one hand, presenting itself as the norm enshrined in the law, the touchstone which you need to meet in order to claim the same rights, including human rights and privileges, and on the other hand:

1. having an exclusive and exclusionary status as well as
2. not being perceived as the norm by non-white people

China Men illustrates how whiteness stakes a claim both to universality and particularity. The oxymoronic construction of whiteness exemplifies what Foucault calls the "simultaneous individualization and totalization of modern power structures" (*Power* 336). Whiteness dresses itself in the garb of universality in *China Men* through its legal construction exposed by Kingston primarily in "The Laws," the chapter which also highlights the exclusive and exclusionary character of whiteness embedded in its legal construction. The legal particularization and universalization of whiteness is coeval with its socio-historical construction. The law helped to sanction and perpetuate an earlier assumed position of dominance in relation to racial minorities. What originated in the transportation of the first slaves to the future United States in 1619, when first slaves arrived in Jamestown, Virginia aboard a Dutch slave ship, was later consistently reaffirmed through social and legal practices.[1]

The second revelation of the oxymoron of whiteness present implicitly in *The Woman Warrior* and explicitly in *China Men* is captured by Ruth Frankenberg's characterization of whiteness as an "*unmarked marker or neutral category, in relation to which others are named or marked other*" ("Whiteness and Americanness" 66, emphasis added). Voicing similar thoughts on the tendency of whites to unmark themselves and mark people of other colors, Richard Dyer notes that "There is no more powerful position than that of being 'just' human" (2). According to Dyer, white culture is overwritten by the "assumption that white people are just people, which is not far off saying that whites are people whereas other colours are something else" (2). As demonstrated in Chapter 1, Kingston reverses this dyad, placing whites in the position of others, ghosts in *The Woman Warrior* and demons as well as devils in *China Men*. Yet the reversal of the above mentioned dynamic is not a mirror reflection because Chinese immigrants do not remain totally unmarked either. They are placed by Kingston in the position of signifying subjects assigning meanings, but they are also marked by the very experience of oppression and by some of the narrator's unflattering descriptions. Overall, however, it is primarily white people, in particular white men, who find themselves in the positions of marked objects: devils and demons. Apart from registering the negative othering of difference, Kingston records the rare moments of meaningful mutual encounters and fetishization of difference. For some whites, Chinese immigrants are not only objects of exploitation and ostracism, but also of ethnographic interest. The following chapter devoted to the representation of whiteness in *China Men* is composed of three parts: the first dedicated to the representation of white people as demons and devils, the second to the oxymoronic construction of whiteness in the legal and socio-historical sphere and the third one to the toppling of the myth of white people as sole founders of the United States.

White Devils and Demons

The label "demon" and "devil" has a two-fold signification in *China Men*. On the one hand, it is a designation applied by mainland Chinese to foreigners and exported to the United States by Chinese immigrants. On the other hand, the very classification of "devils" and "demons" reaches a deeper, more engaged level of signification on American soil in the context of American labor relations in which Chinese immigrants had to negotiate their subject positions. In Kingston's portrayal of Chinese immigrants, white people supervising Chinese workers in the cane fields of Hawaii and in the mainland United States during the construction of the Transcontinental Railroad display brutality stripping them of their humanity and adding much more tangibility to the labels "demons" and "devils."

Nomenclature

As mentioned in *The Woman Warrior* chapter of this study, Kingston's translation of the Chinese term applied to white people sparked an animated debate in the Chinese American community. In particular, Ben Tong and Jeffrey Paul Chan were critical of Kingston's referring to white people in *The Woman Warrior* as "ghosts" rather than "devils" or "demons" as, according to them, the Chinese term "Kuei" or "Gwai" would require (Wong 32). Their claims were countervailed by Cynthia Sau-ling Wong, who was skeptical about translating the term by only one English denotation and barring all other "overtones" of meaning (Wong 37). Gayle K. Fujita Sato explains the difference in translation between *The Woman Warrior* and *China Men* by drawing a distinction between a female vision of reality propounded by *The Woman Warrior* and much more male centered world of *China Men* (199). As I argue in *The Woman Warrior* chapter, one may assume that the term "Kuei" was translated as "demon," "devil" in *China Men* because whiteness carries a much more demonic charge in the novel. White "ghosts" hovering around the immature narrator's house in *The Woman Warrior* are much more innocuous and less tangible to the narrator than white "devils" and "demons" supervising Bak Goong in Hawaii, Ah Goong in the Sierra Nevada Mountains, chasing China Men on completion of the Transcontinental Railroad or interrogating the narrator's father on Angel Island. White oppressors of China Men are much more visible and tangible. While the narrator of *The Woman Warrior* also sees and exposes oppressive faces of whiteness, white oppressors of *The Woman Warrior* are usually not presented as coming in direct contact with Chinese American subjects, but practicing what Slavoi Žižek terms as "racism with a distance" (Žižek cited in Prashad 61). The mature narrator of *The Woman Warrior* directly confronts representations of corporate whiteness in the figures of her racist employers. Yet in most of the narrative situations in *The Woman Warrior*, white power operates from a safe distance. The dispossessing whiteness of urban restructuring that claims the narrator's family laundry never materializes itself in the form of white officials physically performing an act of overtaking. The reader can never see white officials come to Brave Orchid's house in order to claim the laundry. Brave Orchid does express her indignation at "urban renewal ghosts" offering the family "moving money" to start a business elsewhere, but the features of "urban renewal ghosts" are never drawn. They remain ephemeral figures representing a larger power structure. What receives emphasis is the system of oppression in which whiteness maintains its hegemony, hovering in the background in the ostensibly pluralistic society while at the same time arraying racialized subjects in preordained subject positions.

White demons of *China Men* are much more gender-specific than the ghosts of *The Woman Warrior*. In most of the cases the demons and devils of *China Men* are clearly defined as men. When on one occasion the label is extended to proselytizing white women, they are referred to through a gendered construction as white demonesses. While in *The Woman Warrior*, the pronoun he or she is used in reference to ghosts, in most of the cases their gender is not clearly identified. No gendered construction appears, for example, when Brave Orchid complains about the Noisy-Red-Mouth-Ghost haunting the family laundry (123).

The label demon applies consistently in *China Men* even when the narration is focalized through the female point of view. Both Brave Orchid and the narrator also call white people demons. An exception to naming whites as demons occurs in "The Brother in Vietnam" section, in which the label demon no longer applies. Nomenclature may change in "The Brother in Vietnam" because in the face of war, differences between people become diluted. The narrator goes as far as to note the attenuation of differences between the warring sides, claiming that in the fervor of the battle it is difficult to decide on which side one is. The narrator's brother perceives himself as the "other" in relation to the native inhabitants of Taiwan. It is also only in the Taiwanese section of the narrative that the phrase "white devils" is employed when the narration is momentarily focalized through the native Taiwanese's point of view, that is when the brother imagines that he would be reproached by the Taiwanese for "living with a gang of white devils" (296). The brother himself never refers to his white fellow soldiers as demons or devils. Yet he can imagine the native Taiwanese perceiving white people as "devils" or "demons" and extending the terms to him as well. Another term which he imagines as used hypothetically in reference to himself by the native Taiwanese is Ho Chi Kuei, the term applied by first generation Chinese Americans to the second generation Chinese Americans, the term already discussed in this study in *The Woman Warrior* chapter. All of the scolding remains in the realm of the brother's imagination because *China Men* presents a much more lenient attitude towards the younger generation of Chinese Americans.

The narrator of *China Men* refrains from the classification of whiteness as "other" only when it shows its positive face. An instance comes in the description of Chinese massacres through the reference to "a good white lady" hiding the Chinese away from white rampagers. The juxtaposition of the "good white lady" with "demons" signifying bad whites positions "demons" on the margins of whiteness, making them a subspecies of whiteness.

The label "demon" does not apply to whiteness in *China Men* when white people are positioned as equal in relation to Chinese Americans, which takes place for example when the narrator's father shows his family an album of "gray and white photographs" presenting himself and white immigrants of various nationalities (245). The photograph earning the father's special attention and commentary presents a group of multiracial students attending an English class. Reminiscing on his life in the 1930s, the father is emphatic about the fact that all of the students "came from another country" (246). Whiteness no longer invites the classification of "demons" when Chinese American subjects find themselves in parallel positions to white people, who are also first generation immigrants rather than native Americans.

The discussion of nomenclature pertaining to whiteness in *The Woman Warrior* and *China Men* requires an observation that in *China Men* there are many more ghosts on American soil featuring in their most frequent signification of dead people. In particular, there is a proliferation of the United States based ghosts in "The Making of More Americans" chapter, which provides further testimony to the theory that Kingston was originally planning to publish *The Woman Warrior: Memoirs of a Girlhood among Ghosts* and *China Men* as one book. One can find barely any ghosts on American soil in their most frequent popular signification of dead people in *The Woman Warrior*. Apart from "whites" and "the dead," the term "ghosts" stands in *The Woman Warrior* for unrevealed secrets and traumas of the narrator's childhood.

White Beasts

The figuration of whiteness invites the most graphic metaphors when the narration is focalized through the viewpoint of the very first Chinese immigrants into the United States, represented in the narrative world of *China Men* by Bak Goong of Hawaii and Ah Goong of the Sierra Nevada Mountains. Seen though their eyes, white "demons" and "devils" receive the signification of "beasts," "savages," "snakes" and "monsters." Bak Goong's exhortation against "demons" resembles the 1960s black nationalists rant against white devils: "Take-that-white-*demon*. Take-that. Fall-to-the-ground-*demon*. Cut-you-into-pieces. Chop-off-your-legs. Die-snake. Chop-you-down-stinky-demon" (112, emphasis added). In another passage a white supervisor fuses into one with a beast, a horse, to the extent that the qualities of the horse are transferred onto the white man: "when a demon galloped toward him [Bak Goong], boss and horse both with cavernous nostrils wide open" (113). The narrative strategy employed by Kingston at this point approaches what Toni Morrison terms as *metaphysical condensation* (*Playing in the Dark* 68, emphasis added). Morrison argues that "collapsing persons into animals prevents contact and exchange" (68). Yet in this instance it is not the Chinese immigrants who are responsible for the lack of the aforementioned exchange. It is the white supervisors of the Sandalwood Mountains who limit themselves to exploitation and ordering their Chinese subjects about, not only foreclosing the avenues of interracial exchange but also silencing the Chinese, forestalling their self-expression and mutual communication. The above-cited passage comparing the white supervisor to his horse unfolds in the context of whip wielding whites forcing sick China Men of the Sandalwood Mountains to work irrespective of their physical state.

At certain points of the narration animal metaphors are extended to China Men as well, but their context is different. China Men are depicted as displaying some affinity with animals because of the arduous labor they perform and the defenses they need to develop in order to protect themselves against white overseers. Introduced into the sugar cane plantation, Bak Goong is advised by other China Men: "work like an ox," "Keep your machete sharp ... when you smell a demon near you" (97). An act of "smell[ing] the demon out" gives China Men the verisimilitude of animals, but the metaphor is not in any way underlain by bestiality on the part of the Chinese immigrants, as is the case with the white people. The "white scar" revealed by Bak Goong of the Sandalwood Mountains is a remnant of his contracted "coolie" labor reducing him almost to the status of a slave (39). Cooliesm[2] was popular not only in Hawaii but on the mainland American continent as well. In "Is Yellow Black or White" Gary Okihiro explains that cooliesm was very convenient to white Americans, who could replace manumitted slaves with cheap workers from Asia. They did not need to jockey for their votes, so they could pay them less than African Americans and they could use them as a bargain card against African Americans (Okihiro, *Margins and Mainstreams* 44). The narrator of *China Men* overtly reflects on a similar dynamic: "Some of the banging came from the war to decide whether or not black people would continue to work for nothing" (125).

Slave-like conditions of labor in Hawaii sugar cane fields validate the labeling of whites as "devils" and "demons." Kingston's fictional representation of China Men's life in Hawaii corresponds to socio-historical accounts delving into the nature of the Chinese presence in Hawaii. 18,000 Chinese laborers worked in Hawaii between 1850 and 1885 (Shih-Shau Henry Tsai cited in Linton 43). Many Chinese workers had to wear plantation tabs (Takaki cited in Chiu 200). Monica Chiu argues that "nowhere in *China Men* is labor redemptive" (196). Alfred S. Wang identifies the system of labor presented in *China Men* as "collective slavery" (18). Ronald Takaki cites an account by William Hooper, a New England businessman visiting Hawaii, going as far as to claim that labor conditions on the island of Kauai exceed those of slavery: "They [Chinese immigrants] have to work *all* the time—and no regard is paid to their complaints for food, etc., etc. Slavery is nothing compared to it" (21, original emphasis). Takaki also cites unnamed white missionaries, observing that Chinese men were "living like 'animals' on the plantations" (38). Monica Chiu notes that despite their unequivocal contributions, the Chinese were still "the swine of the labor market" (195). In "The Eye of Power" Foucault speaks of the "triple function of labor: the productive function, the symbolic function and the function of dressage, or discipline" (161). By denying the input of Chinese immigrants in the sugar cane fields of Hawaii and in the Sierra Nevada Mountains, white overseers, white owners of the plantations and of the Transcontinental Railroad, as well as white civil subjects, denied the symbolic function of their labor. Chinese immigrants were treated as bodies for labor or working beasts. What white employers and overseers did not take into account was that "power, after investing itself in the body, finds itself exposed to a counterattack in that same body" (Foucault "Body/Power" 56). The "counterattack" in question never assumes the form of a direct physical rebellion in *China Men*, but it reveals itself in diverse, subtler forms of protest such as the protest of the Sandalwood Mountains China Men against enforced silence and the strike of the Sierra Nevada China Men.

In spite of dehumanizing labor conditions stemming mostly from the dehumanizing treatment by their overseers, China Men drawn by Kingston in her narrative resist dehumanization and preserve their civility brought to the North American continent from China. Emphasizing their table manners, Kingston dubs Bak Goong and other China Men of the Sandalwood Mountains as "civilized" (96). The same reversal of an ethnographic gaze and textualization of whites as uncultivated and Chinese Americans as cultured takes place in the case of Ah Goong of the Sierra Nevada Mountains. White "demons" are represented as never having "seen theatre before" until they had an opportunity of seeing Chinese theatre in California (148). Kingston reverses the white Anglo-Saxon discourse, casting Chinese Americans as propagators of culture and placing white people on the receiving end.

The demonization of whiteness transposes the stereotypes attributed in the second half of the nineteenth century to Chinese immigrants. Labeling whites as demons, Kingston inverts the nomenclature applied to the Chinese. In *Never One Nation: Freaks, Savages and Whiteness in U.S. Popular Culture*, Linda Frost cites the examples of the demonization of the Chinese in poetry, press and short fiction writing of the period. In Ned Buntline's story "Dream Elmore" (published in an early 1869 *Golden Era* issue), the Chinese are referred to as "Vandals," "dirty Vandals" and as "opaque-eyed" (Frost 155). Buntline stereotypes the Chinese as disorderly, living in dirt, drinking excessively, smoking, eating opium, gambling and quarreling (Frost 155). In "Traveling Editorial Correspondence" (also published in the *Golden Era*), Buntline calls the Chinese "pagan creatures" (Frost 156). Frost also cites Bret Harte's poem "Plain Language from Truthful James," which in popular parlor circulated under the title "The Heathen Chinee" (Frost 141). In his commentary on Genthe's *Pictures of Old Chinatown*, Will Irwin dubs a section of the San Francisco Chinatown inhabited by elderly and unemployed Chinese men as the "Devil's Kitchen" (Moy, *Marginal Sights* 70). Irwin identifies a vendor of the "Devil's Kitchen" as a "hop fiend" (Irwin cited in Moy 70). The Chinese emerging from Irwin's description are still "beasts" lurking behind the masks of their civility (Moy 73):

> as they drank and played ... something deep below the surface came out in them. Their shouts became squalls; lips drew back from teeth, beady little eyes blazed; their very cheek bones seemed to rise higher on their faces. I thought as I watched of wars of the past; these were not refined Cantonese, with a surface gentility and grace in life greater than anything our masses know; they were those old yellow people with whom our fathers fought before the Caucusus was set as a boundary between the dark race and the light; the hordes of Genghis Khan; the looters of Atilla [Irwin cited in Moy 73].

The passage establishes a clear distinction between what was believed to be the high traditional Chinese culture and the low Chinese culture looked down upon by the Orientalists. Ning Yu argues that the Chinese workers of Hawaii featured in *China Men* reject the high-low categories of the Orientalist discourse, resisting white attempts at classification and rendering them speechless (2). The scene in which Bak Goong and his fellow sugar cane workers refuse to work, dig out a hole in the ground, shout into a dug out pit, to later cover it up and draw a wheel of spokes above, illustrates their rebellion against enforced silence and their ability to reclaim their voice and the right to speak during labor.

The portrayal of whiteness in *China Men* not only inverts the stereotyping of Chinese immigrants, but also the discourse valorizing whiteness. In *Whiteness Visible: The Meaning of Whiteness in American Literature and Culture*, Valerie Babb enumerates "hard work, piousness, civility, cognitive ability, physical beauty" as the features ascribed to whiteness (87). To present themselves in this light, white people needed racial "others." Kingston undermines the afore-cited portrayal of whiteness, attributing most of the above-mentioned features to Chinese American railway constructors cast as mythic forefathers and the pioneers of the American West. White people constructed by Kingston lose their aura of the champions of progress, cultivation and "civilization." Even if they are indirectly named in the narrative as responsible for initiating ground-breaking projects, they are still represented as the ones executing these alterative ventures on the backs of other people without giving them due recognition.

The most demonic features of whiteness are revealed during the massacres of Asian Americans. The narrator of *China Men* enumerates the following Chinese American massacres: the Los Angeles Massacre of 1871, the Denver Anti-Chinese Riot of 1880, the Rock Springs Massacre of 1885, the Drivings out of Tacoma, Seattle, Oregon City, Albania and Marysville. Kingston does not mention the Chico Massacre of 1877 and the Seattle Massacre lasting from October 1885 to February 1886. The patterns of violence against Chinese Americans delineated by Kingston match those described by historian Sucheng Chan, that is, attacks against individuals, outbursts of violence against Chinatown communities and concerted attempts to oust the Chinese from certain towns (48). The narrator of *China Men* reports all of these instances of violence in a matter of fact way, as if she were a historian. While whiteness shows its most demonic face in the violence and atrocities committed against the Chinese immigrants, the narrator does not draw this demonic face in her narrative accounts of the massacres. Violent anti–Chinese events in *China Men* are never fully developed as to expose and figuratively unfurl the bestiality of white perpetrators. The narrator's mythic Grandfather Ah Goong always miraculously meanders between the atrocities against the Chinese immigrants, always hearing about them, but never witnessing them directly. The details of violence against the Chinese immigrants are barely mentioned, reaching merely the level of one-sentence interspersions: "bandits ... would hold him up for his railroad pay and shoot for practice as they shot Injuns and jackrabbits ... he [Ah Goong] hid against the shaking ground in case a demon with a shotgun was hunting from it ... the demons killed for fun and hate. They tied pigtails to horses and dragged chinamen" (144), "demon women and children threw the wounded back in the flames" (146). Anti-Chinese violence is never presented in the form of a personal account bearing verisimilitude to white lynchings depicted in African American fiction. The brief mentions of anti–Chinese attacks do not reach the narrative intensity of description presented by Ralph Ellison in his short story "Party Down the Square," James Baldwin in the short story "Going to Meet the Man," James Weldon Johnson in *The Autobiography of an Ex-Colored Man* or William Melvin Kelley's *A Different Drummer*.[3]

The labels "demons," "devils," "barbarians" are applied in the narrator's contemporary times as well, but on most occasions they do not carry any connotations of wildness or bestiality. In most cases, if any pejorative meaning is hidden under the terms, then usually it implies the distrust of difference, the contempt for the perceived lack of cultivation on the part of white people or at most the presumed ill intentions towards the Chinese immigrants. Brave Orchid applies the term "barbarians" when claiming that they equate all Chinese with communists (193). As in *The Woman Warrior*, whiteness is accepted in the family laundry on sufferance, only as an indispensable part of making a living: "We knew that it was to feed us you [the narrator's father] had to endure demons and physical labor" (8).The ghosts hustling about the narrator's house in *The Woman Warrior* turn into demons. The milk ghost turns into the milk demon, the grocery ghost into the grocery demon. While in *The Woman Warrior* there is the

Garbage Ghost, in *China Men* there is the garbage demon. Unlike the ghosts of *The Woman Warrior*, the demons of *China Men* are no longer capitalized. The demons hovering around the narrator's house stir up similar fears to the ghosts of *The Woman Warrior*. In *China Men* it is not the immature narrator who is traumatized but her Uncle Bun, who shows certain traces of mental instability. Yet at least some of his concerns about the demons parallel closely those of *The Woman Warrior* narrator's about the ghosts. For example, the immature narrator of *The Woman Warrior* and her siblings display the greatest trepidation on seeing the milk ghost because he embodies the most significant accumulation of whiteness. Uncle Bun suspects the milk demon of poisoning the food. He also suspects other "demons" supplying the food of poisoning it. The immature narrator of *The Woman Warrior* does not go so far as to suspect white people of poisoning the food, but she is also uneasy about the fact that whites are the source of their food supply, one of the most basic origins of sustenance: "For our very food we had to traffic with the Grocery Ghosts" (114). Uncle Bun of *China Men* eats only "greens and browns" (200). Interestingly, the poison is to be found only in foodstuffs that are also white in color. Uncle Bun speaks of "white food" being poisoned, identifying the white color as only seemingly pure: "the seeming purity of white food" (195). Significantly for the subject of this study, Uncle Bun brags about seeing through the ways of white people. The visual metaphor of seeing recurs when Uncle Bun recounts how he supposedly "saw" white demons poison his food: "today's evidence is that I saw" (195). Seeing furnishes what he perceives as evidence of whites' invidious actions, approximating the Berkeleyan mode of empiricist reasoning. Emphasizing his visual prowess, his "sharp senses," which he claims to have developed on "wheat germ," Uncle Bun still does not cast whites as totally blind, suspecting them of following, surveying him and hence successfully uncovering his Communist sympathies. The whiteness emerging from Uncle Bun's portrayal resembles the Foucauldian Panopticon.

The construction of contemporary whiteness as bearing verisimilitude to wildness and as reaching the acme of its insensitivity takes place when the narrator presents the story of the Wild Man of the Green Swamp. Doubting the Wild Man's putative wildness, the narrator calls him the Man, while whites remain demons: "he did not look very wild, being led by the posse out of the swamp. He did not look dirty, either. He wore a checkered shirt unbuttoned at the neck, where his white undershirt showed" (224). Never threatening other people, the Wild Man is still hunted like an animal by a posse of hunters and a plane. The Wild Man's ability to survive in the wild terrain of the Green Swamp, Florida totally through his own resourcefulness contrasts sharply with white people's inability to communicate with him successfully. They are able to marshal massive resources to capture and imprison him, but even after enlisting interpreters, they still do not manage to bridge the communication gap and thus prevent his penitentiary suicide, not being able to identify and honor his desire to go back to Taiwan rather than Communist China.

Synecdochic Whiteness

While in *The Woman Warrior* Kingston at one point displays a metonymic approach to whiteness, referring to whites through the elements of their clothing, in *China Men* whiteness is often constructed through synecdoche, in particular parts of white people's body, for example mouth. Bak Goong of the Sandalwood Mountains pays distinct attention to the white supervisor's mouth when the latter tells him to maintain silence during work: "'Shut up, Pakè.' He heard distinct syllables out of the *white demon's moving mouth*. 'Shut up. Go work. Chinaman, go work. You stay go work. Shut up'" (98, emphasis added). The white overseer's "moving mouth" may gain special prominence in order to accentuate the silencing quality of whiteness. Implicitly, the "white demon's moving mouth" contrasts with the China Man's mouth which is supposed to stay shut during work. A similar situation takes place when the China Men of the Sandalwood Mountains note that white female missionaries "spoke a well-intoned Cantonese, which sounded disincarnated coming out of their white faces" (110). Finding Cantonese and white faces mismatched, Chinese immigrants freeze cultural differences. Yet it is also worth mentioning that missionaries do not speak Cantonese solely for the purpose of forging communication but chiefly for the purpose of conversion.

Essentialization of Whiteness and Magnification of White Phenotypic Features

Whiteness is often magnified in the narrative through essentialization of the phenotypic features attributed to white people and through color aesthetics. Such essentialization and magnification of white phenotypic features takes place in the depiction of white female missionaries by Chinese immigrants of the Sandalwood Mountains as "Jesus demonesses with pale eyebrows and gold eyelashes" (110). Pale eyelashes conjure up the connotations of colorlessness. The white women look "strange" to the China Men, who fix them with an ethnographic gaze (110), also perceiving them as sexually titillating because of their racial difference. The China Men's sexual interest in the white women is to some extent a mirror reflection of Edward Said's statement about white people's conviction that the Orient was "a place where one could look for sexual experience unobtainable in Europe" (Said 190). A similar dynamic is at play behind some of the China Men's voyeuristic gaze upon the white women. Still other China Men display an interest merely in the women's ethnographic difference. Their touching of the yellow hair of the white women parallels the interest in the China Men of the Sierra Nevada Mountains shown by some of the white strangers.

The narrator's father also essentializes whiteness, but his essentialization no longer captures whiteness as colorless. During the interrogation of the narrator's father on Angel Island, both the interrogator and the narrator's father subject each other to close scrutiny. Cross-examination is mutual. The interrogator listens for the wrong word and watches for the wrong move on the part of the narrator's father, while the narrator's father also takes the interrogator under a magnifying glass, to the extent of noticing the minute details of his physicality like the yellow hair on the hands of an immigration official (56). The interrogation exposes an invidious side of whiteness when the father undergoes a physical examination: "In a wooden house, a white demon physically examined him, poked him in the ass and genitals, looked in his mouth, pulled his eyelids with a hook" (50). The above cited passage of *China Men* shows the father's terrorizing encounter with whiteness.

Another narrative moment when the father is terrorized by the prospect of an impending confrontation with whiteness takes place during his sea passage to the United States when he hides among cargo crates in the deck of the ship, being able to see a "white trouser leg" of a sailor who otherwise remains invisible to the father: "he saw a white trouser leg turn this way and that. He had never seen anything so white, the crease so sharp. A shark's tooth. A silver blade.... Then, blessedness, the trouser leg turned once more and walked away" (48). The white color and the white person again invite connotations of rapacity. Additionally, whiteness is again represented through synecdoche. A "white trouser leg" is dismembered from the rest of the person whose race would be unclear had they not been identified in the preceding passage as white. It remains to be guessed whether the whiteness of the texture is really so white or whether the father's fear magnifies its whiteness. A similar magnification of whiteness is visible in the representation of white bosses by Bak Goong of the Sandalwood Mountains as "demons in white suits" (102). A "white suit" adds an extra layer of whiteness to the mien of white people, being one more variation on the theme of executive whiteness in Kingston's works. An equivalent of the "white suit" in *The Woman Warrior* is the boss's immaculate white shirt, which the narrator stains with blood in her imagination, unsettling in this way the racial purity to which the boss cleaves so anxiously. "Demons in boss suits" also feature in "The Grandfather of the Sierra Nevada Mountains" chapter, appearing in the context of ruthless exploitation and merciless supervision demanding results irrespective of the casualties and the strain upon human beings (132). Yet in this case the whiteness of the supervisors receives no extra amplification on the aesthetic level of the narrative.

The father essentializes and magnifies white phenotypic features not only in the situations of white dominance over him but also when a white person finds themselves in a similar position to his own. This is how he describes the white man who together with him awaits the draft evaluation. He names whiteness as his most distinctive feature, mentioning it twice and in this way magnifying it: "The *white* man in front of me was *white* and fat—rolls of fat" (271, emphasis added). The perception of a white person mostly through the prism of their racial difference parallels the white perception of racial minorities almost exclusively through the prism of their racial color, approximating what Toni Morrison terms as metonymic displacement or color coding (*Playing in the Dark* 68). Drawing a comparison between his own appearance and the appearance of the white man, the father never mentions his own skin color: "And there I was next to him—skinny with rows of ribs" (271). The essentialist portrayal of the white man contrasts not only with the father's deracinated, deethnicized description of himself but also with the following passage in which the narrator describes a picture of Chinese American soldiers posing on the frontlines in Europe. The picture discussed by the narrator depicts the appearance of the soldiers with no mention of their race and no overt reflection on the fact that the gender of the soldiers was not self-evident because of the military attire, helmets etc. In her own editorial caption to the picture, the narrator is emphatic about the fact that her cousin "did not look peculiarly Chinese" (271). The narrator's construction of the passage may aim at exposing the very nature of racial and ethnic differences as primarily socially constructed rather than essentially biological. Still, the father's earlier representation of the fat would-be army recruit as so overtly white shows the psychological mechanism parallel to that often performed by whites constructing themselves as free of race and ethnicity. In his representation of the fat man, the father plays up the fat man's race, effacing his own.

If in the above cited fat man passage whiteness is presented as a color marking the white man on a par with other of his physical features, a different representation of whiteness is displayed in the already cited "Brother in Vietnam" chapter, which plays down, rather than plays up, the color of whiteness. Apart from being largely free of the demonic charge characterizing whiteness in other passages of *China Men*, whiteness is also implicitly represented as colorless in the passage devoted to soldiers' wives. All of them are characterized as "colorless" although they speak "in the accents of many nations and regions" (288). In the eyes of the brother, who identifies them primarily with their soldier husbands, they represent no one in particular, displaying no distinct identity of their own and no belonging. The race of the women in question remains unmentioned, yet "the accents of many nations and regions" imply diverse ethnicities. The only exception pertains to black women whose race is named, but they are also ranked as "colorless": "even the black women looked colorless" (288). Even though the blackness of black women is textualized here as colorless, blackness implicitly remains a color marker to a greater extent than whiteness.

As in *The Woman Warrior*, the whiteness of *China Men* also invites the connotations of syntheticity and artificiality. Bak Goong of the Sierra Nevada Mountains has an impression that white supervisors of the Sandalwood Mountains "stare" at him with "glass eyes" (102). Glass invokes a clear sense of desensitization and unwillingness to establish a visual exchange. Unlike in *The Woman Warrior*, mechanization of the United States does not necessarily invite negative associations but instills the narrator's father with awe. The immature narrator of *The Woman Warrior* expresses a palpable sense of unease about the extent of automation she stumbles upon at every twist and turn: "America has been full of machines and ghosts" (113). The narrator's father dreams of the Gold Mountain and the family stories of the place highlight automation as a positive aspect, not something to dread of: "'They know how to do things there; they're very good at organization and machinery. They have machines that can do anything.' 'They'll invent robots to do all the work, even answer the door.' ... 'They have swimming pools, elevators, lawns, vacuum cleaners, books with hard covers, X-rays'" (47). The depiction is a far cry from Brave Orchid's complaining in *The Woman Warrior* about the synthetic reality of the United States, in which her children cannot smell flowers or in which automation none the less has not solved the problems of labor and hence "she can't sleep in this country because it doesn't shut down for the night. Factories, canneries, restaurants—always somebody somewhere working through the night. It never gets done all at once here" (*The Woman Warrior* 123–124).

An oxymoronic application of the term "demon" carrying the marks of sacrilege occurs in the representation of Jesus as "a demon nailed to a cross" (110). It remains doubtful that the term "demon" would merely signify a "stranger," "alien," "foreigner" or "white person." The phrase reflects rather the first Chinese immigrants' bewilderment and disenchantment while looking at "Jesus pictures, which were grisly cards with a demon nailed to a cross, probably a warning about what happened to you if you didn't convert" (110). Kingston's construction of the scene stands in direct opposition to Frank Chin's accusations against her that she Christianizes Chinese culture by applying the B.C. nomenclature to speak of the events in Chinese history. Chin compares the practice to saying that Jesus died in the year of the pig. A similar effect is produced in the statement cited above and when missionaries are referred to as Jesus demons who can "sniff out Hawaiians and China Men even in the remotest valleys" (*China Men* 100). The label "demons" also applies to the Chinese immigrants who converted to Christianity (11) and the Chinese who did something wrong, as Ah Goong does when he trades his baby son for a girl. That is when his wife calls him a "dead man," a "dead demon" (16).

Meaningful Encounters with Whiteness and Other Interracial, Transnational Encounters

China Men not only registers enmity towards whiteness and the defamiliarization of whiteness, but also rare moments of meaningful encounters with whiteness, interaction or at least interest on both sides, even if it is marked by ethnographic overtones. An example of the most familiar whiteness comes in the form of two white men living together near the narrator's family Chinatown marshes. On the one hand, the narrator fixes them with an ethnographic gaze, but on the other, she speaks of them as familiar figures resembling lonely elderly China Men living together without families: "Like two old China Men, they lived together lonely with no families.... They were white men, but they lived like China Men" (242). They are familiar whites of the narrative. Unlike most other whites of *China Men* coming in touch with the narrator's family, they escape the classification of demons. Two poor white men living on the fringes of the Stockton Chinatown represent marginal whiteness; however, unlike some other marginal whites of the narrative, for example white railroad workers, they do not reach for what David Roediger terms as compensatory wages of whiteness.[4] Instead, in the spirit of transformational identity politics, they strike an informal alliance with people who may be culturally different to them, but share their marginal socio-economic status. The narrator credits two poor white men with saving her house from robbery and accomplishing it peacefully, "without a fight" (242). Aware of the marginal status of the white men, the narrator is anxious not to offend them, suspecting that they may identify with white burglars attempting the robbery and hence be offended by the label "winos." The marginality of the two poor white men of the Chinatown is accentuated by the fact that both of them disappear so unnoticeably that the narrator barely notices their fading away. One of them is killed by a tractor and the other has to move out when urban restructuring reaches his plot of land. The white man's brush with urban restructuring is one more point of intersection with the history of the narrator's family. Yet the narrator does not consciously reflect on this intersection, not mentioning the dispossession of her family by urban renewal, a point on which she elaborates in *The Woman Warrior*. In the narrator's eyes, the two men resemble mostly her China Men ancestors rather than herself and her immediate family. Unlike it is the case in *The Woman Warrior*, the narrator of *China Men* does not present her immediate family as overtly wounded by whiteness to such an extent as the generations of her forefathers were.

Positive contacts between Chinese immigrants and whites also occur on the sidelines of the railroad construction work in the Sierra Nevada Mountains. The interest in Chinese workers does not come from white people with whom the Chinese immigrants are in touch on a daily basis, that is white supervisors, white co-workers or white railway owners but from the people who specifically approach the Chinese with the purpose of getting to know them: white artists and journalists. Their visual representation of the Chinese shows valorization, fetishization and estrangement of the newly encountered strangers. White artists capture China Men as manly heroes, god-like figures with impressive physiques and eloquent facial expressions as well as elves with pigtails and antennae growing from their heads (139). On the one hand, China Men are idealized, but on the other, they are cast as aliens albeit domesticated and non-threatening.

The above cited encounters of the Hawaiian China Men with white female missionaries provide another example of fairly meaningful contacts between both racial groups. True as it is that some of the Hawaiian China Men fix the missionary women with an ethnographic and lascivious gaze, at least some of them derive pleasure from their very presence in their exclusively male society. While the white women approach the China Men with the intent of winning them over for Christianity, they also represent a different, human face of whiteness. I take an issue with Yiorgos Kalogeras's claim that the white women represent exploitative culture (238). Ulterior as their motives of conversion are in their dealing with China Men, one still needs to draw a line between exploitation and peaceful attempts at conversion.

Contacts between whites and Chinese Americans do not happen in a vacuum, but in the context of encounters with people of other races and ethnicities: Hawaiians in the "The Great Grandfather of the Sandalwood Mountains" chapter, African Americans in the "The Grandfather of the Rocky Mountains" chapter, Africans in "The Adventures of Lo Bun Sun," Japanese Americans and African Americans in the narrator's contemporary times. The Hawaiians of the Sandalwood Mountains are not referred to as demons, but as brown people or as Hawaiians. They enter a whole gamut of social interactions with China Men, ranging from casual social contacts, mutual invited celebrations to entering family relations exemplified by Bak Sook Goong's relationship with a Hawaiian woman and crowned by her emigration to China. While both sides show mutual interest, Hawaiians usually take the initiative, playing the role of an exemplary host society extending an invitation to newcomers. Unlike the white colonizers of Hawaii, the Native Hawaiians are not responsible for the exploitation of China Men. Proclaiming China Men married to Hawaiian women Hawaiians and granting them the right to stay in Hawaii, the king and queen of the Sandalwood Mountains constitute China Men as civil subjects, conferring upon them the rights denied people of Chinese ancestry by white Americans in the United States.

The Hawaiian Islands return in Kingston's *The Fifth Book of Peace*, the last novel analyzed in this study. However, it is no longer the Hawaii of the nineteenth century but the Hawaii of the 1960s. Hawaiians of *The Fifth Book of Peace* are no longer shown as interacting with the newcomers from China but with a particular Chinese American man and his interracial family swapping the position of a non-white minority in the mainland United States for the position of a non-white majority in Hawaii. *The Fifth Book of Peace* offers a much more incisive reflection on the place of Hawaiians in the power structure and the level of their subjection to exploitation. Critics charge Kingston with not devoting sufficient attention to linking the exploitation of the Hawaiian China Men to the exploitation of Native Hawaiians and African Americans on southern plantations. Caroline Yang cites numbers indicating that a relatively high proportion of Hawaiians worked on sugar plantations at the time when the narrator of *China Men* claims that Native Hawaiian workers were already gone from the Sandalwood Mountains: in 1872 over 50 percent of the gross 3,786 and in 1882 around one fifth of the total 10,243 workers. Yang identifies such a portrayal as illustrative of the "power of omission [visible as well] in the narrator's claim that she 'search[es] for [her] American ancestors' in the cane fields in Hawaii" (74). Yang also notes that by naming the Chinese as the "founding ancestors" of Hawaii (*China Men* 76), Kingston diminishes the importance of Native Hawaiians (Yang 76). According to Yang, Kingston erases the "role of capital and empire" in "The Great Grandfather of the Sandalwood Mountains" section (74). Indeed Kingston presents the exploitation of Chinese workers in Hawaii mostly in terms of racial oppression.

Considering that Hawaii did not belong at the time to the United States but was under the influence of American and European capital, Kingston might also have devoted more reflection to the transnational flow of capital and the nexus of intersecting transnational lines of oppression. Kingston's relative neglect of the issue might stem from the fact that when she was writing *China Men*, the focus in the Asian American community was on anchoring Asian Americans within the space of the United States rather than on looking for diasporic connections and transnational links between different types of oppression. She mentions the role of the British only in passing while describing Bak Goong's journey across China prior to the passage to the United States: "Traveling alone, he watched armies march or straggle by ... he flattened like a shadow on the earth, an army silhouetted against the moon. He spied British demons with big noses and guns" (89). In the Sandalwood section, the narrator also stops short of any deeper reflection on the fact that her grandfather Bak Sook Goong has many slaves in China, mentioning it in a matter of fact way (105). *The Woman Warrior* offers much more thought on feudal practices flourishing in China. Yet both works display a certain amount of contradiction, on the one hand, underscoring the relative wealth of the narrator's ancestral families and on the other, speaking of their poverty and the need to look for alternative means of subsistence in America. This is how the narrator of *China Men*, the Sandalwood section ponders on the motivation behind her ancestors' coming to Hawaii and what they find there: "So the ocean and hunger and some other urge made Cantonese people explorers and Americans (88).... You go out on the road to find adventure ... and what you find but another farm where the same things happen day after day. Work. Work. Work. Eat. Eat. Eat. Shit and piss. Sleep. Work. Work" (98).

As noted earlier, at this point of the narrative Kingston does not explicitly connect the racial oppression of Chinese sugar cane workers to the racial oppression of African Americans on the United States southern plantations. Yet one can trace subtle aesthetic innuendos, linking *China Men* and in particular the Sandalwood section of the narrative to the African American heritage of the southern United States through implicit references to Jean Toomer's *Cane*. One can find the echoes of Toomer's work, for example in the above mentioned statement by the narrator: "I have heard the land sing. I have seen the bright blue streaks of spirits whisking through the air. I again search for my American ancestors by listening in the cane" (*China Men* 87). Like the narrator of *Cane*, the narrator of *China Men* was not born in the land of her ancestors, discovering it only in her adult years and listening to the song of the land, which, as it is the case in *Cane*, is also a repository of their spirits and sometimes also bodies. It is while looking at the cane that the narrator of *China Men* formulates the starkest pronouncement on the inequities committed against the people of Hawaii: "Yet the rows and fields, organized like conveyor belts, hide murdered and raped bodies; this is a dumping ground" (85). "Conveyor belts" are a very clear allusion to the landscape of slave-like labor that the cane fields used to be, the cane bearing witness to the injustice unfolding on the land.

African Americans are mentioned overtly in "The Grandfather of the Sierra Nevada Mountains" chapter. Yet unlike Hawaiians, they do not receive any distinct semiotic signification, but are classed together with all other strangers/foreigners and like white people assigned the label "demons": "black demons." China Men building the Transcontinental Railroad are not shown in any interaction with African Americans working on their own team. This may be because of a particular labor situation set up by white owners and supervisors of the construction, an arrangement under which workers of different racial and ethnic groups are supposed to compete against each other on different teams in order to raise the efficiency rate. Although African Americans are not the subjects of exploitation but its objects, they are also labeled "demons." Yet in this case the label denotes "strangers," "foreigners," without carrying pejorative connotations hidden behind the same label when it is applied to white owners and supervisors of the Transcontinental Railroad. The term "demon" receives visible intensification in application to the afore-mentioned whites featuring in the positions of oppressive, exploitative power in relation to China Men: "Pig catcher demons." "Snakes." "Turtles." "Dead demons." "A human body can't work like that." "The demons do not believe this is a human body. This is a chinaman's body" (137). Aware that they are perceived by whites as working beasts, China Men momentarily seem to assume the perspective of white people, speaking of their bodies as if they were separate entities disconnected from the rest of themselves and divested of individual identities. A certain inconsistency in the neutral application of the label "demon" as a "stranger," "foreigner" takes place when initially black co-workers are applied the label "black demons," while white people are referred to as Irishmen, Welshmen or Injuns (137). White workers join the nominal ranks of "demons" after they refuse to participate in China Men's strike: "They would have won forty-five dollars if the thousand demon workers had joined the strike. Demons would have listened to demons" (142).

Black people are briefly invoked in the spirit of interracial solidarity in the section devoted to the narrator's father, "The Father from China." African Americans feature in an impromptu invented poem by the narrator's father, who composes the poem at the request of an illiterate man who spent twenty years in the United States, finding himself on Angel Island together with Chinese newcomers. While he is about to make the journey back home, they await the permission to enter the United States. The poem goes as follows: "'On the Gold Mountain, I met black men black like coal'" (54). Having never encountered poetry, the illiterate man applauds the narrator's father, claiming, together with other literate Angel Island internees, that it provides perfect exemplification. One can speculate that being aware that the illiterate man has had no experience of poetry, the father constructs a poem, which would be illustrative of his own experience. At his entry to the United States the father could not have met black people themselves. He must have been either told about them by the illiterate man or other China Men in their stories of the Gold Mountain. An association of black men with coal suggests that like coal, one of the basic minerals, African Americans are the essence of the American soil. Rather than come across gold on the Gold Mountain, the I-speaker of the father's poem encounters "people black like coal," implying that the people of the United States are its gold to be treasured above everything else. The poem unites two different minerals: gold and coal, both of which can be perceived as a link between African Americans and Chinese Americans. Reflecting on the aesthetics of race, the protagonist of Kingston's third novel, *Tripmaster Monkey*, wonders which color is closest to Chinese Americans. One of his choices is gold, in the end dismissed by him because of the connotations of stereotypes about Chinese Americans that it might evoke, like for example greediness and financial cunningness: "I'm a Gold. We're golds. Nah, too evocative of tight-fisted Chang" (*Tripmaster Monkey* 326). Michel Foucault claims that power always involves the "production and exchange of signs" (Foucault, *Power* 239). The above-cited *China Men* poem shows the Chinese subjects becoming actively involved in this production and exchange of signs: the narrator's father through the very act of composition and his fellow Chinese Angel Island detainees through their understanding and appreciation of the poem. Ultimately, the poem constitutes an alternative to white dominated power dynamics, in which both Asian Americans and African Americans are related to whiteness as if it was a perfect touchstone. Instead, they are juxtaposed in relation to each other.

An interracial connection between African Americans and Asian Americans also features in the section devoted to the narrator's contemporary times. The story of the Wild Man of the Green Swamp makes the narrator think of an African American man living in Chinatown and resembling his counterpart:

> There was a Wild Man in our slough too, only he was a black man. He wore a shirt and no pants, and some mornings when we walked to school, we *saw* him asleep under the bridge. The police came and took him away. The newspaper said he was crazy; it had been *on the lookout for him* for a long time, but we *had seen* him every day [224].

The passage once again reaffirms the trope of seeing and not seeing. For the narrator and her siblings the black man is one of the marginal inhabitants of Chinatown. For the police that are "on the lookout for him" he is just a body to police and subject to the Panopticon of white power, the Panopticon which for a long time has failed. The narrator stresses their casual ability to see the black man and the police's clear failure to detect him despite an apparent intention to do so.

China Man presents encounters between people of African and Chinese origin not only in the continental context of the United States, but also in a transnational one. Such encounters occur in "The Adventures of Lo Bun Sun" chapter whose chief protagonist Lo Bun Sun is a Chinese equivalent of Robinson Crusoe. The very crashing of Lo Bun Sun's ship at sea is implicitly cast as an act of punishment for sailing aboard a slave ship. Figuratively, the disaster is presented as an act of solidarity on the part of the elements with black slaves: "The ocean reared black waves that knocked the sailors off the decks" (225). As in *The Woman Warrior*, the occurrence of black people in the narrative concurs with the occurrence of blackness in the imagery. As it is the case in *The Woman Warrior*, both appear towards the end of the narrative, in the following sequence: first the black man resembling the Wild Man of the Green Swamp, later a mention of the slave ship corresponding to the blackness in the imagery of the narrative and finally black people resurfacing in the section of the chapter devoted to Lo Bun Sun's sojourn on the desert island. Black cannibals visiting Lo Bun Sun's island are identified as "black demons" (231). Unlike in "The Grandfather of the Sierra Nevada Mountains," the term "demons" is not used in a neutral fashion denoting strangers, but carries very clear condemnation and vilification of the black people who engage in cannibalistic practices. The "Adventures of Lo Bun Sun" exempts whites from being the only truly demonized racial group of *China Men*. The narrator calls the black people visiting Lo Bun Sun's island "savages," presenting a naturalistic account of their cannibalistic practices: "They slaughtered one prisoner and dressed the meat in front of the others" (231). The description strikingly resembles above cited Ralph Ellison's account of the lynching in "Party Down the Square." As mentioned earlier, there is no such naturalism of description in the passages pertaining to the massacres of Chinese immigrants by white Americans. The features of the black people visiting Lo Bun Sun's island are never fully developed, ostensibly because Lo Bun Sun can see them from the distance through the spyglass. They remain "black figures against the yellow sand" (231). Lo Bun Sun represents them in his ink drawings as "silhouettes" whose "facial expressions" he could not examine because of the distance (231).

In her characterization of the relationship between Lo Bun Sun and Friday, Kingston does not significantly undermine the original Robinson Crusoe story. In line with the discourse of white colonization, Lo Bun Sun establishes a hierarchy of importance on the island, naming Friday and ordering him to call himself "Teacher." Friday also needs to learn the language of Lo Bun Sun, who teaches him to read and write, spreading the fire of civilization in a similar way to white colonizers. Friday is identified as a savage even before it becomes apparent that he would also be ready to eat human remains. Apart from the above, Friday is textualized in the narrative as Lo Bun Sun's servant and pupil. To a great extent the relation between Lo Bun Sun and Friday follows the pattern of white paternalism, in which Lo Bun Sun assumes the role of a cultivated savior and caretaker whose protectorate Friday highly appreciates. Lo Bun Sun clearly fails in his role of a protector when he endangers and sacrifices the life of Friday by ordering him to talk to native attackers of his ship. It bears mentioning that despite colonial and feudal connotations, Lo Bun Sun is never referred to as master by Friday. Depicting Lo Bun Sun and Friday in the act of writing together, the narrator constructs a demeaning portrayal of Lo Bun Sun, calling him "the Naked Toiling Mule": "the Naked Toiling Mule and Friday" (232). At the same time both are compared to scholars. In *The Woman Warrior*, the narrator identifies herself as a chief knot-maker twisting her stories into designs and yet she performs barely any transformation on the original Robinson Crusoe tale. While in *The Woman Warrior* she transforms female-centered tales in the hope of ensuring liberation for herself and other women, a parallel practice is not employed in male-centered *China Men*, for example there is no reflection on the narrator's part that after the death of his wife, Lo Bun Sun leaves the children behind. The very figure of Lo Bun Sun is also to a degree problematic in the context of the whole novel because at a certain point of his life he chooses the profession of a sugarcane planter in Brazil, finding himself directly on the opposite axis of the labor position to that of Chinese workers on sugarcane plantations in Hawaii. The fact that the national of China chooses to settle momentarily in Brazil amplifies the transnational dimension of Lo Bun Sun's story.

The last non-white ethnic group entering interactions with Chinese Americans is represented by Japanese Americans. The narrator and her Chinese American family have amicable relations with their Japanese American neighbors inhabiting Chinatown, but still preserve their suspicions. An undercurrent of suspicion is visible in the narrator's assuring herself that their neighbors were Japanese Americans, not the Japanese and therefore they should not be linked with the war crimes committed by the Japanese on the Chinese. The narrator and her family respect the intactness of the Japanese American property after they are incarcerated in internment camps. The Japanese Canadian Nakane family of *Obasan* never recovers their property after they are interned because they are never allowed to return to the area which they forcibly had to leave. They also entrust the caretaking of their house into the uncertain hands of a white neighbor, whom they fail to identify as a sexual predator. The *China Men*'s narrator's family shares the Japanese Americans' sense of being abject racial subjects, manifesting itself in their premonition that they may one day follow in the Japanese Americans' footsteps into the internment camps. Mutual insecurity does not shield both sides from mutual prejudices. The immature narrator and her siblings suspect their Japanese American neighbors of displaying amicability out of the fear of being lynched by them. It is interesting that the narrator and her siblings should imagine themselves in the subject positions equivalent to those represented by white oppressors responsible for lynchings. The narrator moderates the strength of her statement by attributing its source to their "peasant minds" (273).

There is also a strong suspicion of hiding heinous crimes by Japanese Americans and therefore showing generosity and amicability out of ulterior motives. Candidly, the narrator also admits the ulterior motives on the part of her family by guessing that her parents try to bribe the Japanese American neighbors into reciprocating their friendliness "when the time came for [them] Chinese to be the ones in camp" (273). Imperfect as the relations with the Japanese Americans are under the surface in *China Men*, they are still superior to the relations with the Japanese Americans in *The Woman Warrior*, where the Japanese American children are identified as the ones attacking Chinese Americans at school.[5] There is no mention of any cross-racial solidarity in *The Woman Warrior* between Japanese Americans and Chinese Americans, but only between Chinese Americans and African Americans, who defend the narrator and other Chinese

American children and whom the immature narrator admires for their exuberant ways.

Chinese Americans' Second Sight, White Blindness, White Gaze and White Supervision

Chinese immigrants' and Chinese Americans' ability to see other racial and ethnic groups in a fairly meaningful way falls within the larger pattern of their second sight, contrasting with the blindness of white people featuring in the narrative. The blindness of white people can be categorized in a two-fold way, on the one hand, as figurative blindness consisting in the inability to recognize racial minorities as active subjects and acknowledge their contribution to building the country and fuelling its economy. This type of blindness could be classified through Ralph Ellison's metaphor of "a peculiar disposition of the eyes of those with whom [the Invisible Man] come[s] in contact. A matter of the construction of their *inner* eyes, those eyes with which they look through their physical eyes upon reality" (*Invisible Man* 3, original emphasis). The other type of blindness at play in *China Men* pertains to literal blindness consisting in literally not being able to see people of color as is the most conspicuous in the above cited passage, when the immature narrator and her siblings can see the Chinatown black man every day, while the police cannot find him despite having been "on the lookout for him for a long time" (224). Chinese immigrants are literally invisible to white people in *China Men* when the latter literally fail to distinguish between particular individuals, homogenizing all Chinese Americans and not being able to tell them apart, which is the case when the narrator's father gives a different name every time when he is arrested by the police on account of conducting illegal gambling (241).

White people's gaze in *China Men* is mostly the gaze of supervision, the gaze that either merely sweeps the surface of one's body to check its subordination or if it penetrates inside, then merely for the purpose of establishing the veracity of what is said. This is the gaze to which white interrogators subject the narrator's father during an interrogation on Angel Island: "They looked into his eyes for lies. Even the Chinese American looked into his eyes, and they repeated his answers as if doubting them" (56). The gaze of white immigration officials is a recurrent theme in Kingston's works, featuring prominently in *The Woman Warrior* as well. As discussed in Chapter 1 of this study, reminiscing on her own experience of being interrogated on her entry to the United States, Brave Orchid compares the gaze of fully assimilated Chinese Americans, in particular that of Moon Orchid's husband, to that of white interrogators. However, unlike in *China Men*, a Chinese American interpreter in *The Woman Warrior* refuses to play a complicit role in the subjugation of Chinese subjects. Rather than fully cooperate, he hints the correct answer to Brave Orchid. It is not without significance that the span of twenty years divides each of the above mentioned entries into the United States. The narrator's father enters as a paper son on fake papers, whereas Brave Orchid enters after the passing of the 1943 Magnuson Act abolishing a ban on Chinese immigration. *The Woman Warrior* Moon Orchid's entry almost another twenty years later looks by far the most innocuous, countering Brave Orchid's premonitions, resembling a mere formality, with no interrogation and "Immigration Ghosts" "stamping papers" (*The Woman Warrior* 133). Comparing her own entry to that of Moon Orchid, Brave Orchid concludes that "These new immigrants had it easy. On Ellis Island the people were thin after forty days at sea and had no fancy luggage" (134). Brave Orchid compares Moon Orchid's entry with her own, but she draws no comparison between her own journey as well as an entrance into the country and that of her husband even though it was by all accounts a much more grueling one, the probable reasons being the focus of *The Woman Warrior* on women and Brave Orchid's proclivity to present herself as the one braving the toughest odds. The moment of Moon Orchid's entry into the country is not specified, but it is either the time of the quotas for particular Asian countries or the period already following the changes in the United States immigration law initiated by John F. Kennedy and enacted several years after his death—in 1965. The reform originated by President Kennedy abolished the system of selecting immigrants on the basis of their national origin. Proponents of the reform did not expect that it would lead to a large influx of Asian population (Hing 39). They anticipated more immigrants from southern and eastern Europe, from countries like Greece and Italy (Kennedy 1).[6]

    The gaze of white people upon Chinese Americans is captured not only at the moment of entrance into the country, but also at the moment of being banished from a particular territory. Whites of *China Men* watch as the Alaskan Indians row away the Alaskan China Men to a nearby schooner, having earlier sealed their fate by voting to drive them out. The position of white people is two-fold. On the one hand, they initiate the driving out of the China Men, supervising its execution, while on the other, they use a different minority group to execute it. The whiteness of the "Alaska China Men" section shows its fomenting face, pitting one minority ethnic group against another. Unlike in the next novel analyzed here, Leonard Chang's *The Fruit 'N Food*, the fomenting face of whiteness remains uncamouflaged, displaying itself in plain sight.

2. Demonic and Oxymoronic Whiteness 93

Another source of the white supervising gaze can be traced in the white overseers watching over the Chinese immigrant workers. Yet this gaze does not remain unreturned. In reaction to the supervising gaze of whiteness and the white supervisors' scolding for working too slowly, the Sierra Nevada China Men "glare" "out of the corners of their eyes" (132). Kingston constructs the above cited scene in such a way as to invert the power dynamics of labor on the Transcontinental Railway. Both the China Men and their white supervisors are immersed in the darkness of the tunnel, but the China Men are placed on scaffolding above the whites, who are the objects of the China Men's gaze rather than its subjects. They are audacious enough to drop some of their tools as a sign of dissatisfaction.

A different spatial and visual arrangement can be traced in the supervision scene on the sugarcane plantation of Hawaii. Bak Goong is on the same level as his supervisors and it is the supervisor rather than Bak Goong that "stare[s]" at Bak Goong with his "glass eyes" (102). If in this scene Bak Goong is the object of the gaze, for most of the work he features as its subject. Already on his way to the United States, during the sea passage, Bak Goong paints eyes on the bow of the ship presumably to prevent the ship from altering the course (90). The scene can be read as a foreshadowing of his visual examination of the new land. Time and again it is emphasized in the narrative that China Men saw the Gold Mountain "with their own eyes" (37). Both Bak Goong and Ah Goong are seeing subjects who can see white people and structures of oppression generated by them. Still, Bak Goong takes a much more decisive stand against the structures of oppression, championing a protest against the ban on speech during work. Ah Goong participates in the strike on the Transcontinental Railroad, yet he is not shown as one of its leaders.

China Men are cast not only as subjects of vision exclusively in relation to white people and the new land, but also in a broader, more metaphysical sense. Working constantly underground immersed in darkness, Ah Goong develops metaphysical vision very similar to Richard Wright's the Man Who Lived Underground. Darkness triggers visions and reflections unavailable to most people. Ah Goong "learned to see many colors in black" (132). He was also able to see time and see "what's real" (132). "See[ing] many colors in black" parallels learning to look into the gourd in *The Woman Warrior*. Looking into the gourd for the very first time, the narrator of *The Woman Warrior* as the embodiment of Fa Mu Lan can initially see nothing but the black surface of water. Only after she learns to look does she discover the magic visual qualities of the gourd. The Ah Goong passage accentuates "black" as a color of possibilities in a parallel way to the textualization of blackness in *The Woman Warrior* black paintings episode discussed in the imagery section of Chapter 1. *China Men* also registers the narrator's experience parallel to that of Ah Goong seeing "many colors in black," when she looks into the black water in the cellar well. The water is alive: "shining, bulging, black water, live, alive, *like an eye*, deep and alive" (237). Associating blackness with vision and the depth of vision, the narrator calls the well "the black sparkling eye of the planet," "an entrance into the other side of the world," "to China" (237). An equivalent encounter with blackness takes place underneath the narrator's family laundry in a network of tunnels explored by the narrator and her siblings in their childhood. Stepping into darkness, into "the inside of the earth, the insides of the city," the narrator, together with her siblings, discovers what is invisible, hidden from the eyes of other people, who "didn't know how incomplete civilization is," who did not "know the secret of cities" (254). The passage again resonates with Richard Wright's "The Man Who Lived Underground." Mesmerized by his underground visions, the Man Who Lived Underground luxuriates in the scope of his visions, displaying willingness to share them with other people.

Penetrating underground in the context of metaphysical vision also features in "The Grandfather of the Sandalwood" section. Clearing the land for future crops, the China Men are represented as the first to explore the entrails of the local territory and "see the meat and bones of the red earth" (100). While Ah Goong and the China Men of the Sierra Nevada Mountains explore the earth horizontally, the China Men of the Sandalwood Mountains excavate it vertically, looking into its very underpinnings. The vertical visual exploration continues when Bak Goong "look[s] up" at the mountains compared to "great stage curtains" "part[ing] or ris[ing]" (102). After the curtains move aside, Bak Goong "would see behind them what really runs the world, whether the gods' faces are kind or evil" (102). The mention of "gods" gives Bak Goong's vision the characteristics of seeing into the realm of the supernal. The textualization of sight in terms of the rising curtain is a recurrent trope highlighted in the black paintings section of *The Woman Warrior* and in the play staging section of *Tripmaster Monkey*.[7]

Since the title of this study is *Visions of Whiteness*, I find it appropriate to briefly allude to the general statements in *China Men* pertaining to the typology of vision although they are not immediately related to perceiving whiteness or extraordinary visual abilities of Chinese Americans as contrasted with white blindness. One of the most profound statements on the nature of human perception is formulated by a Japanese American student of optics encountered by the narrator's brother in Vietnam:

"Clarity was a matter of preference and culture" (295). In other words, how a human being perceives external reality is to a great extent determined by their own subjective predilection and a cultural bias. The statement falls short of the claim that perception is culturally constructed, but it is close to it. A claim which bears an immediate parallel to the one cited above reads: "They asked the man in chains where the gold was, and he said that all they saw was gold" (309). Perception is a matter of individual interpretation. What you see often depends on what you hope to see.[8]

China Men emphasizes that seeing is the first step to embodying particular ideas. Upon the first sighting of the Statue of Liberty, the narrator's father concludes that "the Americans *saw* the idea of Liberty so real that they *made* a statue of it" (49). While "the idea of liberty" on American soil is not in any way questioned by the narrator's father enchanted with the New York skyline, the very narrative construction of the Statue of Liberty scene undermines the idea of freedom because the passage is preceded with the depiction of the father's cramped journey to the United States in a box upon the ship. It is followed by an alternative vision of the father's entrance to the United States, which does not end with the father's walking free off the ship, but with his incarceration in an immigration detention center on Angel Island. The idea of freedom totally evaporates with the father's physical examination in an enclosed space of a "wooden house," giving the scene the semblance of an envelope structure, starting in the cramped space of the box aboard the ship bound for the United States, the box out of which the father wants to look out and ending with the wooden house, in which a white immigration official physically examines him, compromising the intimacy of his body, "pok[ing] him in the ass and genitals" (50). The father's enchantment with the figuration of freedom in the Statue of Liberty contrasts with an equivalent entrance to the United States depicted by Amy Ling in "Whose America Is It?." On the surface, both Ling and the *China Men* father depict the Statue of Liberty in similar terms. For the father, she is "a gray and green giantess" "carr[ying] fire and a book" (49). For Amy Ling as a child, the Statue is "the giant green lady with the torch and book" (27). Invoking the idea of freedom at the sight of the Statue of Liberty, Amy Ling's mother identifies the United States as "the land of the free; the country where everyone was treated equally," "the Beautiful Country," "the land of wealth and opportunity" (27). Yet the mother's reassurance is preceded by a conversation between herself and her three-year-old son. To the son's question "Whose America is it? Theirs or ours?," the mother responds "Theirs," bringing tears to the son's eyes. Ling contrasts an account of her own entry into the country with the 1990s entries denied: the 1992 turning down of the Haitians by President George Herbert Walker Bush, the 1993 Golden Enterprise rejection by President Clinton, and 60 percent of *Newsweek* respondents declaring in 1993 that immigration was not beneficial for the country (27).

While on the whole Chinese Americans are characterized in the narrative as endowed with sharp vision, at some points they are also portrayed as suffering from inability to see others and as mimicking[9] whiteness and the structures of oppression. Their figurative blindness is visible in their approach to some members of their most immediate community. *The Woman Warrior* registers frictions between first and second generation immigrants. *China Men* records equivalent tensions between already established first generation Chinese immigrants and fresh immigrants or so called fresh-off-the-boats. Before starting their own business, the narrator's parents suffer exploitation from their fellow–Chinese employers. Yet after already finding a measure of self-aggrandizement, stability and settlement, they replicate structures of oppression in relation to their nephews from Hong Kong, who sleep in their basement and work at a grocery store for next to nothing. *China* Men also sheds light on the exploitation of immigrants by fellow-immigrants from equivalent backgrounds. Like Leon of Fae Myenne Ng's *Bone*, the narrator's father is cheated out of his laundry business by his partners.

The vision of demonic whiteness emerging from *China Men* exposes its brutality, dehumanization and exploitation of non-white racial groups, all of which undermine its self-assumed position of exemplary normativity. Seen through the eyes of Chinese immigrants, white demons reveal the features that estrange them from the rest of human kind. Devilish as they are, white demons with whom China Men come in touch are first of all the executors of the policies drafted to a great extent by invisible white originators of oppression. Kingston ensures visibility for the laws that helped to propel the ostracism of Chinese immigrants in "The Laws" chapter, rendering the oxymoronic character of whiteness, which presents itself as universal and at the same time cautiously guards its exclusivity.

The Legal and Socio-Historical Oxymoron of Whiteness

The legal and socio-historical construction of whiteness captured by Kingston in "The Laws" exemplifies the oxymoron of whiteness consisting in simultaneous gesturing towards universality and particularity. On the one hand, whiteness dresses itself in the robes of the self-proclaimed standard-bearer, the self-declared legal norm. On the other hand, this self-proclaimed norm rests on the principle of exclusivity and exclusion. Wielding a weapon of exclusion, whiteness has constructed a legally manufactured white identity that bars non-whites, in this case Chinese and other Asian immigrants from citizenship, economic resources, space, the "mainstream" American society and "mainstream" American culture. Kingston not only exposes anti–Chinese and anti–Asian legislation, but also shows Chinese immigrants' responses to this legislation, their failed and successful attempts at countervailing various forms of exclusion and "exclusive" treatment they received.

Kingston calls *China Men* a "history book," claiming that she placed "The Laws" chapter in the middle of the book in order to "educate a reader" ("Coming Home," Paul Skenazy's Interview with Maxine Hong Kingston 108). The central location of "The Laws" as well as the chapter itself has invited a lot of critical attention. Donald Goellnicht argues that the "centric authority of American law is subverted and contested by the 'eccentric' or marginal, but richly imaginative stories of China Men that surround it" (Goellnicht cited in Nishime 70). In line with Goellnicht's sentiments, David Leiwei Li notes that the "section on laws excluding Chinese" "estranges or rather excludes the reader from the customary view of American history" ("China Men" 491). Kingston herself speaks of being able to "see more particularly because she know[s] more of [Chinese American] history" (Kingston cited in Madsen 241–242). By including "The Laws" chapter, Kingston grants an average reader of her day a more particularist point of view. According to Li, Kingston "transform[s]" anti–Chinese laws into a "counter-language," helping to ensure that "history is not conceived as a glorious expansionist epic but as a systemic exploitation of the ethnic minority whose contribution has been appropriated but legal status rejected" ("China Men" 492). Linda Ching Sledge notes that "Kingston has thus included a lengthy central digression in *China Men* containing purely factual testimony of Chinese American legal history ("The Laws") because some detractors have persisted in faulting her works for not being revisionist histories" (2). Sledge goes on to say that "the inclusion of this section balances the remaining chapters on '"invented' or idealized history with substantial documentary material" (2). Observing that facts "acquire a particular meaning in the context of the author's research and writing" (227), Yiorgos Kalogeras claims that on account of the central position, "The Laws" chapter highlights "various facts that are scattered throughout" (236). Brook Thomas reflects on the limitations of the law exposed by Kingston in the chapter. These limitations pertain both to the very construction of the laws and the generic limitations in front of the author trying to shed light on the legal situation of subjects affected by these laws. According to Thomas, "works of the imagination, like Kingston's" "can, more effectively than the law, provide a vision of what constitutes active citizenship" (691). Kingston admits that the writing of "The Laws" section was a challenge to her as an author, going as far as to claim that her editor rewrote that section to "make it sound legal" (179). She also notes that "'There's poetic language and there's legal language.' I was contrasting the language of feeling, where you could make friends with the characters and feel for them, with this formal, distanced language" (Perry's Interview with Kingston 179). Explaining why she placed "The Laws" in the middle of *China Men*, Kingston claims that it was a way of ensuring that the readers would not skip this section, also drawing parallels between "The Laws" section and the psalms placed in the mid-section of the Bible. Kingston argues that like psalms or commandments, the laws were "implacable" (179).

Anti-Chinese laws were a tool of legitimizing white power, constituting what Foucault terms as "instrumental modes" of power (*Power* 344). Most of the laws cited by Kingston in "The Laws" chapter come from the nineteenth and the beginning of the twentieth century, a time which Valerie Babb identifies as best "illuminat[ing] the development of an ideology of whiteness" (45). Apart from directly targeting the Chinese and other Asians, the laws discussed by Kingston reflected the penal regime of the nineteenth century, which displayed concern not so much for "what individuals did"—whether it was lawful or not, but for "what they might do, what they were capable of doing" (Foucault, *Power* 57). Anti-Asian laws show that for the white apparatus of power the Chinese presented a very high level of what Foucault calls "dangerousness," or "potential for crime" (57). However, the main causes of Chinese and Asian exclusion by the white apparatus of power lie in the national ideology of originally white centered America and economic motives.

The "Nordic" Fiber of the Laws

In the very first laws cited by Kingston whiteness constitutes itself as the cornerstone of the American nation, its very essence, reserving the right to define the racial and ethnic make-up of the nation as well as to exclude non-whites. In theory, the Naturalization Act of 1870 invoked by Kingston gave the right to citizenship not only to "free whites" but also to "African aliens" (Kingston, *China Men* 150). Yet in practice, America was to be predominantly white. Kingston cites the Nationality Act Congress debate during which Congressmen proclaimed that "America would be a nation of 'Nordic fiber'" (150). Kingston's reflection on the equation of whiteness and Americanness begins only in connection with the passing of the above-cited 1870 Nationality Act. While whiteness came to be used synonymously with Americanness, it had not always been the case. Citing the *Oxford English Dictionary* definition of whiteness, Gary Taylor dates the first written explication of the term "American" as "an American Indian" or as "an American of European descent" at 1765 (342, 409). Taylor cites European accounts of South American and Latin American Indians whose pale skin startled some of the darker-skinned Europeans: "Some Amerindians may have been shockingly pale" (63). Many of these Amerindians were perceived as white by the aforementioned travellers. Taylor argues that since 1700 the whiteness of "Anglos" came to be taken for granted (7). Native Americans began to be seen as "red" only after the British started to see themselves as white. The same process applied to Asians who were not necessarily at once perceived as "yellow": "Having redefined themselves as 'white' (rather than ruddy or red), Brits on both sides of the Atlantic could, in the eighteenth century, redefine Amerindians as 'redskins' or 'the red man.' The originally 'white' peoples of Asia were recategorized as 'yellow'" (344).

Still, the definition of whiteness and Americanness was not yet entirely crystallized. Envisioning the United States as a nation of white people, Benjamin Franklin went on to say that only Anglo-Saxons were truly white in their complexion (Babb 33). In 1782 Hector Crèvecoeur did not invoke whiteness explicitly, but he defined the American as "either an European, or the descendant of an European," no longer limiting Americans exclusively to Anglo-Saxons (Crèvecoeur cited in Babb 37). Tracing the emergence of xenophobia and nativism,[10] Ali Bedhad cites chief nativist's, Thomas Whitney's, distinction between "native"/"old" immigrants and "alien"/"new" immigrants (138). Bedhad also cites Alexander Hamilton's statement, comparing immigrants to a "Grecian horse" (Hamilton cited in Bedhad 116). Valerie Babb notes that "From the 1700s on, whiteness is key to the maintenance of American nation-state identity" (37). In a similar vein, Bedhad reflects on the "role of xenophobia in the construction of national identity" (116). Anti-alien parties gained in strength in the late 1830s, but xenophobia started to bear the hallmarks of an organized political movement only in the mid-nineteenth century (Bedhad 117). Bedhad attributes the solidifying of nativism to the rise in the number of unskilled immigrants between 1845 and 1854. Three million people entered the United States in that period. Most of the newcomers were Irish and German laborers (Bedhad 118). Even with the intensification of nativist views in the mid-nineteenth century, immigrants of the period were still viewed as political dissidents posing a danger to the ideological underpinnings of the republic. In the late nineteenth century they came to be viewed as polluters threatening the health of the country because of bringing in "dangerous germs and genes" (Bedhad 131). Physicians like Alfred C. Reed and Terence Powderly denied any anti-alien sentiments, but proclaimed their concern for the health of the nation (Bedhad 135–136). Both wrote their treatises at the beginning of the twentieth century. Bedhad traces a distinction between "native"/"old" immigrants and "alien"/"new" immigrants both in the writings of the mid-nineteenth century nativists like for example Thomas Whitney and the turn of the century physicians ostensibly standing guard over the health of the nation (137–138). The medical discourse was incorporated into the public rhetoric of the state. Bedhad notes that doctors of the United States Public Health Service were not only "healers," but also authorities on social and moral issues (132). According to Bedhad, their scientific writings were instrumental in the introduction of quotas of 1921 and 1924. In Bedhad's view, they also contributed to the stemming of immigration from eastern and southern Europe. In 1891 Congress passed an immigration law excluding immigrants "suffering a loathsome or a dangerous contagious disease," the "feeble-minded," "idiots," and the "insane" (Bedhad 132). The term "loathsome" may potentially exclude any disease. Each poor immigrant was marked with a particular letter denoting their state of health (133). The procedure approximated medical triage, the sorting or screening of patients in order to determine which service is initially required.[11] Bedhad claims that a "disciplinary approach to immigration" "where every underclass immigrant" was assumed to be potentially diseased and thus "subjected to examination and discipline" helped to generate "a permanent 'state of emergency' that perpetuates an exclusive and differential form of national identity" (138–139).

The figures of immigrants emerging from the anti–Asian legislation resemble Julia Kristeva's definition of the abject—the other side of the socially sanctified: "For abjection, when all is said and done, is the other side of religious, moral, and ideological codes on which rest the sleep of individuals and the breathing spells of societies" (Kristeva, *The Powers of Horror* 209). Kelly Oliver, the editor of *The Portable Kristeva* defines the abject as that which "calls into question borders and threatens identity. The abject is on the borderline, and as such it is both fascinating and terrifying" (225).[12] This particular definition of abjection matches future stereotyping of Asian American immigrants as on the one hand, model minority subjects, while on the other, "yellow peril." The border metaphor in the definition of abjection also resonates with the above-cited

Bedhad's *A Forgetful Nation: On Immigration and Cultural Identity in the United States* (2005) and Karen Shimakawa's *National Abjection. Asian American Body Onstage. National Abjection* (2002). According to Bedhad, the border "posits a binary and exclusionary relation between a self that obeys the law and an alien who transgresses it" (165). Shimakawa notes that ostracism against Asian Americans facilitated American subject formation, "mark[ing] the 'frontier' of Americanness" (Shimakawa 6). The term "frontier" is very applicable in the discussion of Chinese American exclusion, the construction of whiteness and Americanness. Through their very presence on the American land and the legislation aimed at excluding and circumscribing them, Chinese Americans helped to demarcate the "frontier" of whiteness and Americanness. Through their labor in the American west, they helped to settle and demarcate the physical and geographical "frontier" of the American land.

The third law cited by Kingston in "The Laws" chapter sheds light on the positioning of Chinese immigrants in the frontier land of California. The Californian Constitutional Convention of 1878 barred Chinese immigrants from entering California. Ironically, while introducing the Chinese exclusion from California, Kingston reaches for the term "to settle 'the Chinese problem'" (151). The phrase "to settle" is ironic because they were effectively unsettled by the anti–Chinese legislation, being prevented from settling or setting roots. Kingston is emphatic about the fact that thirty-five out of one hundred and fifty-five delegates voting during the Convention were Europeans, not American citizens, which once again exposes whiteness as not only a passport to Americanness, but also a key to setting benchmarks for other people's Americanness even when those casting votes were not American citizens themselves. The aforementioned legislation gave Californian counties and cities the right to "confine" "within specified areas" or "throw out" Chinese immigrants altogether (151). By physically excluding Chinese immigrants and circumscribing their presence, the American frontier land effectively created a number of micro and macro frontiers.

The question of Chinese immigrants' exclusion and spatial confinement relates directly to the problem of their assimilation. On the one hand, the measures against Chinese immigrants impeded assimilation and were supposed to isolate Chinese immigrants from the rest of American society. On the other hand, whites charged Chinese immigrants with an inability to assimilate, citing their lack of assimilation as a reason for their exclusion from American society. In order to explain discrimination against Chinese immigrants, whites engaged in a tautological reasoning. Chinese immigrants were dubbed as "a race 'that will not assimilate'"

(Kingston, *China Men* 153). In the 1893 ruling of Yue Ting v. the United States, the Supreme Court gave Congress the right to drive out Chinese immigrants, identifying them as a race "'who continue to be aliens, having taken no steps toward becoming citizens'" (153). In the 1889 ruling of Chae Chan Ping v. the United States, the Supreme Court indirectly defined Chinese immigrants as "vast hordes" "crowding in upon" the United States (153). Immigration from China was compared to a military invasion posing a threat to "peace and security" (153). The wording of the Supreme Court's ruling resembles the text of the 1906 petition drafted by the Japanese and Korean Exclusion League. The authors of the petition alarmed American citizens to the danger that "hordes" of Mongolians posed to the white race (in Ichigashi 274). They appealed for the extension of the Chinese Exclusion Act to the Japanese and Koreans. The petition ended with a call: "Stop the Mongolian invasion" (in Ichigashi 274).

Kingston is emphatic about the fact that even after the rescinding of the 1882 Exclusion Act in 1943, the number of the Chinese allowed into the country remained set at one hundred and five a year, a staggeringly low number in light of the fact that China and the United States had already signed a treaty of alliance and the Chinese were decimated at a very high rate by Japanese soldiers. The data cited by Kingston indicates that ten million Chinese died. According to Kingston, the Immigration and Nationalization Service still maintained that it was unable to find one hundred and five Chinese who "qualified" to immigrate into the United States (155). Kingston does not specify what is hidden under the term "qualified," but goes on to say that a "Chinese" was a person "with more than fifty percent Chinese blood" (155). Whites reserved the right to adjudicate on other people's racial and ethnic descent. If in the case of the Chinese, they had to have over fifty percent ancestry to be considered Chinese, in the case of African Americans, the theory of hypodescent established that even very remote black ancestry, identified also as "one drop" or "traceable amount," made a phenotypically white person legally black (Harris 1738, Bennett 5). Depending on what suited white people financially, politically and emotionally, they adjusted the definitions of non-white racial and ethnic groups. The legal situation of Native Americans was and remains directly opposite to that of people with black ancestry in the past. Very remote Native American ancestry is not enough to define oneself as a Native American before the law. It was and is much more complicated to define oneself as a Native American because anyone who proves one-eighth of Native American descent is entitled to financial benefits from the state (Piper 427).

The afore-cited "Nordic fiber" originating at the inception of the

2. Demonic and Oxymoronic Whiteness

American nation persisted in various forms in the laws passed already in the modern day era (150). Until 1968, the Chinese and other Asian ethnic groups usually received a separate exclusionary treatment. The Refugee Act passed in 1948 applied only to Europeans. The Chinese were covered by a separate Displaced Persons Act (155). Since 1968 the number of immigrants allowed to enter the country was allocated by hemisphere, not by race or nation: 120,000 allowed to enter from the Western Hemisphere and 170,000 from the Eastern Hemisphere. Still, the 20,000 per-country quota remained in effect for the Eastern Hemisphere. These inequalities between hemispheres were removed in 1976, when the Immigration and Nationality Act Amendments applied a 20,000 per country limit to the Western Hemisphere as well (157).

Economic Hegemony of Whiteness Enshrined in the Laws

Whiteness captured by Kingston in "The Laws" chapter is also the whiteness that guards access to economic resources, creating legislation and adjusting existing laws in such a way as to preserve economic hegemony. Chinese immigrants were either consistently excluded from economic resources or unjustly punished through various fiscal punitive measures. Economic policies towards Chinese immigrants reflected other practices employed by the white apparatus of power, which either excluded Chinese immigrants or offered them an "exclusive" treatment in a pejorative sense of the term. Citing the fiscal measures against Chinese fishermen, Kingston notes that although they pioneered the fishing of certain fish varieties, they were the only Californian fishermen who had to pay fishing and shellfish taxes (151). The same principle of "exclusive" treatment applied to those Chinese immigrants who were expected to pay a "police tax" to cover super-ordinary police supervision incurred by their very presence (151). In 1884, the 1882 Exclusion Act was perfected in order to eliminate Chinese competition in such areas of business as for example fishing (152). The economic repercussions of the anti–Asian and anti–Chinese laws illustrate Valerie Babb's phrase "conservation of whiteness" (12). Consecutive laws show how the white apparatus of power perfected the system of exclusion in such a way as to maximize its own economic advantage and pluck all the loopholes that might facilitate the aggrandizement of Asian and Chinese capital in the United States or potentially spur the creation of such capital with new waves of Asian and Chinese immigration. A measure aimed at stemming Chinese immigration was the Scott Act of 1888 that proclaimed the certificates of return invalid.

The 1954 ruling of the Supreme Court on Mao v. Brownell maintained the law "forbidding Chinese Americans to send money to relatives in China" (156). Whatever Chinese Americans earned in the United States they were supposed to spend in the United States, fuelling the national economy not only with their labor but also with their capital. Kingston cites numbers in line with which Chinese Americans sent $70 million during World War II. If one accepts Linda Frost's statement that "American identity ... has historically been defined by way of property ownership" (157), then various forms of economic disempowerment have been one more way of excluding Chinese Americans and Asian Americans from the national narrative.

"Vast hordes" "crowding" "upon" the United States and cited by Kingston in connection with the recurrent revocation of the certificates of return on the part of the United States as well as Chae Chan Ping's 1889 legal appeal after the recall of his certificate (153) were problematic for the American government and broader American public not only on account of their potential unsettling of the earlier cited "Nordic fiber" of the nation, but also because of presenting competition on the labor market. While Chinese Americans were indispensable labor, especially at the very beginning of their immigration, the growing numbers of Chinese American population made them much more of a threat in the eyes of the white labor force. Kingston claims that the Exclusion Acts dramatically reduced the number of Chinese immigrants in the United States from 107,000 in 1882, the date of the passing of the first Exclusion Act to 70,000 in the 1920s (155). Sucheng Chan estimates the number of Chinese immigrants' arrivals in California and Hawaii between the late 1840s and early 1880s at 370,000 (Chan 3). Citing Takaki's statistics in line with which "by the end of 1870, there were three workers—two white and one Chinese—for every job in San Francisco," Linda Frost argues that the numbers of Chinese immigrants in California "ensured their position as the region's most visible, exploitable, and consequently threatening cultural other" (Frost 141). Tòmas Almaguer calls the competition in which whites were locked with Chinese immigrants "frenzied" (Almaguer cited in Frost 141). The job stealing argument is one of the persisting arguments against new immigrants, not only against Chinese immigrants, the other three arguments being that they do not match the standards of the host culture because of their racial and cultural inferiority, that they do not assimilate and finally that they fuel "political crises" for the government (Feagin cited in Bedhad 140). Virtually all of these arguments arise in one way or another in the anti–Chinese and anti–Asian legislation cited by Kingston in the "Laws" chapter.

2. Demonic and Oxymoronic Whiteness

CROSS-RACIAL AND CROSS-ETHNIC APPLICATION OF THE LAWS

The focus of "The Laws" chapter falls on anti–Chinese legislation, yet Kingston puts this anti–Chinese legislation into broader perspective, tracing interethnic and interracial patterns of oppression and probing the othering practices applied by whites in relation to other races as well as other ethnicities within Asian diaspora. The nineteenth-century school legislation in California cited by Kingston had a cross-racial application, excluding Mongolians, Indians, and Negroes from public schools (151). Presumably covering various Asian ethnicities, the term "Mongolians" is very general, failing to give credit to the heterogeneity of Asian immigrants and conflating all of them. In the strictly legal context of a court appearance, the distinction between the Chinese and Mongolians is clear: "No 'Chinese or Mongolian or Indian' could testify in court 'either for or against a white man'" (151). The law is a good illustration of a situation described by David Roediger in the autobiographic section of *The Wages of Whiteness* (1991), the section in which he reminisces on his childhood in the segregated Cairo of the 1960s. Many of the decisions taken by the city council, like the decision to "close Cairo's swimming pool rather than integrate it," negatively affected white people, but whites still bent over backwards to cautiously guard the exclusivity of their whiteness as if this exclusivity was a value in itself, even without any conspicuous benefits (*The Wages of Whiteness* 4). Whites were determined to protect the exclusivity of their whiteness and the rights reserved for it even if the very exclusivity compromised their own interests.

Interethnic exclusion of racial minorities comes up again in "The Laws" chapter when Kingston cites the 1906 decision of the San Francisco Board of Education to segregate all Chinese, Japanese and Korean children into an Oriental school (154). The same decision shows whites' readiness to allow the existence of cracks within their segregationist policies since at the request of President Theodore Roosevelt, after the complaints of the Japanese government, the rule of school segregation in San Francisco was lifted for Japanese students. Making an exception for the Japanese also exemplifies swinging moods towards the Japanese and the Chinese. At the time Japan was one of the new superpowers, having just emerged victoriously from the Russian War, while China was in a state of an internal disarray, suffering the plunder of foreign powers. Finally, an allusion to interracial exclusion laws can be indirectly traced in 1943 laws, already after the signing of a treaty of alliance against Japan together with China. Kingston quotes the definition of a Chinese as anyone with a higher percentage of "Chinese blood" than fifty percent (155). As mentioned earlier, different rules applied to African Americans and Native Americans.

Immigrant Acts—Agency Exercised by Chinese Americans in the Struggle Against the Laws

"The Laws" chapter registers not only the exclusion laws, but also legal challenges of these laws by Chinese immigrants. Kingston lists the challenges chronologically, interweaving them with anti-Chinese and anti-Asian legislation. Kingston entitled the chapter of her book "The Laws," yet like Lisa Lowe, the author of *Immigrant Acts* (1996), she shows immigrants' responses to the exclusion laws, empowering immigrants and placing them in the position of active subjects. Chinese immigrants may or may not have been citizens of the United States, but they demonstrated agency in trying to decrease the cleavage dividing them from citizenship.[13] Kingston claims that federal courts pronounced part of the state and city legislation unconstitutional, sporadically leading to the rescinding of the most drastic anti-Chinese legislation, which was often still re-introduced in altered forms.[14] Chinese immigrants undertook a concerted effort to fight exclusion laws in court, for example by collecting money for legal representation (153). Even if the legal challenge was unsuccessful, as it was the case with the above-cited Chae Chan Ping's challenging of the nullification of his certificate of return in 1889, the very act of standing up for their rights was still significant in itself. For the purpose of fighting the legislation targeting them, Chinese Americans also founded the Equal Rights League and the Native Sons of the Golden State (153). To avoid being trapped outside the United States, Chinese Americans called to have their citizenship verified before leaving the country. A crucial immigrant act and a legal victory came in 1898 in the ruling of the United States v. Wong Kim Ark. The ruling of the Supreme Court acknowledged that the Fourteenth Amendment of 1868 should apply to Chinese immigrants born in the United States as well, granting them the right to American citizenship on account of the jus soli citizenship classification prevailing in the United States (153). Kingston does not go into the details of the Wong Kim Ark case, but she identifies it as a legal landmark for Chinese immigrants' claims to their American citizenship.[15] The Wong Kim Ark ruling was the first definitive challenge to the white only or "Nordic fiber" only rule applied in reference to Chinese Americans and other Asian Americans. It was also the Wong Kim Ark ruling that paved the way for the 1952 McCarran-Walter Act abolishing all racial bars to American citizenship.

Reporting other legal victories on the part of Chinese immigrants,

Kingston mostly does not probe the details of these cases either, recording the breakthrough which they brought about, but stopping short of unveiling the situational context leading to the undermining of white supremacy. For example, she introduces the 1886 Yick Wo v. Hopkins case with one word: "A victory" (153). What follows is a brief outlining of the ramifications of the Supreme Court's ruling on the matter—toppling San Francisco ordinances as aimed at hounding Chinese laundrymen. The date appearing beside the Yick Wo case in the 1986 edition of *China Men* is faulty, 1896, not 1886, the date of the Supreme Court's ruling ("Yick Wo v. Hopkins—Case Brief Summary" 1).[16] The immediate reason for Yick Wo v. Hopkins was the imprisonment of Yick Wo for running his laundry in a wooden building and hence violating a San Francisco statute. Prior fire and safety inspections over the twenty two years revealed no violations. Apart from skipping the details of the case, Kingston does not mention the fact that in legal analyses, Yick Wo v. Hopkins is often related to another case preceding it only by one year—1885 Tape v. Hurley (Ngai 138). In both of these cases, the United States Supreme Court ruled that the law was implemented in a racially biased manner. Tape v. Hurley originated in the denial of admission to the Spring Valley School to the Chinese American eight-year-old Mamie Tape. Both the Superior Court and the California Supreme Court ruled in Tape's favor. Yet at the same time the San Francisco school board pressured for separate education for Chinese and "Mongolian" children, bringing about the creation of the Oriental Public School in San Francisco. An immigrant victory significant for the shape of the Chinese American community and reported by Kingston in "The Laws" was The United States v. Mrs. Cue Lim, allowing wives and children of treaty merchants to come to the United States (154). The final immigrant victory comes in the last sentence of "The Laws," in which Kingston announces that "The 1980 census may show a million or more" Chinese Americans living in the United States (158), a stark contrast to the numbers earlier cited by Kingston: 107,000 in 1882, the year of the passing of the first Exclusion Act and 70,000 in the 1920s (155).

Gender Specificity of the Laws

As mentioned above, whiteness is gender-specific and in relation to it other races and ethnicities are treated gender-specifically, which is visible in the anti–Asian laws. An example of such a law comes in the form of the 1870 Act and 1875 Page Law both banning the immigration of Chinese women for the purpose of prostitution (Chan 54). Bill Ong Hing argues that such legislation almost equated all Chinese women with prostitutes (Hing 45). According to Patti Duncan, one of the ramifications of anti–Asian laws was the "destruction of Asian family systems and traditional gender and familial roles" (Duncan cited in Zhang 14). An at least partial reconstruction of Chinese families was a corollary of anti–Asian legislation, the primary motivation of the bans on female immigration being to prevent Chinese immigrants from setting roots in the United States, to forestall an increase in Chinese population and to force Chinese immigrants into an eternal sojourner category. In her catalogue of anti–Asian laws, Kingston does not explicitly mention the 1870 ban on female immigration or the 1875 Page Law, but she notes the unequal treatment of female immigrants, observing that only after the passage of the 1952 Immigration and Nationality Act did the same rules of the immigration law pertain to Chinese women and men.

Socio-Historical Mechanisms Behind the Construction of Whiteness

Most of the mechanisms behind the construction of whiteness are exposed in "The Laws" section, yet it is also worth looking at "The Brother in Vietnam" chapter in order to see the process of constructing Americanness and the factors that significantly facilitated the verification of one's Americanness if a person belonged to a minority group. The youngest brother's military service in Vietnam helps to clarify the narrator's family's immigration status and ensure their safety from deportation. In recognition of the brother's participation in the Vietnam War, the government declares the brother's family as safe, adjudicating at the same time on their Americanness: "The government was certifying that the family was really American, not precariously American but super–American, extraordinarily secure—Q Clearance Americans" (299). Making a link between the brother's military service in Vietnam and the clearance of her family, the narrator indirectly refers to "The Laws" section of the narrative, noting that the government had every power to adjust the law in such a way as to prevent the brother's return from Asia to the United States: "The government had not found him un–American with divided loyalties and treasonous inclinations. Though he was conveniently close to China, the United States government, *which could make up new laws, change the law on him*, did not dump him there. While his services were needed for the undeclared American-Vietnam war, the family was safe" (300, emphasis added). By speaking about "mak[ing] up new laws" and "chang[ing] the law," the narrator implicitly invokes the nineteenth century practice of revoking Chinese immigrants' certificates of return. The pas-

2. Demonic and Oxymoronic Whiteness 109

sage also reverberates with echoes of the narrator's comments on the Japanese internment camps and her family's fears that one day their turn will come (274). The narrator enumerates a long litany of activities in the history of her family that could potentially render them un–American and susceptible to deportation. Some of the facts brought to light by the narrator and including distant family details, for example her Great Uncle's river piracy, seem to be barely within the scope of the government's verification, testifying to the Althusserian interpellation being at play both in the case of the narrator and her brother. On hearing that their family was exposed to the government's investigation, both instantly relate themselves to the terminology of law and crime. Before learning of the outcome of the investigation, the brother instinctively thinks for a moment that his family has been deported, while the narrator assumes more issues to be the subject of investigation than there really were. The marginalization that her family suffered over the decades suffices to solidify in the narrator's mind the idea of the panoptic power of whiteness,[17] the power to penetrate all minutiae of her family's life. Yet all possible trespasses of her close and distant relatives are trumped, rendered null and void by the brother's army service in Vietnam.[18]

The formation of one's consciousness and Americanness in the above cited passage of "The Brother in Vietnam" follows a different track than it does in "The Grandfather of the Sierra Nevada Mountains," the chapter which the narrator also recalls while speculating that the Citizenship Judge from whom Ah Goong purchased his citizenship might have been real after all. While in the case of "The Grandfather of the Sierra Nevada Mountains" and Ah Goong, the narrator does not need external confirmation of Ah Goong's Americanness, declaring that even if the Judge was fake and sold Ah Goong false papers, Ah Goong was still an American because his labor on the railroad made him an American, in "The Brother in Vietnam" section the narrator is much more prone to look outside for the confirmation of their Americanness, displaying much more tentativeness. This sense of trepidation and tentativeness may stem from a different narrative moment in which the narrator finds herself—the end of the narrative. Having guided the reader through the meanders of Chinese American history in the United States, including anti–Asian legislation leveled at Chinese Americans and the cases of Chinese Americans being trapped outside the United States, unable to return, the narrator is acutely aware that one's self-perception and sheer will to be perceived as an American were often not enough to be identified as one. In the army the brother is reminded time and again by an instructing officer that he is an American as if the officer was trying to reassure himself, afraid that the brother may have "divided loyalties and treasonous inclinations" (300): "'Remember you're not from Vietnam. Remember which side you're on. You're no gook from Vietnam'" (286). Considering the emerging panethnic consciousness[19] championed by Asian American activists in the 1960s, the loyalties indeed might have been divided among Asian American soldiers not only on the grounds of the pacifist bent which many of them displayed, but also because they were in a sense forced to fight against their own roots, to metaphorically uproot themselves. According to the narrator, the Vietnam war finally gave whites an opportunity to send Asian Americans back where they belonged, that is, to Asia: "And 'Orientals' belonged over there in Asia fighting among their own kind" (277). "They'd send a gook to fight the gook war" (283). In the spirit of transformational identity politics and solidarity with other racial and ethnic groups, the narrator claims that they were seen as cannon fodder and therefore dispatched to the infantry.

The narrator's observations on the relation between Asian Americans' participation in war efforts and their acknowledgement as American citizens correspond to critics' reflections on the subject. Rachel Lee notes that "the only sanctioned means of proving one's citizenship" for Chinese Americans was "through war-like engagement and endangerment" (150). Writing from the perspective of 2010, Jutta Gsoels-Lorensen declares that the trend of increasing immigrants' rights still goes hand in hand with attempts to draft as many of them as possible (6). Gsoels-Lorensen cites the Development, Relief and Education for Minors Act of 2009, known as the DREAM Act, first introduced to the Senate in 2001. The Act assumed the granting of a temporary residency status in exchange for two years of military service or two years at a four-year institution of higher education. As of 2013, the bill had not been passed on the federal level, but diverse versions of the bill have been passed on the level of state legislatures by twelve states ("DREAM Act" 1–6). Gsoels-Lorensen contends that the provision of military service in the DREAM Act

> shows remarkable consistency with the brother's path to citizenship, as in both cases the adjustment of immigration status is negotiated over the body. Moreover, the body is placed on the line first and foremost for the life of the polity, not that of the subject. It is as though somewhere in this process of legalization the step of assuming one's subjectivity actively was deemed unnecessary, if not entirely forgotten [7].

Gsoels-Lorensen's debate on subjectivity and citizenship is worth confronting with Brook Thomas's observation on the distinction between subjects and citizens. While Gsoels-Lorensen looks at the term "subject" mostly in the context of consciousness and identity formation, Thomas considers the term mostly in the legal context, claiming that being a

2. Demonic and Oxymoronic Whiteness   111

subject does not necessarily make one a citizen (702). Reflecting on the brother in Vietnam's civic empowerment through the Vietnam War, Gsoels-Lorensen observes a different dynamic at play, pointing out that it is as if thanks to the brother's and other minorities' participation in the Vietnam War that the state affirmed their right to citizenship without approaching them as subjects first. In the above cited passage, Gsoels-Lorensen discusses the second half of the twentieth century, whereas Thomas primarily delves into the legal cases of the second half of the nineteenth century. Apart from analyzing the link between the military service in Vietnam and acquisition of citizenship, one may also ponder on the link between the United States' military engagement in South East Asia and the state's immigration policy. Historian Neil Gotanda argues that the American engagement in South East Asia effected a change in the immigration policy towards the citizens of South East Asian countries (146). The United States' engagement in South East Asia did not play well with its national origin quotas on immigrants from Asia, including refugees from the Vietnam War.

"The Brother in Vietnam" chapter illustrates the construction of whiteness not only by exposing the techniques employed by the white apparatus of power, but also by showing Chinese American soldiers' interactions with Chinese people and their attitudes to Chinese people. Devoting most of the chapter's narrative attention to the brother's engagement in the Vietnam War, the narrator confronts his experiences in Asia with her Chinese American relatives' experiences on the Chinese front during World War II. Chinese American World War II soldiers featured in "The Brother in Vietnam" chapter do not necessarily display any mental bonding with indigenous people of China. Ironically, to some extent they mimic whites in the performance of their uniqueness and othering of the people who are culturally different from them. Chinese American soldiers do not directly express their views in the narrative, yet the third person narration is clearly focalized through their point of view. The nomenclature employed by the narrator in reference to the indigenous Chinese mimics the discourse of colonization: "What they found in Chungking was a city of primitive natives who did not understand Cantonese" (272). The presence of the people who are more Chinese than themselves reaffirms their Americanness, shedding light on the othering practices on which it is built. "Thousands of natives" (272) build the road for Chinese American army truck drivers, performing the activities similar to those of the nineteenth-century Chinese immigrant pioneers in the United States. The overt performance of their Americanness originated in the army continues for some time after they return home to the United States:

> For a while after the soldiers in the family came home, they looked like their photographs; they wore the uniforms visiting. But then they put on their regular slacks and white shirts. Their hair grew out, and their wives trimmed it with home clippers. Their noses rounded out, the bridges receding, and their tight jaws softened. They did not walk from the shoulders like football players and boxers any more. They started speaking Chinese loud again [273].

It is to be assumed that immediately after their return from the war, they do not speak Chinese loud because in their perception it could compromise their Americanness. Interestingly that despite their strenuous attempts to get the narrator's father off the draft, the narrator's most immediate family still inadvertently fetishizes the war by dressing its male children in uniforms, symbolically readying them for the future war in which they are to participate. The only color mentioned as a descriptor of one of these uniforms is white: "white middy collar and white shorts" (272).

Revelations of whiteness also come in the section of "The Brother in Vietnam" chapter pertaining to the American school-time experience—both that of the narrator as a child and that of the narrator's brother as a teacher. Othering practices employed by whites are visible in the classification assigned to racial minorities at the narrator's elementary school. The dog tags worn by the narrator and all other racial groups except for blacks and whites bear an inscription "O," which the narrator correctly deciphers as "Other" "because neither black nor white[20]" (276). The "O" tag episode is a very good exemplification of how whiteness reserves the right to name, classify and define racial minorities as others. The brother's encounters with his high school pupils are one of the narrative moments showcasing compensatory wages of whiteness. Undereducated and underprivileged pupils use their whiteness and Americanness as the only compensation against all the drawbacks and misgivings of their lives. The only comfort of a low IQ pupil is that he is "no dumb Mexican from Mexico" and that he has "been speaking English all [his] life" (281). Mexicans are not the only non-white minority singled out for ostracism by the brother's students. They also identify him as the "other," assuming that he is a Communist since he looks "Oriental," "like a gook" (278). Any criticism of the American reality or the Vietnam War on the brother's part entails an instant suspicion of Communist propaganda. Even if the students themselves or their parents are negatively affected by the very policies which the brother dares to question, they still blindly defend them, suspecting the brother of representing external, hostile forces, of being "gookish," (278) or of being what Robert G. Lee identifies as an alien threat from within[21] (190).

In *China Men*, Maxine Hong Kingston exposes the contradictions underlying the legal and socio-historical construction of whiteness. The basic contradiction is that through the laws and socio-historical practices, whiteness accords itself the status of the norm, at the same time creating an air of rarity and exclusivity around itself. The norm usually entails commonness and accessibility. This was not, however, the case with whiteness. The discriminatory laws and concomitant socio-historical practices of othering and exclusion were to guarantee whiteness the status of a rare, unique, exceptional and exclusive quality, which one still had to possess to pass the test of admission to the privileges of the American democracy. Being non-white equaled being non-normative, different, inferior, unworthy of belonging in a full sense of the term. Being white meant being legally and socio-historically normative and at the same time special, unique, exceptional, worthy of rewards stemming from American citizenship. In *China Men*, Kingston shows what legal measures and socio-historical mechanisms had to be employed to hedge the oxymoron of whiteness as normative and yet unique, difficult to obtain. Without a whole battery of laws, as well as socio-historical devices of othering and stereotyping, whiteness would have quickly crumbled, inevitably exposing the fact that its self-ascribed qualities and self-assigned status of normative exception or exceptional norm by no means inhered in whiteness, but were meticulously manufactured.

Toppling the Myth of White Exclusivity in Founding the Nation

Apart from presenting in *China Men* Chinese Americans' perception of whiteness as well as the legal and socio-historical construction of whiteness, Kingston undermines the long-persisting myth of white Americans as sole founders and pioneers of the United States. The ethos of a white Anglo-Saxon man as a sole originating and sustaining force behind the creation and development of the country is one more manifestation of white exclusivity and its propensity towards exclusion of racial and ethnic minorities. Shedding a spotlight on her Chinese American ancestors' significant contribution to building the country, Kingston aims at reconstructing the official version of American history and recentering her Chinese immigrant ancestors from the margins to the center. Still, any recentering carries its own pitfalls, entailing the danger of replicating some of the dominant structures of power that one tries to undermine.

On the very first pages of the narrative the narrator identifies Chinese Americans as "*eccentric*" people in the United States (9, original emphasis).

As if trying to transcend this eccentricity, the narrator's father inscribes each nook and cranny of their family laundry with the term *Center*. In the last section of the narrative, "The Brother in Vietnam," China (also known as the Middle Kingdom) is implicitly identified as center in relation to Taiwan, the place of "emigrants, rejects and misfits" (302). China is also identified as center in a tale about an exiled Chinese poet, Li Sao, who had to leave the Center and "roam in the outer world" (256). The Center signifies China, while the outer world stands for other countries or outer most territories of China ruled by barbarians. The subchapter on Li Sao, the exiled Chinese poet, is placed strategically at the end of the "The American Father" section of the narrative, establishing a clear link between the modern day Chinese immigrant poet—the narrator's father and China's ancient, oldest poet. The last sentence of the Li Sao tale reads that he is remembered not only by the Chinese, but also by the Koreans, the Japanese, the Vietnamese, the Malaysians and the Americans, the nations that either Li Sao or his fellow Chinese immigrant poets of the later day might have roamed in.

In *China Men*, Kingston inverts the marginality of Chinese Americans in the historical narrative of the United States, asserting their Americanness and emphasizing their input into the growth of the country. Therefore she lends mythic, "Godlike" qualities to her Chinese immigrant ancestral pioneers constructing the railway in the Sierra Nevada Mountains, presenting them as the ones who "enter the sky," "change the face of the world" (129) as well as "mark the land" (136) albeit the marking does not take place through traditional methods of cartography and map charting, but by dropping their dead along the way, the numbered track sections being the only grave markers of the Transcontinental Railway casualties. The constructors of the railroad are cast as founders of the nation who "banded the nation North and South, East and West, with crisscrossing steel, being the binding and building ancestors of this place" (144). Ah Goong features as father of the nation cradling in his arms the American children who gather around him during his lonely enforced trek across the United States when the driving out begins. The narrator also speculates that he might have become a biological father in the United Sates, breaking anti-miscegenation ordinances and "father[ing] citizens" (149).

The narrator offers an equivalent portrayal of her great grandfather's generation of China Men, toiling in the Sandalwood Mountains. Bak Goong and other China Men of the Sandalwood Mountains appear as pioneers, founding ancestors winning the land from the wilderness, great explorers participating in geographical discoveries and being wooed into

2. Demonic and Oxymoronic Whiteness 115

coming to Hawaii by the spell of the faraway land. Reaching for catalogues while accounting for the succession of male generations travelling to the United States, the narrator creates a semblance of a heroic epic in which China Men are the driving forces behind the making of America and the Chinese American presence in America. The narrator makes it evident at the same time that each of her male ancestors wins America his own way.

Proactive plotting on the part of whiteness to create white spots in the history of the American nation and efface non-white contribution to the development of the country is the most conspicuous in the photograph scene at the completion of the Transcontinental Railroad in 1869. Only white people feature in the picture, while China Men along with African Americans and Mexicans are strategically excised. The narrator of *China Men* claims that only seventy Chinese immigrants out of more than ten thousand who constructed the railroad were allowed to ride it. While before and during the construction of the railroad, Chinese immigrants were indispensable labor (138), after its finalization, they become dispensable and hence subjected to expulsion and violence: "The Driving Out had begun" (143). Kingston constructs the railroad inauguration scene in such a way that Chinese immigrants are associated with the real, whereas white Americans with the fake: "A white demon in top hat tap-tapped on the gold spike, and pulled it back out. Then one China Man held the real spike, the steel one, and another hammered it in" (143). The photograph scene has been the subject of ample critical investigation. Li very aptly comments on the exclusion of Chinese immigrants from the photograph by claiming that "the linking of the continent fails to make the hoped for connection between the Chinese and the American" ("China Men" 491). Teresa Zackodnik points out that photography not only "record[s] the past," but also "invents it, lending authenticity and notability to its images" (5). According to Zackodnik, Kingston attaches too much importance to photography as a tool of documentation, risking the reification of photography as "document in service of the corrupt regulation of information, identity, history and power that has refused to validate Chinese American experience" (5). Making her observations on the danger of magnifying of the status of photography, Zackodnik juxtaposes Ah Goong's excision from the photograph with Bak Goong's presence in the annual end of the year communal photograph in the Hawaiian photo studio. Zackodnik does not reflect on the fact that Bak Goong and his fellow Chinese immigrants in Hawaii exercise agency to commemorate visually their presence in Hawaii, whereas in the case of Ah Goong, the agency to commemorate the occasion rests with whites, not Chinese immigrants. The annual end of the year photographs are presumably exclusively Chinese, while the Transcontinental Railroad commemoration photograph would have been multiracial and multiethnic, had it included Chinese Americans, African Americans and Mexican Americans.

In *Racial Castration* (2001), David Eng looks at the 1869 Promontory Summit photograph discussed by Kingston through the prism of "the influential status of the image and the ways in which visual representations significantly constitute our sense of everyday reality" (29). Assuming a psychoanalytic approach, Eng argues that Kingston "rework[s] dominant narratives of national history through an emphatic shifting of the visual image ... teach[ing] us how to resist what Lacan terms 'the given-to-be-seen' of the visual order so as to see something else," the practice which Eng terms as "vigilant looking" (30). Interestingly, Eng analyzes "vigilant looking" in the works of the authors who usually found themselves at odds over many issues concerning Asian American literature and the Asian American community: Kingston's *China Men* and Frank Chin's *Donald Duk* (1991) (30). In particular, Eng shows the protagonist of *Donald Duk* correct his history teacher's (Mr. Meanwright's) vision of history and his perception of Chinese Americans when the latter treats his students

Completion of the Transcontinental Railroad at Promontory Summit, Utah, on May 10, 1869 (photograph by Charles Roscoe Savage).

to a slide show excluding Chinese immigrants from the Promontory Summit celebration.[22]

As noted at the very outset, any act of recentering carries the danger of replicating structures of oppression and mimicking the dominant discourses since usually there are no centers without margins. This is the problem which many of the critics have noticed in Kingston's act of recentering of Chinese male immigrant ancestors in *China Men*. According to some critics, in *China Men* Kingston became overly concerned with the criticism of her first narrative *The Woman Warrior* and fell into a trap of the nationalist ideology promoted by Asian American activists Frank Chin, Jeffrey Paul Chan, Lawson Fusao Inada, Shawn Hsu Wong and Ben Tong. In the hope of bringing Asian American people together, they opted for the centrist approach, trying to debunk stereotypes of Asian Americans as aliens, spies and effeminate eunuchs. Therefore they accentuated their American nativity, masculinity, and heterosexuality. Fighting against discrimination, they became embroiled in discriminatory practices themselves. Their model of authentic racial identity was based to a great extent on the exclusion of people who did not match their paradigm of an Asian American. As a result, fresh immigrants, women and homosexuals found themselves on the perimeter of Asian American identity. It is quite paradoxical that while aiming at the undermining of white supremacy, Asian American nationalists included so many white dogmas in their own ideology. Patriarchy, apotheosis of masculinity and heterosexuality are no less a part of whiteness than racial oppression is. This hardly comprehensive critique of whiteness on the part of Asian American nationalists may stem from the fact that nationalist movements saw whiteness as a monolith, a homogenous bastion. To be fully successful in their analysis of whiteness, they would need to differentiate between its constituents. In the 1976 Afterword to *MELUS*, Chin says "[I] have no idea what whites think is beyond whiteness into the universal mode" (14). Universal as whiteness in many ways claims to be, it rests on other universals to which Asian American nationalists and other nationalist movements often remained blind. The apotheosis of masculinity, heterosexuality and American nativity has been a part of whiteness too and Asian American nationalists incorporated these universals into their ideology as well. While Kingston anchors Chinese Americans in the domain of Americanness and reappraises Chinese American men in *China Men*, she cannot be charged with ostracizing any of the aforementioned groups. It is also difficult to assume that she wrote *China Men* in response to any of the nationalist criticisms of *The Woman Warrior* since in many of her interviews she claims to have originally planned to publish *The Woman Warrior* and *China Men* as one book.

Even though Kingston does not overtly become ensnared in any of centrism's traps, critics still charge her with inadvertently replicating some of the dominant discourses. Lei Lani Nishime argues that Kingston offers somewhat essentialist visions of gender and history that may leave some of her readers with an impression that "Americanness translates into masculinity" (76). Indeed, the book that makes a concerted effort to claim America for Chinese Americans is *China Men*, not *The Woman Warrior*, in which she foregrounds the female perspective and the stories of Asian American women, but in which the narrator is still in the process of answering the question what her village is. Nishime also claims that at certain points Kingston mimics "the writing about Western expansionism and the Frontier" (78). In a similar vein, David Leiwei Li invokes the Manifest Destiny associations while discussing sections of *China Men* devoted to the Chinese American presence in the American West. According to Li, Chinese constructors of the railway unwittingly contributed to the propagation of the Manifest Destiny—the westward expansion in the United States and colonization of Asian countries: "the Chinese ironically became accomplices in the exploitation of their ancient empire" ("China Men: Maxine Hong Kingston and the American Canon" 490). Rachel Lee notes that China Men are implicated in the destruction of the land since claiming America entails various "physical harnessing acts performed upon the land" (Lee 148). Lee goes on to say that "Crossing boundaries to establish claims involves the violent restructuring of both settlers and the soil" (148). A different perspective on China Men's relation to the land emerges from Brook Thomas's critical essay. Observing a distinction between the political and material making of the country, Thomas states that *China Men* supplements the question "What makes an American" with "Who made America?" (709), noting further that the claiming of the land and China Men is mutual because China Men figuratively claim the American land and the American land figuratively claims them, commemorating their input of labor with the whisper of the cane (710).

The aesthetics employed by Kingston in *China Men* seems to indicate that she is aware of the pitfalls of the centrist approach. In his opium induced vision, Bak Goong can see "an amazing gold electric ring connecting every living being" (92). All human beings of his vision appear to be located on the margins of the ring, leaving the core empty. Another unifying device featuring in Bak Goong's vision is "a gold net or a light" (92). All of the above provide an alternative to the centrist imagery and the discourses valorizing the center, anticipating Kingston's reappraisal of the margin proposed in her 2011 memoirs *I Love a Broad Margin to My Life* and evoking some of the alternative ways of imagining reality proposed by scholars specializing in ethnic literature. A certain portion of scholars refuse to shift themselves to the center and draw our attention to the potential dormant in the margin. bell hooks speaks of "the spaces that the margin opens," distinguishing between two kinds of marginality: "imposed by the dominant structure" and "marginality one chooses as site of resistance" (hooks cited in Hooper and Soja 191). hooks's reasoning resembles the conclusions reached by David Palumbo-Liu in his introduction to *The Ethnic Canon* (1995), Palumbo-Liu argues that once we shift the minority discourse to the center, it "loses its latitude as a counterdiscourse and its ability to designate a shifting open space outside the hegemonic" (17). Valuable as all these reappraisals of margins are, it is important not to glamorize margins. Margins are a site of resistance only if they challenge existing power relations rather than settle for marginality.

Beyond toppling the myth of whiteness as the exclusive foundation stone of the United States, Kingston also demotes the white concocted myth of the working class as exclusively white. In *Black Reconstruction* (1935), W.E.B. Du Bois notes that the American worker has been traditionally presented as white (711). Kingston dismantles this perception by shining light on Chinese immigrants' labor in the Sandalwood Mountains of Hawaii and the mainland western United States, where she shows Chinese workers side by side with African American, Mexican and white workers. Kingston also undermines the perception of Chinese American workers as obsequious, submissive and willing to work for next to nothing without any questioning. Both in "The Great Grandfather of the Sandalwood Mountains" and "The Grandfather of the Sierra Nevada Mountains," the narrator's ancestors initiate a protest against labor conditions and unsatisfactory remuneration. Bak Goong of the Sandalwood Mountains mentally revolts at slave-like wages he is offered upon arrival in Hawaii and together with other China Men of Hawaii he wins their right to speak and sing during labor. Perceiving themselves as "free men," not "coolies," Ah Goong and other China Men of the Sierra Nevada Mountains stage a strike against their wages and a disproportionately long day of labor. China Men fail to convince white workers to join the strike. Their reasoning: "Eight hours a day good for white man, all the same good for China Man" (139) does not persuade white workers that they have mutual interests worth fighting for. White labor's refusal to join the strike is the best exemplification in the narrative of Du Bois's compensatory wages of whiteness. Du Bois employs the term mainly in the context of labor relations between whites and African Americans, yet the same rule operates in the context of labor relations between whites and workers of other races and marginalized ethnicities. In *Black Reconstruction*, Du Bois argues that the discrimination against black people not only gave members of the working class comparatively higher wages, but also offered a significant boost to their ego. Du Bois terms the phenomenon "compensatory wages of whiteness" (*Black Reconstruction* 700). Working class whites derived a considerable comfort from the fact that there was still someone lower in the hierarchy. Exposed to class oppression, they were free of racial oppression and apparently that was enough to keep them from identifying and targeting those responsible for their exploitation and those drawing the largest dividends. The result of such a reasoning on the part of the white working class was that "the wages of both classes could be kept low, the whites fearing to be supplanted by Negro labor, the Negroes always being threatened by the substitution of white labor" (*Black Reconstruction* 701). Cheryl Harris observes that the white working class was much more likely to identify with the bourgeoisie than with fellow black workers, playing up their racial status rather than class identification (1741). Elaborating on Du Bois's concept of compensatory wages of whiteness, David Roediger avers that "status and privileges conferred by race could be used to make up for alienating and exploitative class relationships, North and South. White workers could, and did, define and accept their class positions by fashioning identities as 'not slaves' and as 'not Blacks'" (*Wages of Whiteness* 13). A parallel psychological wage is at play during the railroad strike in *China Men* when in response to China Men's pleading to join the strike, white workers racially slur Chinese workers by calling them "Cheap John Chinaman" (139). Rather than choose class solidarity and strike out for higher wages, they assiduously cherish the color line and guard their racial separateness.

Kingston's undermining of the myth of white exclusivity in founding and developing the nation complements *China Men's* unraveling of the paradox of whiteness in line with which whiteness presents itself as universal yet at the same time exclusive and exclusionary. A parallel practice operates in the myth of white exclusivity in founding the nation. On the one hand, whiteness universalizes the socio-historical narrative behind the creation and sustenance of the United States, while on the other, it once again builds this narrative on the exclusion of non-white racial and ethnic groups. By inserting Chinese Americans into the bland, white picture of the origins and growth of the United States, Kingston intervenes in the official version of the United States history, changing the status of Chinese Americans from that of virtual historical non-existence to that of playing a vital role in the construction of the nation. The recentering of Chinese Americans in *China Men* involves inadvertent masculinization of Americanness and at least partial replication of the dominant discourse of colonization and settlement. Yet overall, Kingston manages to avoid the ostracism of other marginalized groups that often occurs in the course of recentering.

Conclusion

Maxine Hong Kingston's *China Men* exposes and dismantles the oxymoron of whiteness in a three-fold way. By presenting whiteness through the eyes of the very first Chinese immigrants into the United States who construct whites as brutal "demons" and "devils," *China Men* demotes the self-perceived normativity of whiteness, casting a shadow on its self-ascribed features of impeccable morality, magnanimity, love of another human being and selfless devotion to the upgrading of non-white races. The dismantling of the oxymoron of whiteness is amplified by the scrutiny of its legal construction hinging on the paradoxical juxtaposition of its self-assumed normativity and exclusivity. Finally, the deconstruction of the oxymoron of whiteness reveals the loopholes in the socio-historical narrative behind the creation and development of the United States. The exposure of whiteness in *China Men* takes a much more direct form than it does in *The Woman Warrior* or the next work analyzed here, Leonard Chang's *The Fruit 'N Food*.

3

Dreaming and Living White Terror in Leonard Chang's *The Fruit 'N Food*

> yet for all these accumulated associations, with whatever is sweet, and honorable, and sublime, there yet lurks an elusive something in the innermost idea of this hue, *which strikes more of panic to the soul than that redness which affrights in blood.*—Herman Melville, Moby Dick 189, emphasis added

Introduction

Most of the revelations of whiteness in Leonard Chang's *The Fruit 'N Food* (1996) occur through the Korean American protagonist's (Tom Pak's) dreams. Dreams compose a crucial layer of imagery in the novel, providing a significant commentary on the present, past and future events within and outside the narrative. Dreams are inextricably linked with the textualization of whiteness, which is a recurring trope of Tom Pak's nightmares. Unfolding against the background of the 1990s conflict between African Americans and Korean Americans, *The Fruit 'N Food* establishes whiteness as a socio-historical and racial category. Tom Pak's dreams show whiteness as omnipresent, albeit seemingly absent from Tom's life as well as the lives of other Korean Americans and African Americans, who ostensibly battle it out among each other in the inner city conflict. Working as a hand in the Queens neighborhood of Kasdan, Tom barely ever comes into contact with white people. It is only in his nightmares that he has visions of whiteness. Dreams feature in the novel as a particular way of seeing, seeing through the mind's eye, rather than one's physical eyes. Revealed through the prism of Tom Pak's dreams and recollections, the terror of whiteness assumes a much less overt form in *The Fruit 'N Food* than it does in the previous work analyzed here, Maxine Hong Kingston's

China Men. White people are never portrayed as whip cracking "demons" or "devils." They are mysteriously missing from Tom's oneiric landscape and the topographic landscape in which he moves about before the physically blinding attack. They are not the ones to violently charge at Tom. Their role in the conflict between African Americans and Korean Americans is signaled only by the recurring whiteness of Tom's dreams and Tom's reflections on the reasons behind the conflict. The events of *The Fruit 'N Food* take place some one hundred years after a narrative scene unfolding in *China Men*, a scene in which whites orchestrate the removal of Alaska China Men. They watch from the shore how Native Americans perform their orders and row away Alaska China Men. Irrespective of a different socio-historical moment and two different racial and ethnic minorities involved in *The Fruit 'N Food*, white people perform an equivalently vital role in setting up the situation in which African Americans and Korean Americans find themselves battling each other. Yet the role of whiteness in the unfolding events is on the surface much less visible. Leonard Chang's subtle and at the same time extremely powerful mode of revealing the role of whiteness in the African American–Korean American dyad through Tom's dreams renders the ostensible invisibility of whiteness in the conflict, its uncanny ability to camouflage and remove itself from the picture while being the orchestrating force behind it.

Inner Sight Vision

Revelatory dreams of whiteness are in *The Fruit 'N Food* a state of increased awareness, of being able to see what may not be within the immediate reach of one's eyesight. They foreshadow Tom's loss of sight and the clinical whiteness in which he wakes up after being blinded with a firebomb during the racial unrest in the neighborhood:

> he woke up enveloped in that whiteness he had dreamed about, a whiteness that stayed around him for what seemed like forever, an ever-lasting blinding coldness like a cruel sun, and though this reminded him of his nightmares, he was not in pain, nor was he struggling in the midst of this. He was calm. He was quiet ... and the noises around him were bodiless, formless [215].

Time and again whiteness and brightness blind Tom, both in his nightmares and in his waking life. In the incipient stages of his recurrent nightmares, he dreams of a "bright, white light shining into his eyes, hurting him" (10). Brightness literally impairs Tom's vision when he struggles with exhaustion caused by insomnia and the toil of his everyday labor: "His vision was playing tricks in the low sun. Objects wavered under his gaze—

telephone poles, street signs, parked cars—and he had to blink a few times, violently, for everything to keep still" (102–103).[1] The images of the blinding whiteness and the sun are a clear foreshadowing of Tom's physical blindness.

Tom's dreams and his blindness are to a great extent parallel states, in which Tom looks through his inner eyes. Dreams give Tom inklings of what may elude his eyesight. In the nightmare phase of the narrative, Tom does not yet have a full picture of what is going on around him. Only after the inner city racial upheaval and after the blinding incident does he gain a composite picture of the events. At hospital he can put everything into perspective: "Now, while going over those events, Tom understands more, that the lack of sleep and the stress of the grocery, of June [Tom's girlfriend, the daughter of his grocery store employers, the Rhees], were converging on him, pushing him. All he knew at that time, though, was that something was wrong" (101). If the events in Kasdan interspersed with Tom's nightmares constitute the body of the narrative, it is only his hospital flashbacks that frame the work, which starts with Tom in hospital and ends with Tom seemingly in the same location but in a very different position if we consider his broader perspective of the events after he takes a retrospective look at everything that has occurred. Neil Smith and Cindi Katz contrast "location" with "position," claiming that "position" "implies location vis-à-vis other locations and incorporates a sense of perspective on other places" (69). Reliving his Kasdan days, Tom sees the events of the immediate past in the context of his whole life, in the context of other places in which he lived and other people with whom he interacted. Ironically, after losing his sight, he can see everything in a sharper focus. The detachment from other people and almost complete withdrawal inside himself make him see what was not entirely visible to him before.

Tom's inner sight vision can be compared to the Duboisian second sight. In his 1897 essay "Strivings of the Negro People," republished in 1903 in *The Souls of Black Folk*, Du Bois uses the term second sight to describe black people's prescience counterbalancing the alienating power of the veil, which stands primarily for the color line. African Americans are not the only minority endowed with second sight. As a Korean American suffering multiple marginalization, Tom is equally predisposed to the gift of second sight. While during the Kasdan racial unrest he displays greater insight and impartiality than most participants of the events, his clairvoyance is not yet fully fledged. It rises to the highest point only after the blinding incident. Tom's hospital ruminations are equivalent to Du Bois's rising above the veil into his own reflections liberating him from the dividing power of the color line. Unlike Du Bois, however, Tom intends to stay above the veil definitely, withdrawing inside and permanently shutting out the outside world.

Dreams in *The Fruit 'N Food* approximate the Jungian rather than the Freudian definition of dreams. Freud interprets dreams archeologically, searching for an explanation of dreams in the past, whereas Jung perceives dreams teleologically, looking for their objective in the future (Adams 77). Tom's nightmare visions of terrorizing whiteness have their roots in the past experiences of white racism. Still, these experiences are never fully articulated. They are only to be inferred when Tom reflects on the racist slur hurled at him: "'Go fucking home, chinks!' 'You don't belong here!' 'Go fucking back to Korea!' Tom tried to ignore them but he felt his head pounding and his eyes blurring with anger, listening to these taunts which he hadn't heard since he was a child" (157). While Tom's dreams have some anchorage in the past, they first of all anticipate the terror which he will need to confront in the future.

The Socio-Historical Context of the Conflict Between African Americans and Korean Americans

It is impossible to neglect the socio-historical context of the narrative if one considers the events against whose background Tom dreams his nightmares of whiteness. The urban unrest depicted by Chang is not totally the product of the author's imagination, but derives from historical events of 1991 and 1992—the Latasha Harlins incident[2] and the Rodney King rebellion.[3] Leonard Chang[4] published *The Fruit 'N Food* in 1996, only several years after the aforementioned events. The book is classified in the front matter as social fiction, the recipient of the 1996 Black Heron Press Award for Social Fiction. Leonard Chang makes it clear that Korean Americans and African Americans who skirmish with each other in his fictional and yet in many ways so real world are only pawns within a "larger problem of inner city discontent" (Chang 219).

To understand this "larger problem of inner city discontent," we need to look at the history of Korean American and African American relations. Korean Americans and African Americans come into immediate contact with each other mostly during customer-merchant relations in black neighborhoods, since a large portion of Korean American grocery stores is located in black districts. Korean Americans began to enter those districts as traders in the 1970s and took over after Jewish merchants who were moving out at the time. Korean Americans came to play a similar role in minority districts as Jews used to play—namely the role of a "middleman minority." I borrow the term "the middleman minority" from Pyong Gap Min and Andrew Kolodny. According to Min and Kolodny, the middleman minority has the following characteristics:

1. a concentration in small business
2. a focus on providing services to minority customers
3. a dependence on U.S. corporations for supply of merchandise
4. a strong ethnic cohesion
5. a subjection to stereotyping (Min and Kolodny 132).

Middleman minorities are usually hated by both sides of the racial spectrum of a given society. The middleman merchant is an intermediary passing on corporate products to minorities. Korean Americans opened their businesses in minority neighborhoods because of low rents and because they would not have survived competition in white neighborhoods. Whites, on the other hand, found minority neighborhoods unattractive as potential business venues because they feared violence and the prospect of robbery.

Different historical, social and economic experience of both groups contributes to the tensions in their relations. Korean immigrants who came to the United States after the 1965 changes in American immigration policy were mostly highly educated white-collar workers (Kwang Chung Kim and Shin Kim 28). The language barrier and discrimination made it impossible for them to find white-collar employment. They were able to open small businesses because of the support of their own communities and thanks to the Korean American financial system called "kye." Because of their relative cultural homogeneity, Korean Americans are a much more cohesive group than Afro-Americans (Min and Kolodny 143). Most Korean American merchants opened their stores in black districts in the 1980s, at a time when the state was withdrawing capital from those areas, leaving them impoverished.

The Reagan policy of the 1980s led to further degradation and impoverishment of those already underprivileged areas. Trying to deprive minorities of the gains won during the Civil Rights era, Reagan proclaimed the United States a color-blind country, where everyone supposedly had equal opportunities (Omi and Winant 2). Such a declaration amounted to a virtual war on affirmative action. In the color blind state there was no need for affirmative action. The withdrawal of capital from inner-city areas consisted of:

- migration of business to the margins of the city
- cutting back of the funds for various community organizations

3. Dreaming and Living White Terror   127

- the cessation of federal programs extended to impoverished areas (Park 63).

Leonard Chang raises most of the above mentioned issues in *The Fruit 'N Food*. Through the eyes of Tom Pak the third person narrator of the novel registers the changes which occurred in the inner city neighborhood of Kasdan. He notes the growing ethnic homogeneity in the area and the fading away of community spaces which make room for the hallmarks of urban restructuring, for example a multi level parking lot:

> He remembered when this had been a well-kept, lower-middle-class area, with Italians and small pockets of blacks, Latinos, and Asians. Now, after seeing more of this neighborhood these past few days, Tom saw that everything had become older, more run down, and ethnically it seemed that the majority of residents were black, West Indian, and as he went further north, more Latino. Or maybe he had remembered things wrong, though he distinctly recalled a larger Korean community, especially near Michaelson Park, with a Korean church that his father had attended, and even a few stores next to it with Korean signs and their English translations. But the church wasn't there anymore. Neither were the stores. Instead, these had been torn down and replaced by a three-level parking structure, with a thick chain-like fence on the lower level and indecipherable graffiti decorating the smooth, dirty grey concrete face. A thin layer of grime had descended on Kasdan [43].

The passage above depicts only a small portion of the changes which took place in inner cities. The planned restructuring of city centers destroyed many of those communities. Mom and pop shops as well as low-rent apartments inhabited by people of color often had to make place for high-rise projects, financial centers, highways connecting the suburbs to daytime offices of people who worked there during the day and left the city core by night. As a result, communities of color found themselves displaced, caught in the middle of urban restructuring.

The Fruit 'N Food traces the intricacies of the relations between Korean Americans and African Americans. In a conversation with Tom, his employer Mr. Rhee explains why Korean Americans open their grocery stores in predominantly African American inner city areas. Tom asks: "'What do you look for in locations?,' to which Rhee responds: 'If other grocery nearby, if many *hanguk-saddem*.' He paused. 'Korean people.' ... 'If the keh[5] gives the money, and if this store does good, then we expand.'" (23). The word "expand" exerts a special impact on Tom Pak, a Korean American exploited by other Korean Americans in their store. "Expansion" may conjure up colonial connotations of conquest, domination and exploitation. African Americans boycotting Korean American stores in the novel perceive Korean Americans precisely in such terms, accusing them of draining the neighborhoods and taking profits elsewhere, outside the neighborhoods:

> "You come in here and *suck* the money from the neighborhood and take it to your Long Is–land house and treat us African brothers and sisters like we nothing. Like we nothing."
> "What're you talking about? I—I don't live—"
> "But we are *something*. We are everything. We are your money, your customers, your nice car, your college education. So we want to be treated right. We want the respect we deserve" [118].

Ironically, African Americans vent their frustration on Tom, who himself is the target of exploitation. African American protestors do not realize that grocery trading is not for Korean Americans a job of their dreams. Nor do they realize that Korean Americans are usually unable to open their stores in a different location. Asked by Tom why he pursues the grocery business if he does not enjoy it, Mr. Rhee answers: "'I don't like this,' he said. 'But we have nothing.' ... 'This is everything'" (18). The Rhees' American dream goes up in smoke together with their plundered store. Their failure is a part of Chang's demystification of Asian Americans as a model minority.

Dreaming in White: Haunting Whiteness of Tom's Dreams as an Articulation of the Missing Link in the Inner City Discontent

The missing link in the conflict between African Americans and Korean Americans is articulated only through the pervasive images of whiteness in Tom's dreams. Physically absent from inner city areas, the invisible white[6] cartographer[7] keeps significant numbers of minority citizens in their particular locations, making it difficult for them to live or do business in other areas. The invisible cartographer sets up the situation in which African Americans are largely confined to inner cities, while Korean Americans enter these districts as middle-man tradesmen/women, often distributing merchandise provided by large corporations. Karen Tei Yamashita hints at the existence of the invisible cartographer in her novel *Tropic of Orange*: "Somebody else must have the big map. Or maybe just the next map. The one with the new layers you can't even imagine" (82). The missing component behind the cartographic design is revealed in *The Fruit 'N Food* through Tom's dreams. In *Ghostly Matters: Haunting and the Sociological Imagination* Avery Gordon claims "that which appears to be not there is often a seething presence" (8). Whiteness is a seething presence in Tom's life and the lives of other minorities inhabiting the urban core although it is seemingly "not there."

Whiteness haunts Tom throughout the narrative in his dreams, anticipating the whiteness in which he wakes up after losing his sight. The whiteness in which Tom wakes up after his blinding is not only the hospital whiteness that envelopes him but also the whiteness that he can see with his mind's eye, having lost his physical sight. Blindness is usually textualized in terms of darkness, while in *The Fruit 'N Food* it is represented as whiteness. The passage depicting Tom's sensations after the loss of sight captures the images parallel to those which Tom can see in his dreams:

> he woke up *enveloped in that whiteness he had dreamed about*, a *whiteness that stayed around him* for what seemed like forever, an ever-lasting *blinding coldness like a cruel sun*, and though this reminded him of his nightmares, he was not in pain, nor was he struggling in the midst of this. He was calm. He was quiet ... and the noises around him were bodiless, formless [215, emphasis added].

Whiteness triggers associations of "blinding coldness." Coldness and whiteness also recur together in Tom's dreams. Whiteness has conjured up associations of coldness both as a color category and as a skin color.[8] Aristotle calls coldness "the mother of whiteness" (Aristotle cited in Taylor 394). In the above cited passage of *The Fruit 'N Food*, an attribute of whiteness, namely its ability to blind, is transferred onto coldness: "an ever-lasting blinding coldness." The metaphor "blinding coldness" is an example of synesthesia, of mixing dichotomous sense impressions of touch and sight. The simile "an ever-lasting blinding coldness like a cruel sun" renders an oxymoronic quality of whiteness haunting Tom in his dreams and revisiting him once again on his awakening after the blinding incident. If coldness and whiteness match each other, coldness and the sun are in sharp contrast. The "cruel sun" stands in sharp opposition to the benevolent sun, which gives light and warmth. The cruel sun, on the other hand, blinds and burns. Combined with the implicit redness of the "cruel sun," the imagery of blinding and burning mirrors the injuries received by Tom during the firebomb explosion. At the moment of the explosion he can see a "flash of light" and feels "pain all over" (214). A prelude to the firebomb incident comes earlier during the racial unrest when Tom is punched on the face. Before passing out, he can see a "flash of red and white," having a sense of an "explosion" landing on his face (189).

Consciously reflecting on the recurrence of whiteness in his dreams, Tom is emphatic about the fact that whiteness is a defining feature of his nightmares, blotting out everything else. Prodded by June to tell what else he can see apart from whiteness, he cannot distinguish any further details because there is nothing but whiteness:

> "All I remember is everything being white," he told her. He was trying to explain his nightmares.
> "But what else? What was white?"
> "Everything was. Everywhere I looked, it was really white. I don't know, maybe I was in Heaven."
> June laughed through her nose. "A nightmare in Heaven? That's perfect" [77].

Tom's speculation that he might have been in Heaven is odd, considering how mentally and physically exhausting his dreams are. The association of whiteness with Heaven may be explained through two different theories. The first would assume the archetypal valorization of whiteness over blackness, while the other would suppose the internalization of racial stereotypes of the black and white color. Archetypal (or transcultural) theories of the color perception derive from the research of Tzvetan Todorov, Robert Bosnack, Victor Turner and James Hillman. Todorov looks for the opposition in nature that contributed to the creation of the dichotomy of black vs. white across cultures (Todorov cited in Adams 20). Whiteness is associated with light and day, while blackness with darkness and night. Robert Bosnack speaks of "Thanatos blackness," that is archetypal or universal images of blackness connected with the night and the fears unleashed by the night (Bosnack cited in Adams 22). Victor Turner conducted research with the Ndembu tribe of Zambia, for whom whiteness invited positive associations, while blackness negative (Adams 24–25). Drawing on ethnographic, etymological, lexical, mythological, historical and literary evidence, Hillman concludes that both white and black people tend to prefer the white color to black (Hillman cited in Adams 27). Hillman's conclusions invite some doubts if we consider that depending on the context, whiteness may have negative or at least ambivalent associations for white people as well, for example predominantly white interiors may conjure up the images of hospitals and medical centers—places of healing, but also of pain, trauma, injections etc.

The socio-historical explanation for Tom's speculation about the heavenly provenance of his white nightmares is grounded in particularism rather than universalism, deriving from the negative stereotyping of darkness and blackness. Negative stereotypes of blackness are closely related to the prejudice against dark skinned people, the prejudice backed up by various pseudo-scientific theories flourishing in the second half of the nineteenth century and the beginning of the twentieth century: theories of polygenesis and monogenesis, Arthur de Gobineau's theses, social Darwinism and the eugenicist movement initiated by Darwin's cousin—Francis Galton.[9] Although Franz Boas, Horace Meyer Kallen and Robert E. Park undertook the first attempts to undermine the pseudoscientific notions of race already at the turn of the nineteenth and twentieth century, those theories were still alive and well in the 1930s and they circulated in a variety of forms in the southern United States until the 1960s.[10]

June's extempore remark on Tom's dream memories of all encompassing whiteness bears special significance: "A nightmare in Heaven? That's perfect" (77). Rather than being a manifestation of the American dream, Tom's life in the United States resembles a nightmare. He feels trapped, whether awake or asleep (177). The phrase "a nightmare in Heaven" brings up yet another oxymoronic association of whiteness, further illustrating its role in the conflict between African Americans and Korean Americans. Posing African Americans and Korean Americans in their particular positions of the inner city neighborhood and setting up the conflict situation, whiteness remains largely invisible. "That's perfect" may be referred to the perfect arrangement in which whites stay largely away from the scene of the conflict, while at the same time playing an instrumental role in drawing the cartographic design and setting up the stage for the conflict. The only white people present at the site of the clashes are white policemen who are merely instruments, not the controlling forces. Usually there were too few police officers in the conflict zone to protect Korean American grocery stores and keep both sides apart.

In some of Tom's dreams whiteness is shaded with blue. The blue-white dreams are less traumatic than all pervading whiteness dreams. Tom contrasts "warm blue" with "cold whiteness" (165). C.L. Hardin, the author of *Color for Philosophers: Unweaving the Rainbow*, classifies blue as "the last of the psychologically primary hues to be distinguished by a basic linguistic color category" (167). Red is the first chromatic category. Next come green, yellow and blue (Hardin 166–167).[11] Blue is perceived as a soothing color. Hardin draws a contrast between the effect produced by blue and red. When a person moves from a neutral to a blue environment, their blood pressure, temperature and breathing rate fall down immediately. A diametrically opposite result is produced for the red (Hardin 166). Therapeutic qualities of blue account for the soothing effect it exerts on Tom. Apart from calming him down, the blue also "darken[s] him" (Chang, *The Fruit 'N Food* 165). The darkening effect of blue may be seen as an indication that all pervading whiteness of his dreams poses a threat to his Korean American racial heritage.[12] The blue of his dreams is also a foreshadowing of the blue which he can see with his mind's eye in hospital, after losing his sight. The blue visiting Tom's consciousness in hospital represents the oceanic, the perfect reality of his childhood, the brief spell of happiness, the dimension with which he would like to merge definitely.

Throughout the narrative Tom is caught between sleep and sleeplessness, dream-like states and conscious states of mind. During the nights he suffers from insomnia, staying awake until daybreak or sleeping in spurts, dreaming his white nightmares. Tom's insomnia stems from grueling physical labor and the tense atmosphere of the Rhees' Fruit' n Food grocery store, Mrs. Rhee's overblown expectations and the burgeoning conflict between African Americans and Korean Americans. At the Rhees' store he is constantly on edge, expected to perform several jobs at once, working extremely long hours for below a minimum wage and suffering hunger. At night he ends up staring at the ceiling or mindlessly watching TV. Whiteness not only enters his dreams, but also haunts him during his sleeplessness. Gazing at the ceiling, he can see white paint peelings dangling in the air: "white tongues hanging down at him" (48). The stupor of the night extends into the daytime, when he cannot focus his mind or vision, being in constant state of confusion, having doubts about what is real or imagined: "nothing was what it appeared anymore" (102). It is during his semi-conscious states of mind that Tom has premonitions of something being wrong (101). The full realization comes later.

A myriad of factors frustrates Tom's desire to be able to "sleepwalk through life and not mind" (9). Even if he literally sleepwalks, he cannot figuratively "sleepwalk through life and not mind" (9). Orphaned by his mother at a very young age, he spends most of his childhood with distant relatives. When his father dies, he is left completely to himself. Having graduated from college, he never obtains white collar employment, always working in menial jobs. The question why Tom never takes up a white collar job is left to the reader to answer. Partly, it can be blamed on Tom's lack of resourcefulness, his own inaptitude. The reader never finds out if Tom ever seeks work outside the narrow range of sales and services jobs in which he works. We are never told if Tom's Korean American ethnic heritage ever plays a role in the limited spectrum of opportunities he has in his professional life. Tom is an antithesis of an Asian American model minority overachiever. He is also an odd choice for work at a family run Korean American grocery store. The employees at such stores are usually not Korean American college graduates but fresh immigrants taking up the employment because of a very narrow horizon of possibilities. None of the jobs undertaken by Tom provides a stable place of work. Being constantly forced to move, he craves for a sense of belonging, for settlement, for setting roots in one place definitely (8).

Towards the Embrace of Transformational Identity Politics in the Patchwork of Inner City Allegiances

Tom's blinding is the direct result of his positioning in a network of complex allegiances.[13] Suffering exploitation at the Rhees' Fruit' n Food store, Tom is still perceived by African Americans boycotting the store as a parasite in their community, as a drainer of African American resources. Protestors outside the Fruit' n Food vent their pent up frustration on Tom, hurling racial slur at him, spitting on him and in the end physically attacking him (188–189). He faces animosity outside the store and the space of the store itself cannot be seen as his safe place either. The relationship with his employers, the Rhees, is very complex. Tom's exploitation is only one of the factors that complicate the relationship. First of all, Tom displays clear unease about Mrs. Rhee' s prejudice against African American customers and her expectations that he should watch them lest they steal anything. Tom does not know how he should behave should any problematic situation arise. Mrs. Rhee's prejudice and her excessive precautions trigger the conflict situation—namely the boycott of the store. Still, she does not perceive herself as the culprit but pins all the blame on Tom. The last complicating factor in the relationship with the Rhees is a liaison between Tom and the Rhees' daughter June. Even though June is the initiating party in the relationship, Tom is again perceived as the main culprit.

The final irony of Tom's positioning in the patchwork of inner city allegiances is the fact that he is blinded by four Asian youths attacking an elderly black man, Mr. Harris, whom Tom remembers as a patron of the Rhees' store and a decent man. At this point of the narrative Tom no longer sleepwalks but takes decisive action. Standing up to Harris's defense, he proves that his identification is primarily with humanity, be it African American, Asian American or any other racial origin. The defense of Mr. Harris and the reproach directed at his attackers: "Four to one. Punching him, four to one. Tough guys. Real tough guys to pick an old man" (212) are a good illustration of an espousal of transformational identity politics and transcendence of conventional identity politics. While supporters of conventional identity politics overly concentrate on their own difference, proponents of transformational identity politics seek similarities between themselves and other marginalized people. They do not pursue universalism or sameness, but at the same time they realize that divisions between identities are not set in stone, because all identities are fluid. Cherishing their particular experience, they are still aware of what they have in common with other people. Rather than identify with the color of oppression, Tom sympathizes with the victims of oppression, irrespective of their racial or ethnic origin.

Tom's experiences culminating in his blinding leave him enriched with sharp insight into interracial relations but at the same time resigned and totally withdrawn from the outside world. Only immediately after waking up in hospital does he want to move and establish verbal contact with people approaching him (216). Still, initially, he is not able to either move or speak. Later, even if he could, he no longer cares to reconnect. Believing that he has no outside world to return to, Tom "withdraws more into his world of dreams" (226). His hospital dream-like, semi-conscious condition is an extension of his earlier mental state, yet his hospital dreams are no longer nightmares. Instead, they resemble languor, reminiscence, mental wandering between particular stages of his life, piecing together a fragmentary, postmodern narrative that does not give him unequivocal answers. In hospital Tom understands more (101), but he is still confused, for example he is not sure where he is. If we accept Gary Taylor's statement that "Every who implies a where" (12), the question "Where is he?" (*The Fruit 'N Food* 218) also resonates with "Who is he?"

The distinction between the real and imagined remains tenuous for Tom, who is not certain if the voices come from without or within (218). The voices inside Tom's head correspond to the statement from Don Delilo's novel *White Noise*: "To remember would be like having voices inside your head" (315). Remembering the events of the past, Tom also hears voices inside his head. The voices make more sense than before the blinding incident, but they do not fall into a coherent whole. External voices reaching Tom in hospital are "bodiless" and "formless" because he cannot trace their source (215). Parallelly, the source of racial dissonances in Kasdan is not easily traceable either.

Unlike earlier nightmares, Tom's hospital dreams or rather his daydreaming is soothing. Periodically, Tom is gripped by the "pounding" and "throbbing" pain in his head, the pain comparable to the "fire in his head" (19). The "fire in his head" is a clear reference to the fire raging across the Kasdan community. The fire consuming the inner city neighborhood is one more manifestation of James Baldwin's prophecy made in *The Fire Next Time*. However, African American anger does not turn against the people responsible for their oppression but against those who suffer exploitation themselves and who open their businesses in inner city neighborhoods because they have nowhere else to go.

Pills bring Tom relief from the fire inside his head and from the sense of literal "immobility," plunging him in whiteness "shaded with blues" (216). "The blues and whites mixing together" imitate "the sound of the ocean nearby, the lulling waves repeating their rhythmic crashes in his mind" (216). Concluding that there is no place he can belong to, Tom finds ultimate peace and anchorage in his dreams. The work at the Fruit' n Food store is his last ditch attempt to belong. Starting his work at the Fruit' n Food, he thinks that he may finally belong somewhere. With the store closing down, he finds his work "meaningless" (225). Tom's regrets indicate that he does not treat the Fruit' n Food employment simply as a means of subsistence but as part of a larger whole. His hopes once again being dashed, he decides to belong nowhere but to his dreams. When the outside world finally displays some interest in Tom through doctors, rehabilitators and his visitors, he shows no more will to reciprocate their interest, cooperating only to a degree he has to, resisting being led to various rehabilitation rooms. The hospital dreams transport Tom back to the brief bliss of his childhood, to the beach, to playing in the sand at the seaside and to his dead mother. Tom's return to the childhood stage of his life is further accentuated when a caretaker addresses him as a "big boy" (218). In the final phase of his dreaming Tom merges with the oceanic, which stands for the ideal, for the perfect reality unmarred by any want or longing.

The last stage of Tom's narrative life marked by his physical immobility[14] and mental indifference may symbolize the pacification of the people involved in the inner city discontent. They live out the scenario written by the invisible white scriptwriter. Tom's physical immobility underscores his social immobility and the social immobility of other inhabitants of the urban core. Cut off from major resources of the American economy, most of them are incarcerated in their positions.

Conclusion

Whiteness of *The Fruit 'N Food* barely ever features directly in the narrative as an explicitly articulated socio-historical category. White people practically never enter the dyad of Korean American and African American interactions presented in the novel, except for the presence of white police who play a marginal role in the dispute. Unnamed expressly in the main plot as the originating force behind the African American—Korean American discord, whiteness enters the picture only through Tom Pak's dreams, providing a significant commentary on what remains unstated directly. For Tom, dreams are an alternative way of seeing, of striving for understanding, of seeking his way out of confusion. Pervasive images of whiteness in his dreams expose the responsibility of whiteness for initiating the circumstances of the inner city conflict. In the context of the "larger problem of inner city discontent" (219), Tom's white nightmares prompt the reader to think of the forces seemingly absent from the clash between African Americans and Korean Americans, yet playing a crucial role in setting the stage for it.

4

Representation of Whiteness in Joy Kogawa's *Obasan*

Introduction

The criticism of whiteness is much more explicit in Joy Kogawa's *Obasan* (1981) than it is the case in the previous work analyzed here, Leonard Chang's *The Fruit 'N Food*. Kogawa overtly names white people as responsible for oppression of Japanese Canadians during World War II and in the postwar years. At the same time she avoids essentialist characterizations of whiteness to be encountered in the sections of the first two works probed in the book: Kingston's *The Woman Warrior* and *China Men*. Pointing explicitly to whiteness as responsible for the oppression of Japanese Canadians, Kogawa also hints at the potential of whiteness for transformation. Yet this potential is never stated so expressly as in the next and last work explored in this study—Maxine Hong Kingston's *The Fifth Book of Peace*. Just as Leonard Chang is very refined in indicating the implication of whiteness in the African American–Korean American conflict, encoding the meanings in the imagery of the narrative, so is Joy Kogawa in hinting at the potential of whiteness for transformation, revealing this potential only through the aesthetic layer of the narrative.

Set against the background of World War II internment of Japanese Canadians and post–World War II memories of internment, *Obasan* presents whiteness as the color of death, betrayal, domination, separation and distance. Overall, however, whiteness invites double-edged associations in *Obasan*. On the one hand, whiteness emerges clearly as a site of dominance and repression. On the other hand, it is associated with light, brightness, the promise of liberation and salvation, albeit liberation and salvation at a price. My analysis of whiteness in *Obasan* centers mostly on color imagery employed in such a way as to illustrate the position of Japanese Canadians in a predominantly white society and to render their attitudes to whiteness. Mixed associations of whiteness in *Obasan* stem from

Kogawa's defiance of clear-cut binaries and her search for the space in between, the safe niche between the oppressor and the oppressed. This twilight zone is represented by "murkiness" or the color of gray. While the focus of the chapter falls on whiteness, it is impossible to analyze whiteness without placing it in a wider spectrum of colors featured in the novel. All these colors are brought together in the final liberating scene in the act of triumph over different kinds of oppression exposed by Kogawa.

The most striking images of whiteness in the novel are:

- white paper
- a white hen destroying its own yellow chicks
- images of bones and skeletons
- whiteness of the nuclear explosion
- the biblical white stone inscribed with the names of people who are to be saved
- light and brightness standing in opposition to shadow and darkness symbolizing death, invisibility and emptiness.

For the first-person narrator whiteness is also firmly linked with sexual exploitation and military aggression which in some of her nightmares merge into one.[1]

The Historical Context

To understand why whiteness invites particular aesthetic associations in *Obasan*, we need to take a brief look at the socio-historical context in which the novel unfolds. The first person narrator, thirty-six-year-old Naomi Nakane, speaks from the perspective of 1972, looking at the events of World War II and post-war years. In Canada of the 1940s whiteness was a site of normativity, a visible marker of belonging to the Canadian nation, while Japanese Canadian ethnicity was a visible marker of difference and alienness. The tenuous standing of Japanese Canadians became conspicuous in all its bluntness after the attack on Pearl Harbor on December 7, 1941. On the same day the Canadian government ordered Japanese Canadians to register with the Registrar of Enemy Aliens by February 7, 1942 (Lo 101). Earlier such measures were also applied to German Canadians and Italian Canadians. However, the similarities end here. On February 25, 1942, the Canadian government ordered all Japanese Canadians to leave a hundred mile protected area along the Western Coast (Lo 101). Their property including homes and fishing boats was impounded never to be recovered again. Before being relocated further inland, Japanese

Canadians were sent to the Hastings Park Exhibition Grounds, where they had to live in adapted livestock stalls.[2] After the relocation they were thrown into wild uninhabited areas, into virtual ghost towns, forced to live in squalid conditions, often in wooden cabins or tents.[3] The measures taken against Japanese Canadians expose the status of whiteness as a marker of normativity. No internment orders were issued against German Canadians or Italian Canadians. The official explanation of the internment was that Japanese Canadians posed a military threat, although Chief of General Staff, Lieutenant General Ken Stuart, declared otherwise (Adachi cited in Lo 101). The most probable cause for the internment was the fear of racial difference and economic competition, mostly from Japanese Canadian fishermen (Goellnicht "Minority History as Metafiction" 188). The Canadian citizenship of the internees was selectively revoked. After 12,000[4] Japanese Canadians had already settled in the interior of British Columbia (in such towns as Slocan or Kootenay Lake) and set up their own farms, they were uprooted again by the Canadian government in 1944. Pursuing the policy of dispersal, the government forced them to either migrate to Japan, a strange country for most of them, or to move still further from the Pacific Coast, east of the Rocky Mountains. Out of 14,000 Japanese Canadians only 4,000 chose to repatriate to Japan (Goellnicht "Minority History as Metafiction" 289). Those who went east of the Rockies were forced into the most sordid forms of employment like sugar beet farming (Lo 101).[5] Only in 1949 did the government allow Japanese Canadians to return to the West Coast. In reality they had nothing to return to since all their property was liquidated.

At the time when Naomi constructs her narrative, whiteness remains the marker of normativity. Three decades after World War II, a white Canadian man still asks Naomi where she comes from, placing her outside the perimeter of Canada and assuming that she cannot be a Canadian citizen. Canada as a country is represented in *Obasan* as a figure with "pale arms" (290). A representative of an older generation of Japanese Canadians—Naomi's aunt and de facto foster-mother named Obasan is equally alienated in Canada. There would be no place for her in a "white-walled, white-washed and totally white old folks' home" (269).

White Paper

Double-edged associations of whiteness in *Obasan* are the most conspicuous in the image of white paper. As a vehicle for the word, paper is a powerful witness of Japanese Canadian history, the "history in black and white" (40), to cite Naomi's activist Aunt Emily, also referred to as "one of the world's *white blood cells*" (41, emphasis added). Papers in Aunt Emily's collection include: letters, legal documents, memoranda, pamphlets, newspaper clippings as well as her diary. All these papers impart a documentary quality to the novel. They document successive relocations, internment, expropriation, expulsions from Canada as well as the dispersal and splintering of families. Gurleen Grewal identifies some passages of the novel as documentary prose (7). While Kogawa herself was exposed to enforced relocation during World War II and her own experience of relocation inevitably found its way into the text, she cannot be identified with the first person narrator of the novel. Unlike Naomi's fractured family, Kogawa's own family managed to stay together during successive relocations into the interior of Canada (Lo 100).[6] Constructing the narrative, Kogawa drew to a great extent on the letters and journals of Japanese Canadian activist, Muriel Kittagawa,[7] who served as a prototype for Naomi's activist Aunt Emily (Lo 102). Aunt Emily's papers and Naomi's recollections complement each other, amplifying the documentary quality of *Obasan*.

The power of print[8] and paper cuts both ways in the novel. Paper becomes a tool both for oppressors and their victims. It is a material inscribed with internment orders, sequestration letters and anti-Japanese propaganda of newspapers. Print gave an air of legality to all the measures leveled against Japanese Canadians. Print also helped to obfuscate history or to "whitewash it," to use Donald Goellnicht's term ("Minority History as Metafiction" 296). The white newspaper shows Japanese Canadian internees "grinning and happy" after their forced resettlement to Alberta (230). The caption in the newspaper stands in sharp contrast to Naomi's reflections on life in Granton, Alberta. Before relating the conditions in which they live, the back-breaking toil, the heat and cold, Naomi states that their life in Alberta is beyond remembering, resembling a nightmare "from which there is no waking, only deeper and deeper sleep" (232). The concealment of oppression is visible in the terminology employed by the Canadian government to cover up oppression. Internment camps are referred to as "interior housing projects" (41).[9]

Papers collected by Aunt Emily resemble *"white wafers"* in the priest's silver box, "symbols of communion," "the materials of communication," *"white paper bread for* the mind's meal" (217, emphasis added). Significantly, Naomi describes Japanese Canadians as "unwilling communicants" (217). "Unwilling" can invite several interpretations. It may be connected to the complex relationship that people of Japanese descent have with Christian missionaries.[10] They are also "unwilling communicants" because they often communicate through silences rather than actual words.[11] However, most significantly, they are "unwilling communicants" because they are reluctant recipients and followers of government internment orders and segregation letters, because they mentally resist the propaganda of white newspapers. The communion offered by Canada to its fellow-citizens cannot be called any other way but "loveless" if it sacrifices its own children (217). In Aunt Emily's words what Canada "did to [Japanese Canadians], it did to itself," swerving from the path of democracy and mimicking the totalitarian practices which it ostensibly combated during the war (46).[12]

Paper circulates both ways in *Obasan*. Japanese Canadians may be "unwilling communicants" of government directives but they write back in an attempt to defend themselves. Paper symbolizes both the fragility and endurance of Japanese Canadian lives. "Aunt Emily sends letters to the Government. The Government makes paper airplanes out of our lives and files us out the windows. Some people return home. Some do not. War, they all say, and some people survive" (291). Even if "the government makes paper airplanes out of [their] letters," people like Aunt Emily persist in their efforts and in the end succeed in exposing suffered injustices and obtaining their redress, symbolic as it is. The first step to the full redress was the 1946 memorandum sent by the Co-operative on Japanese Canadians to the House and the Senate of Canada. It was signed by three Canadian citizens who belatedly listened to Japanese Canadian complaints, declaring the internment orders illegal and demanding their revocation.[13] Kogawa chooses to close the novel with the text of the memorandum, emphasizing the need for justice, cooperation and reconciliation.

Paper is the only material link between the living and the dead, those who survived and those who died during the internment or in the Hiroshima and Nagasaki bombings as Naomi's mother did when Naomi was a small child. The narrator compares her dead mother's letters to "skeletons" and "bones" (292), the only remainder of the mother's bodily presence, the "bone marrow" that remains after the flesh is gone. The *whiteness* of paper corresponds to the *whiteness* of bones, both standing for remnants of the spent life. "All that is left is your word" (291), Naomi declares. The mother's words were passed down to her only two decades after her death, the intention of the mother being to protect the daughter from the horrors of the Nagasaki nuclear explosion. Through her mother's word she envisions her world after the bombing, narrowing the gap between the living and the dead. Letters written by the Japanese deported to Japan are a release from their silence and loneliness. Grandma Kato writes because she does not want to be the only one to dream the nightmare of living through the nuclear attack.

The comparison of white paper to white bones or skeletons is not the only moment in the text when bones are explicitly mentioned. The narrator also visualizes the recovery of the bones belonging to Japanese Canadian fishermen who were forced to leave the coast of Vancouver and settle on the prairies of Alberta. Symbolically, their bones rest in the northwest corner of the local cemetery. Naomi wonders how the future genealogist will react to the presence of so many fishermen's bones away from the seacoast, on the prairies (270). Like paper, bones are a testimony to Japanese Canadian history. According to David Palumbo-Liu, bones have the "potential to speak" provided that they indeed are discovered by some future genealogist (223). No signs of Japanese Canadian presence are visible in former places of their residence in the interior of British Columbia. Retracing their own genealogy, Naomi and her relatives discover that their lives in the area of Slocan are white spots on the map: "We looked for evidence of our having been in Bayfarm, in Lemon Creek, in Popoff.... Where on the map or on the road was there any sign? Not a mark was left" (121). They used to be pioneers conquering the wilderness of the area only to see it return to the forest. Naomi's memory of spectacular Japanese Canadian gardens of Slocan remains just a memory. The only familiar site of the place is a "small white community" existing already before they arrived (121). Whiteness survives, removing unwanted intrusions out of its way.

As mentioned earlier, *whiteness* of *Obasan* and in particular *whiteness* of white paper also stands for emptiness and erasure. In one of her dreams Naomi can see a book composed exclusively of blank *white pages*. White pages of the book parallel the above-cited *white spots* on the map, symbolizing the attempted erasure of Japanese Canadians from Canadian history. The dream foreshadows the deaths inside and outside Naomi's family. Empty pages of the book stand for "erased victims" (Banerjee 114). Constructing the narrative and filling empty pages with her own accounts as well as the accounts of her relatives, Naomi partly undoes the erasure, acting on her aunt's precept to make Japanese Canadians visible and "knowable" (Kogawa 49). Some of the documents that find their way into Naomi's narrative used to be white, but in the course of time they turned yellow or brown. Overwritten with Japanese Canadian experience, they also show signs of wear and time.

Mourning in White: Whiteness as a Harbinger of Death, Loss and Destruction

In the Japanese tradition whiteness is the color of death and mourning. Whenever the narrator remembers or dreams of her dead mother, it is against the background of whiteness. She dreams of the mother as a sea tide drawing her away from the shore to the *"white distance*, skyward and away from this blood-drugged earth" (290). The Nagasaki bombing which leaves the mother severely mutilated is also described in terms of whiteness[14]:

> there was a sudden *white flash*, brighter than a bolt of lightning. She [Naomi's grandmother] had no idea what could have exploded. It was as if the entire sky were swallowed up. A moment later she was hurled sideways by a blast. She had a sensation of floating tranquilly *in a cool whiteness* high above the earth [284, emphasis added].

Whiteness is the harbinger of death and destruction. Kogawa anticipates the whiteness of the nuclear explosion in the opening fragment of the narrative through synesthesia. Visual and auditory impressions merge in the image of the *white sound*. The white sound muffles everything else. To arrive at the truth about her mother's disappearance, Naomi needs to reach beyond the clatter of white propaganda and to excavate the hidden meaning symbolized by the underground stream (V).[15] She pictures separation from her mother and father also in terms of whiteness, colorlessness and winter:

> The sadness and the absence are *like a long winter storm*, the *snow falling in an unrelieved colorlessness* that settles and freezes, burying me beneath a growing *monochromatic* weight. Something *dead* is happening, like the weeds that are left to *bleach and wither in the sun* [240, emphasis added].

Once again whiteness evokes death, separation, emptiness, sadness, insipidness and monotony. Naomi craves for color to return to her life. Color does return into her life in the final scene when she discovers the symphony of colors in the woods. In the forest Naomi experiences a symbolic reunion with her dead relatives.

White Dominance: Canada Devouring Its Own Children

The representation of whiteness as the color of domination and oppression of Japanese Canadians is the most conspicuous in the fragment presenting a white hen destroying yellow chicks (70).[16] Describing the pecking of the chickens to death, Naomi employs the military register. The hen is "bayoneting" the chicks (70). Analogically, the white Canadian government destroys its own people by subjecting them to multiple relocations, arduous labor and forced expulsion. Japanese Canadians identified adamantly as Canadian citizens but they were denied the rights stemming from their citizenship. It is significant that the pecking of chickens to death takes place in Naomi's own backyard. As Naomi observes: "outside, even in the backyard, there is an infinitely unpredictable, unknown, and often dangerous world" (69). The safe space of home protects Naomi from anti-Japanese Canadian sentiments of the outside world.[17] Outside her own house she falls prey to sexual exploitation at the hands of her white neighbor and to harassment from white children.

Reflecting on the yellow color of the chickens, Naomi concludes that in popular imagery, "yellow," unlike white, stands for cowardice and menace—"Yellow Peril" (180). "Yellow Peril" is a pejorative term applied to people of Asian origin. They supposedly present a threat to white civilization—either a military or cultural threat. People of Asian origin living in the United States and Canada were seen as potential spies and as inassimilable aliens, who might pollute "white" Eurocentric culture. As mentioned above, they were also perceived as an economic threat and competition. Kogawa highlights the blind spots of the anti-Japanese Canadian discourse. Aunt Emily aptly notes that, on the one hand, they are labeled as inassimilable, while on the other, they pose a constant threat of assimilation (47). Naomi's brother makes similar observations, pointing out that Japanese Canadians are both the "enemy and not the enemy" (84). Naomi's own reflections on the question of "Yellow Peril" are focalized through the child's point of view and through her memories of the cardboard game called "Yellow Peril." The fact that in her childhood Naomi associates the yellow color with negative features like being cowardly, weak and small indicates partial internalization of white people's racism. It may also point up yet another inconsistency in the "Yellow Peril" discourse. People of Asian origin were at the same time portrayed as a threat and as weak, incapable and fearful. To some extent Aunt Emily mirrors these claims by reproaching Japanese Canadians for their lack of decisive resistance to internment orders: "What a bunch of sheep we were. Polite. Meek. All the way up the slaughterhouse ramp" (45). Aunt Emily's words may seem controversial because they contradict her own efforts and they reinforce the stereotype of Japanese Canadians as passive victims. Kogawa herself admits that her portrayal may appear problematic, creating an impression that she constructs Japanese Canadian identity around the experience of "powerlessness and loss" (Kogawa cited in Goldman 364). The reinscription of Japanese Canadians as a minority sacrificed by the majority is the most visible in Naomi's conversation with Aunt Emily: "the fears of the collective can only be calmed by the sacrifice of a minority" (Kogawa 42). The sacrifice that is at stake goes beyond the hardships suffered by Japanese Canadians during World War II. It also involves the sacrifice of Japanese Canadian identity. Naomi observes: "When the yellow chicks grow up, they turn white" (181), indicating that some Japanese Canadians equate assimilation with the effacement of their racial and ethnic heritage. Naomi's brother Stephen is the example of a yellow chick who grows up and turns white, rejecting the Japanese heritage completely. Naomi grows up to be Momotaro in her family. Momotaro is a traditional Japanese hero who saves his people and their tradition. In the pages of the narrative Naomi also performs a figurative act of saving Japanese Canadians from oblivion and indifference. She has kept her Japanese Canadian identity but like other Japanese Canadians, she nonetheless bears the consequences of her community's break-up. Apart from losing her parents and suffering physical as well as psychological trauma, she no longer has any Japanese Canadian friends: "None of my friends today are Japanese Canadians" (46). According to Aunt Emily, the "destruction of community" equals for Japanese Canadians the "destruction of life" (Beedham 144).

The biblical epigraph to *Obasan* foreshadows the prominence of whiteness in the novel and the promise of salvation at a very high price:

> To him that overcometh
> will I give to eat
> of the hidden *manna*
> and will give him
> a *white* stone
> and in the stone
> a new name written[18]
> [emphasis added].

It is significant that the epigraph is virtually steeped in whiteness, the whiteness of the hidden manna and the whiteness of the stone with a new name. Survival and salvation in predominantly white Canada demand a significant erasure of survivors' identity. "Stone" can be a foundation, but it is also a desensitized object. Many of Naomi's relatives "rest in the world of stone" (295). In the prologue section of the narrative Naomi claims that "The word is stone" (V). The word will remain "stone" only until it is spoken, until it "bursts with telling" and becomes the "freeing word" (V). Suspended between the living and the dead, between her aunt's torrents of words and steadfast silences of other members of her community, Naomi can reach the "freeing word" not only by breaking her own silence, but also by learning to listen and read silence.[19] When Naomi visits the woods in the epilogue section to pay homage to her dead relatives and to re-establish the link with them, the moon is "pure white stone" (296). The whiteness of the moon has positive connotations. The stone is no longer a desensitized object because now it is animated by its shimmering reflection on the surface of water, the symbol of life. Gurleen Grewal maintains that "the final immersion indicates a psychological restoration, the harmony of emotions in a balanced dance of life" (155). Watching the dance of water and the moon, Naomi experiences a spiritual rebirth and reconnects with her dead relatives.

Positive Connotations of Whiteness: Light and Brightness in Opposition to Darkness and Blackness

If whiteness itself has ambivalent associations in *Obasan*, light and brightness are unambiguously positive, standing in opposition to death, shadow and darkness. "The *white light* from the stars" (202) portends the joy of reunion. The quietness of "the white light from the stars" and of the falling snow symbolizes the calm withstanding the chaos. "The faint shaft of light" (202) separates the "living from the dead" (296). In opposition to light, darkness symbolizes separation, invisibility, death and emptiness. The blackness of the night intensifies Naomi's sense of invisibility and insignificance, magnifying an ever-present threat of disappearance, of vanishing into space: "Sometimes when I stand in a prairie night the emptiness draws me irresistibly, like a dust speck into a vacuum cleaner, and I can imagine myself disappearing off into space like a rocket with my questions trailing behind me" (222).[20] It is in the darkness of the "predawn hour" (295) that Naomi feels the acme of her isolation: "How thick the darkness behind which hides the animal cry. I know what is there, hidden from my stare. Grief's weeping. Deeper emptiness. Grief wails like a scarecrow in the wild night" (295). The Japanese Canadians who leave their family and friends forever disappear "into the night and dispersal" (214). Blackness is the most distinctive feature of the train that takes them away to Alberta in 1944:

> The day we leave, the train station is a forest of legs and bodies waiting as the train jerks and inches back and forth, its *black* hulk hissing with steam and smelling of *black* oil drops that drip onto the cinders. We are all standing still, as thick and full of rushing as trees in a forest storm, waiting for the giant woodsman with his mighty ax. He is in my grade-two reader, that giant woodcutter, standing leaning on his giant ax after felling the giant tree [215, emphasis added].

The giant woodcutter resembles an executioner, waiting to mete out a punishment at the guillotine.

The accumulation of darkness and blackness around the lives of Japanese Canadians does not extinguish their inner light, the light brought to the surface through the activism of people like Aunt Emily. Japanese Canadians are portrayed as "networks and streamers of light dotting the country" (38). Remembering the relocation of 1942, Naomi depicts her people as descending into the "middle of the earth," expelled "into the waiting wilderness" "for the sake of light" so that they "may bring sight" (132). Implicitly, it is the white Canadians who need to see and recognize Japanese Canadians as their own people. Ironically, by trying to render them irrelevant and invisible, the Canadian government pushes Japanese Canadians further inland, on the one hand, condemning them to hardship and privation, on the other, anchoring them even more firmly inside the land. Darkness also envelopes the prologue of the novel. Only after silence has been broken and attended to,[21] is the darkness of the prologue illuminated in the epilogue. The underground stream becomes the source of brightness and "the brooding light," linking the living and the dead (295).

Although Naomi herself attaches unequivocally positive associations to light and brightness, she does not have a clear-cut vision. She remains dubious about her aunt's commandment: "Write the vision and make it plain" (Habakkuk 2:2 in Kogawa 38). For Naomi the truth is "more murky, shadowy and gray" (38). Memories are "gray shapes in the water ... passing shadows" (25). Murkiness and gray imply the color in between black and white, in between clear cut definitions, interpretations and visions of events. Rather than settle for a one-sided account of the past, Naomi embraces the postmodern definition of reality, the reality which is always constructed, contestable, hybrid and polyvocal. As mentioned earlier, she juxtaposes her own memories with her aunt's diaries, official documents and newspaper clippings. For Aunt Emily it is important to "get the facts straight" (219). Naomi comprehends the enormity of the task, realizing that many of the facts, especially the most personal, will never see the light of the day and will forever remain unspoken. Facts are very different for the four-year-old Naomi who goes through several relocations marked by personal traumas. Facts are different for Aunt Emily who spends most of the war in Ontario. They are different for Naomi's musician father forced to work as an ordinary laborer on road construction teams. They are different for Naomi's mother who survives the horror of the Nagasaki bombing and dies several years later from her mortal wounds. Facts are different for each and single Japanese Canadian and they are different for white Canadians, those who were directly involved in the internment, those who watched passively, and those who staged a protest against singling Japanese Canadians out for different treatment. Reflecting on the politics of memory in *Obasan*, David Palumbo Liu speaks of the "possibility of truth" ("The Politics of Memory" 215). According to Palumbo-Liu, "the possibilities of truth are intimately tied to memory" (215). In her narrative Naomi records convergences and divergences of memories contingent on a particular person's location, age, gender, race, power. While she focuses on racial injustice, she places it on the broader map of oppressions, identifying their individual strings in the hope of achieving at least partial catharsis.

It is significant that the final scene, which gives the heroine a measure of liberation, brings together the whole gamut of colors: "the colors all meet—red and yellow and blue" (295). Apart from symbolizing the reunion with dead relatives, the symphony of diverse colors stands for transformational identity politics, uniting people from various oppressed groups, distinguishing between their unique experiences of oppression, yet at the same time seeking commonalities instead of excessively stressing differences.[22]

Conclusion

Joy Kogawa exposes whiteness as a site of dominance and oppression, but she also avoids an essentialist approach to whiteness. Rather than see whiteness as a monolith and slot all whites into one category, she differentiates between various shades of whiteness, conjuring both negative and positive images of whiteness. Implicated as whiteness is in Naomi's personal exploitation and collective exploitation of other Japanese Canadians, it has potential for transformation. Analogically to the final passage encounter between the pure white stone moon and the dark river, whiteness can cooperate with people of color. For this to happen, however, it must recognize and redress the injustices perpetrated against these people.

5

Towards Transformation of Whiteness in Maxine Hong Kingston's *The Fifth Book of Peace*

Introduction

This study begins and ends with the analysis of whiteness in the writing of Maxine Hong Kingston. *The Fifth Book of Peace* marks the evolution of Kingston's vision of whiteness and the very definition of racial categories in her works featured here. In *The Fifth Book of Peace*, Kingston assumes a much more transnational perspective, reflecting to a greater extent on the enmeshment of whiteness in imperialist and colonizing practices beyond the perimeter of the mainland United States and the territory of the United States as a whole. While in *The Fifth Book of Peace* Kingston notes the implication of whiteness in colonization and imperialism, she also to a greater extent stresses the potential of whiteness for transformation. This potential was hinted at in *The Woman Warrior*, but it is much more explicitly elaborated on only in *The Fifth Book of Peace*.

As in Joy Kogawa's *Obasan*, whiteness reveals itself to the reader in *The Fifth Book of Peace* through a whole array of images, bringing up its positive and negative associations. On the one hand, it signifies death, mourning, loss, destruction, expansive nationalism and colonization. On the other hand, it stands for opulence, plenitude, luxury, comfort, empowerment, light, brightness and visibility. All of Kingston's works are written in the spirit of transformational identity politics and intersectionality. In all of her works, Kingston notices the intersection of diverse types of oppression, going beyond exposing the stripes of exploitation that immediately affect the major characters of her works. Yet it is only in *The Fifth Book of Peace* that she underscores the need for cooperation between individuals affected by diverse types of trauma stemming from different kinds of oppression. It is also in *The Fifth Book of Peace* that Kingston envisions the possibility of white Americans cooperating with people of other races and nationalities on behalf of peace rather than in the name of war, expansion and colonialism symbolized in the narrative by the wars in Vietnam, Iraq and the colonization of Hawaii.

More than any other work by Kingston analyzed here, *The Fifth Book of Peace* exemplifies her message to inspiring writers, encapsulated in an epigraph opening this study:

> You're not just a writer in an ivory tower. You are a citizen of this country and of this world, and so what are your responsibilities? As Norman Mailer puts it, are you a participant or are you an observer? How distant are you going to be from the material, from the readers, from the doings of your time? (Lim's Interview with Kingston 168).

It is *The Fifth Book of Peace* that to the greatest extent blurs the lines between fact and fiction, the author and the narrator, giving the reader the most palpable sense of Kingston's own involvement in the quest for peace and her egalitarian drive to include as many as possible in her narrative enterprise and in her communities of healing patterned on Buddhist sanghas. *The Fifth Book of Peace* encompasses all of Kingston's major works, interweaving thematic, generic and aesthetic threads and yet still reaching beyond anything attempted in any of her previous narratives and in broader literature. Opening with the death of the narrator's father and closing with the death of the narrator's mother, Kingston establishes a clear link with *The Woman Warrior*, the book of women and *China Men*, the book of men, drawing a circle around her artistic output and imparting an impression that "the end is in the beginning" and "lies far ahead," to cite Ralph Ellison with whom Kingston felt an affinity after also losing the original manuscript of her book in a fire (*Invisible Man* 5). The middle "Water" section of *The Fifth Book of Peace* tracks the descendant of the narrator's maternal and paternal generation of fresh immigrants into the United States, the protagonist of her third major work *Tripmaster Monkey*, Wittman Ah Sing, who "has to break open Chinese American consciousness that he built with such difficulty" (Kingston, "The Novel's Next Step" 40). The narrator of *The Woman Warrior* marches to change the world, wondering what her village is, only to conclude in a conversation with Brave Orchid that "'We belong to the planet now, Mama. Does it make sense to you that if we're no longer attached to one piece of land, we belong to the planet? Wherever we happen to be standing, why, that spot belongs to us as much as any other spot'" (125). In another passage of *The Woman Warrior*, the narrator states that "[her] job is [her] own only land" (58). Both passages anticipate *The Fifth Book of Peace*. It is only in *The Fifth Book of Peace* that the philosophy of these passages becomes fully fledged.

In *China Men* and *Tripmaster Monkey*, Kingston keeps claiming America for Chinese Americans. In *The Fifth Book of Peace*, she goes beyond claiming any particular territory, instead trying to claim the individuals who need healing, most of them on account of the pursuit of the imperial and colonial warfare for the control over land and its people.

After losing the original manuscript of her book and before venturing upon the composition of a new one that was to become *The Fifth Book of Peace*, Kingston spoke extensively on what she hoped to achieve in and through her narrative. In a 1993 interview with Neila C. Seshachari, Kingston declared that in *The Fifth Book of Peace* she would like to "claim evolution"—the evolution of the human species (210). Ideally, according to Kingston, "reading and writing should expand and transform the self" (ibid 213). This transformation and expansion of the self is possible only if one "go[es] beyond" "family, tribe, Chinatown, gang, nation—into a larger selflessness or agape" (ibid 213). Reminiscing on the beginning of her writing career, Kingston remembers that she initially envisioned herself as avoiding explicitly political discussion and didacticism, being even close to embracing the concept of art for art's sake (Skenazy's Interview "Coming Home" 109–110). Later she concluded that it was incumbent upon writers to "have a vision of a future" and she claimed to have the "power to envision a healthy society, healthy human beings" (ibid 110). Noting that "the imaginative life and the real life intertwine" (ibid 110), Kingston envisions her writing as interventionist, asserting "I want to be able to manipulate reality as easily as I can manipulate fiction.... What if I could strongly write peace, I can cause an end to war" (Seshachari's Interview 196). In *The Fifth Book of Peace*, everyone is supposed to be a "star" and a "spectator" (ibid 212), an observer and a participant. Making all these bold claims, Kingston takes the concept of a writerly text one step further, not only including readers in the very act of composition, but also exhorting them to do certain things, to transpose the concepts of her fiction to the extratextual reality.

The Potential of Whiteness for Transformation

The transformation of the self that Kingston envisions through reading and writing inevitably involves the transformation of whiteness in her writing. Double associations of whiteness and the potential of whiteness for transformation are best encapsulated in the narrative through Kingston's representation of two different flags: the flag of the United States and the flag of the United Nations. In Kingston's portrayal, the "Red, White and Blue stands for competition and nationalism" (12). She openly declares her desire to resignify the red, white and blue of the American flag in such a way as to make them "stand for peace and cooperation" (12). The reflections on the flag come in the section of *The Fifth Book of Peace* in which the narrator of "Fire" visits the site of her burnt down house, being able to see the singed American flag waving opposite the empty space of her former house. The white elements of the flag are further underscored by the whiteness of the "white metal flagpole," adding to the sense of desensitization evoked by the narrator[1] through her associations of the flag with competition and nationalism. It also bears noting that the narrator identifies the red, white, and blue of the American flag as "its primary colors," observing that they "don't occur much in nature," (12) a claim which may be startling considering that one can find a lot of red, white and blue in nature. Yet on a moment of reflection one must indeed agree that while they do occur separately, they barely ever appear together, amplifying the narrator's metaphor of competition and nationalism as well as the need for cooperation. The label "primary colors" invites not only the sociohistorical connotations specific for the United States, but also the optical context of color theories. The Optical Society of America distinguishes between primary basic colors and derived basic colors (Boynton 137). Together with green, yellow and black; red, white and blue are also defined as "unique" or "elemental" color categories (Wooten and Miller 75). They are identified as "unique," "elemental," or primary because "non-unique" or derived colors are derived from them or in other words "compounded of them" (ibid 75).

The flag of the United States is juxtaposed in the "Fire" section of *The Fifth Book of Peace* with the flag of the United Nations, which the narrator mentions in connection with the outbreak of the first war against Iraq, identifying herself together with her neighbor as the only ones to fly a flag of peace at the inception of the war. The white and blue of the United States flag recur on the United Nations flag, but they are reconfigured in such a way as to signify peace and cooperation rather than earlier mentioned competition and nationalism. In juxtaposition with the white dove, the symbol of peace, whiteness no longer stands for competition and nationalism. Another recurring color is blue. Still, it is also a different kind of blue than that on the United States flag, being qualified as "sky-blue" (13). Depicting the United Nations flag, the narrator returns blue to its most frequent positive signification. As mentioned in *The Fruit 'N Food* chapter of this study, blue is usually perceived as a soothing color. Blue is also the last primary color, red being the first one (Hardin 304). Both blue and red are often perceived in opposition to each other. While red features on the United States flag depicted by Kingston, it is no longer a part of the description of the United Nations flag that follows. The only recurring colors white and blue are accompanied by another primary color—green and derived colors—orange and brown: "a white dove on a sky-blue silk field, UN colors plus orange beak, green leaves, brown branch, brown eye" (13). Orange is a compound of yellow and red (Wooten and Miller 78), while brown is compounded of black and yellow (Wooten and Miller 81). In the multicultural context of the United States, derived colors imply racial and ethnic mosaic, cooperation desired by the narrator rather than competition, nationalism and separatism.

The narrator's preference for the United Nations flag to the United States flag epitomizes not only her quest for peace, but also her embrace of a much more transnational perspective than in the previous works by Kingston. This transnational perspective is explicitly delineated in some of the pronouncements on race, nation and ethnicity in *The Fifth Book of Peace*. Reflecting on the aesthetics of race in the "Water" section, Wittman concludes that race is a matter of perception: "But race is in the eyes of the beholder; if you look at her [the Hawaiian beauty] and think Black, then she looks Black. You think Italian, your eye searches out the features that are to you Mediterranean, such as olive skin, aquiline nose. Noses and lips are a degree more or less flared or flat or wide. We differ but shades and fractions of an angle from one another. Whatever race you're thinking, you can see it" (110). A similar line of reasoning occurs when Wittman declares "Free-choose your ethnicity" (77), claiming to be "almost a Hawaiian," arguing that he could trace Hawaiian ancestry in his lineage and averring that he would vote against Hawaii becoming another state of the United States of America (77). Such a declaration is a stark divergence from Wittman's mentality in *Tripmaster Monkey*, in which he bent over backwards to emphasize his own Americanness, as well as trying to change the mindset of first generation Chinese Americans who perceived themselves as Chinese rather than Chinese Americans. The evolution of Wittman's mentality fulfills Kingston's afore-cited design to "break open" Wittman's Chinese American consciousness (Kingston, "The Novel's Next Step" 40). Now he is close to embracing the mentality of a transnational, diasporic subject.

The Perception of Nation and National Belonging

The narrator's own reflections on nation and national belonging become conspicuous in the "Earth" section at the time of her visit to the

Vietnamese sangha community, Plum Village, together with Vietnam veterans participating in her writing workshops. Attracting people from all over the world, Plum Village "cross[es]," "erase[s]" and "broaden[s] boundaries" (390). A visit to Plum Village also in a sense completes the textual search for her own village initiated by Kingston in *The Woman Warrior*. While the narrator of *The Woman Warrior* grapples with the question about her village, in the end concluding that "'Wherever we happen to be standing, why, that spot belongs to us as much as any other spot'" (125) and '[her] job is [her] own only land'" (58), the narrator of *The Fifth Book of Peace* seems to be aware that assigning oneself physically and mentally to one particular place may be more and more challenging for postmodern subjects with personal histories of migration or migration of their families. "Crossing, erasing, broadening boundaries" of which the narrator speaks in the context of Plum Village matches Alejandro Portes's definition of transnationalism as "goal-oriented initiatives that require coordination across national borders by members of civil society" (186). Portes emphasizes that these activities "are undertaken on their own behalf, rather than on behalf of the state or other corporate bodies" (ibid 186).[2] The encounter between the narrator's community of peace and healing operating in the United States and Vietnam based Buddhist sangha exemplifies transnational cooperation between members of civil society across national boundaries on behalf of peace. Peace that is at stake is not only global peace in a broader sense of the word, but also internal peace that according to the narrator and the Vietnamese Buddhist monks is essential for the achievement of global peace.

Asked about the definition of "nation," the narrator is dumbfounded, proclaiming it to be one of the "abstract terms" which "put [her] into despair" (390). Defining "nation" as an abstract term, the narrator is still aware that this abstraction is backed up by very concrete acts such as choosing a ruler, inventing an ideology, making money, amassing weapons etc. (390). The definition of "nation" as an abstract term approximates Benedict Anderson's definition of nation as an "imagined community" (6). Still, like the narrator of the "Earth" section in the afore-cited passage, Anderson's *Imagined Communities* traces the concrete steps that accompanied the process of imagining. Transnationalism also finds its way into the narrator's definition of Americanness. For her, being an American is to be from everywhere: "'When you hug Americans, who are from everywhere, you hug all the people of the earth'" (396). An equivalent of Vietnamese Plum Village on American soil comes in the form of creative writing workshops organized not only for veteran soldiers of various wars, but also for survivors of other traumatic events like domestic violence.

The participants are predominantly yet non-exclusively American men since the workshops include women of diverse ethnic and racial origin and Vietnamese soldiers too, bringing together in the spirit of transformational identity politics people of various races and ethnicities with diverse histories of oppression. While American soldiers may be seen as a tool of imperialism and colonialism in Vietnam, they were also the victims of imperialist and colonial policies. The inclusion of white American soldiers in creative writing workshops, which are about to bring healing and nurture peace is also part of the striving for the transformation of whiteness. The Sanctuary created by Wittman and Tana in the Hawaii based "Water" section of the narrative is a refuge for all draft dodgers who hope to evade the Vietnam war and defy the imperialist and colonial policies. Like Plum Village and the narrator's veteran creative writing workshops, the Sanctuary brings together individuals across the racial and ethnic divide.

The Colonizing, Imperialist Face of Whiteness That Is to Be Transformed

Whiteness and in particular the elements of the discourse of the white national narrative discussed in part three of the *China Men* chapter lie at the core of oppression from which communal organizations like the Sanctuary, veteran creative writing workshops or Plum Village try to escape, or which they try to heal. Traces of this white national narrative are visible in President Johnson's speech to American soldiers at Cam Ranh Bay, the speech cited by the Hawaiian woman Poly in a conversation with Wittman in the "Water" section of the narrative. The speech attributed to Johnson displays a minoritizing face of whiteness, whiteness that presents itself as a "minority identity," to use Robyn Wiegman's term (116), fearing lest it be swept from the surface of the Earth by non-white races: "'The trouble is that there are only two hundred million of us and nearly three billion of them and they want what we've got and we're not going to give it to them'" (78). Wittman's reaction to Johnson's speech is as follows: "Who are the Them he's talking about? He can't come up with three billion unless he's counting every Oriental on earth" (78). The whiteness of Johnson's speech is a site of power that assiduously clings to its entitlements afraid lest some non-white intruders weaken them.

While in the above cited passages whiteness embodies power presenting itself as being under siege, in another passage of the "Water" section whiteness is identified as a source of empowerment and a status booster. The narrator presents the whiteness of Wittman's wife, Tana, as a marker of empowerment and entitlement: "Spoken like the White woman she is.... One reason you espouse yourself to a White person: access to more of the world" (71). "A habit that the Ah Sings had gotten into was that the White person in the family did the negotiating, went out ahead into America, particularly the rental market" (85). "Going out ahead into America" implies progress and ability to bring about certain results. It is not accidental that Kingston mentions the rental market since minorities have been perennially discriminated against in the real estate market and the legislation designed to achieve residential integration of racial minorities was successfully blocked in Congress (Massey and Denton 234).

Another aspect of colonizing, conquering whiteness appears in *The Fifth Book of Peace* in the context of the colonization of Hawaii. More than once in the narrative, native Hawaiians express their grudge against "haoles." The "ghosts" of *The Woman Warrior* and the "demons/devils" of *China Men* turn in *The Fifth Book of Peace* into "haoles," although "haoles" does not occur in the narrative with the intensity of "ghosts" of *The Woman Warrior* and "demons/devils" of *China Men*. In her anthropological study of whites in Hawaii, *The Mainland HAOLE*, Elvi Whittaker observes that the term "haole" originally denoted a "stranger," yet since most strangers were whites, it started to pertain to whites (197). Because of the context in which whites appeared in Hawaii, it also came to be linked with white conquest, white reign or white supremacy. Even if the term is used in the neutral context, many whites still see it pejoratively. Whittaker notes that if Hawaiians wish to express their negative attitude to whites, they usually do it through their intonation or by adding a pejorative adjective: "'God damn *haole*,' 'stupid *haole*,' 'fuckin' lazy *haole*'" (53). *The Fifth Book of Peace* registers the following exchange between above mentioned Poly, native Hawaiian woman educated in law, and Wittman—Tana duo while the latter are flying into Hawaii: "'haoles come over and make us wear clothes; now they laze on the beach with no clothes on, and we do the labor. The slavebor.' Though she wasn't directly name-calling, her listeners felt sticks and stones" (78). Although Wittman is not white and he goes as far as to trace remote Hawaiian lineage and identify himself as Hawaiian, he also seems to be an addressee of Poly's statement because he is a newcomer from the mainland. Tana treats Poly's words as directed overtly at her, which is why she feels compelled to emphasize that she is not "Anglo haole," but a person of "Dutch and Indonesian descent" (78). In the mainland United States she resents being called "an Anglo" or "English." The narrator's follow-up on Tana's disidentification in the

Hawaiian context is that "now she would have to start saying, 'Don't call me haole'" (78). In her attitude Tana fits into the race-traitor-school within whiteness studies, which "advocates the abolition of whiteness through white disaffiliation from race privilege" (Wiegman 122). Tana's disidentification from the Anglo centered identity clashes with her attitude displayed in afore-cited passages in which she very consciously draws benefits from white privilege. Tana's disidentification from "Anglo haoles" can also be explained through Elvi Whittaker's anthropological observations on Caucasians' dissatisfaction with the fact that in Hawaii their "ethnicity" becomes the most defining characteristic. Whittaker observes that for many it is their very first confrontation of the issue of their own "ethnicity" (153).[3]

Non-native inhabitants of Hawaii, mainlanders, not exclusively whites but all people from the mainland United States, are portrayed in *The Fifth Book of Peace* as exploiters of the Hawaiian land, violating "aloha," the Hawaiian tradition of giving and receiving: "'You mainland people ... you take advantage of our aloha. You come to our country with the prejudice that we give, give, give, and you take, take, take. 'Aloha' does not mean only giving. It is giving and receiving. Giving and receiving love. Reciprocal generosity.' Wittman had been told: Cold hard English does not have a word for 'aloha'"(75). Indirectly, whiteness is again associated with coldness. It received similar associations in the section of *The Woman Warrior* in which the narrator speaks of the icicle in the desert, the passage of *The Fruit in Food* in which the white imagery of Tom Pak's dreams gains a semblance of "blinding coldness like a cruel sun" (Chang 215), "cool whiteness" of the Nagasaki bombing (Kogawa 284) and Naomi's representation of the separation from her parents in terms of whiteness, colorlessness and winter in *Obasan* (Kogawa 240).

The colonizing and imperialist face of whiteness appears in the Hawaiian context of *The Fifth Book of Peace* also in connection with the Hawaiian land "aina" defined by Kingston as "land, earth, property, estate. Not just any land, but the sacred land that is Hawai`i" (79).[4] For native Hawaiians of *The Fifth Book of Peace*, the land is a sacred feature that needs saving and protection from foreign inroads. Poly casts herself as someone who thanks to her law degree can protect the land. The land provides in the narrative a staging ground for the maneuvers of the United States army before its redeployment to Hawaii: "The U.S. Army were on maneuvers, occupying Hawaii. On their way to Viet Nam" (117). In Kingston's portrayal, the United States army is an occupier of Hawaii, which becomes a stop in a colonial enterprise of the government of the United States: "The island was an aircraft carrier, a launching pad, an armed satellite, and its purpose was to funnel our every destructive resource to Viet Nam" (119). Wittman's analysis of the scope of the military presence on the tourist map reveals an incommensurately large appropriation of Oahu by the military. Ironically, the presence of the army is marked in pink, the color perceived as feminine, not masculine.

The presence of the United States army on the island is presented in *The Fifth Book* as anything but innocent. The acts perpetrated on Hawaiian soil during the military maneuvers parallel those depicted in *China Men* and performed in the name of conquest and civilization. The citations below reveal this correspondence: "They [China Men] were the first human beings to dig into this part of the island and see the meat and bones of the red earth. After rain, the mud ran like blood" (*China Men* 100). "He [Wittman] saw the green skin of a section of mountain to his right explode, blow apart, fly apart. Underneath the green skin was red earth like meat.... Pieces of green skin and red-meat dirt chunks broke apart and fell" (119). While the purpose of China Men's work on the land is its cultivation albeit through what Rachel Lee terms as the "violent restructuring of both settlers and the soil" (148), American soldiers' military exercises bring about exclusively destruction. Both constitute a version of Manifest Destiny performed in the name of democracy and progress ostensibly championed by the propagators of the white national narrative. Both China Men and the American soldiers play the role of the executors of this design.

The soldiers of the United States Army exercising in Hawaii are by no means identified as exclusively white. Watching the soldiers pass by, Wittman can also spot African Americans, Chinese Americans and Japanese Americans. With all his pacifism he does not perceive them as aggressors, but as victims themselves: "They should be in college. It's the poor, the uneducated who have to go to war, the poor fighting the poor" (117). The racial differences of the soldiers in question are made almost indistinct because of the blackening covering their faces, including the faces of African American soldiers. "The poor fighting the poor" obfuscates racial and ethnic divisions in favor of class solidarity.

Whiteness is not the only site of racial oppression in the Hawaiian context of *The Fifth Book of Peace*. The Hawaiians themselves become implicated in racial oppression on the basis of reverse power dynamics, misdirecting their anger at two black Peace Corps welfare workers from the mainland United States: Sheraton and Clifton. Having received all kind of assistance from Sheraton and Clifton, the Hawaiians show no gratitude, but instead drive them out of the island, behaving as if the black social workers presented an affront to their pride: "'Who they think they are?' 'Fuckeeng Popolos, Welfaring us'" (188). The reasoning of the Hawaiians runs along the following lines: "'Black haoles. Bad enough White haoles—we get Black haoles'" (188). Since they cannot run out whites, they will at least run out blacks. The Hawaiians spout all kinds of racist slurs against black people, essentializing their physical features: "'You should see their Popolo eyes—so big and round and sked.' 'Pop eyes like Rochester and Buckwheat.' 'They get white eyes shine in the dark.' 'They fuzzy-wuzzy hair stand up in air. No more Popolo in Kahalu'u forevah now.' 'Popolos go stay back to Main Land.' 'Da *black*, da buggahs'" (189). The pidgin spoken by the Hawaiians brings remote echoes of the white Southern racial slurring of African Americans. In Wittman's imagination, the driving out scene gains the semblance of a lynching, exposing the dehumanization of human condition close to that traced in white "demons" and "devils" in *China Men*. It is interesting that the most graphic scene of racial prejudice involves representatives of two racial minorities excluding whites. In a similar vein, Kingston mentions anti–Asian American racial massacres in *China Men*, but never employs her artistic imagination to describe one.

Imagery of Whiteness: From the Negative Representation of Whiteness towards Its Valorization

A substantial portion of the representation of whiteness in *The Fifth Book of Peace* takes place through the imagery of the work, illustrating Mieke Bal's claim that imagery can be a tool of subversion and counterdiscourse (1290). Like Joy Kogawa's *Obasan*, *The Fifth Book of Peace* reflects an ambivalent attitude towards whiteness, also registering the transformation of whiteness in the course of the narrative. While in the initial sections of *The Fifth Book of Peace* the imagery of whiteness reveals whiteness as associated with death, mourning, loss and destruction, in the course of the narrative whiteness comes to signify opulence, plenitude, luxury, comfort, empowerment, peace, light, brightness and visibility.

As it is the case in *The Woman Warrior*, whiteness often features in *The Fifth Book of Peace* together with blackness. At the very outset of the narrative Kingston establishes the tandemic connection of whiteness to blackness, claiming that both black and white have negative connotations in the Chinese tradition, signifying death and mourning. Red stands in opposition to both, being the vibrant positive alternative, the color of life (15). Black and white prevail in the depiction of destruction following the fire of the narrator's house. The color of the narrator's burnt house turns from red to white: "Its paint had been seared from red to white" (12). Looking at the scorched landscape surrounding her former house, the narrator can see "a black-and-white *Guernica* of trees—black skeletons, negatives of trees, caught in poses of agony, killed and reaching for air" (22). Approaching the fire zone, the narrator notes that she "[has] entered the black negative dimension where things disappeared" (10). She goes on to compare her former house to "the black space" that replaced it (18). The original manuscript of *The Fifth Book of Peace* lost in the fire also turns white: "a book-shaped pile of *white ash* in the middle of the alcove.... The *ashes* of my Book of Peace were *purely white, paper and words gone entirely white* ... the edges of pages, like silvery vanes of feathers, *like white eyelashes* ... this *ghost of my book*" (34, emphasis added). Apart from standing for death, destruction and in this case the spent life of the book, whiteness also signifies in the above cited passage, as it does in *The Woman Warrior* and *China Men*, insipidness and blandness. "The ghost of my book" is one more whiteness related application of the term "ghost" in Kingston's works, embodying a remnant of a once living thing.

Kingston's representation of the fire is an exemplification of what E. San Juan, Jr., terms as "anti-imperialist aesthetics" (11). Whiteness evoked aesthetically in the fire of the narrator's house reverberates once again as implicated in the colonial or semi-colonial ventures, which the narrator visualizes while watching and later surveying the destruction of her neighborhood. For the narrator, the fire triggers an instant association of the fires of war ravaging in the past Vietnam and in her contemporary times Iraq: "God is showing us Iraq. It is wrong to kill and refuse to look at what we've done. Count the children killed, in 'sanctions': 150,000, 360,000, 750,000. 'Collateral damage' ... we are given this sight of our city in ashes. God is teaching us, showing us this scene that is like war" (13–14). In the narrator's portrayal, the fire becomes a visualization of the war in Iraq. Taking a bird's eye view of the fire, a Vietnam veteran remembers "the shock and horror of Vietnam" (14). Seeking communion with the survivors of other traumas caused by "firewinds blow[ing] over the top of the earth," the narrator displays understanding for those living underground in Vietnam and Okinawa (12). Although the Oakland fire is the making of a natural force, in *The Fifth Book of Peace* it becomes a focal point for establishing a connection with survivors of man-made disasters. Explaining the significance of the fire episode, Hsu shounan cites the Badiouian typology of an event, claiming that every event is significant, a "situation is a 'presented multiplicity' ... 'compel[ling] [a person] to decide a new way of being'" (1). After the fire the narrator concludes that stripped of her possessions, she can appreciate the sphere of "idea" to a greater extent.

"Touch[ing] the ashes again and again," the narrator resembles the I-speaker of Anne Bradstreet's "Upon the Burning of Our House," when the latter repeatedly reminisces on the things that were no more. Leading expeditions to the fire site, the narrator rejects the position of a passive victim, placing herself in the position of an active subject. The Oakland fire interfered with the publication of the original manuscript of *The Fifth Book of Peace* and another fire almost got in the way of the publication of the recreated manuscript. Kingston delivered the first draft of *The Fifth Book* when September 11 occurred only to hear from the editor, Deborah Garrison, that her book was too pacifist and outdated since in the current political climate everyone had to be more "sensitive" in order not to hurt the majority's political feelings (Lim's Interview with Kingston, "Reading Back, Looking Forward" 167).

With the progression of *The Fifth Book of Peace*, negative representations of whiteness give way to its valorization. Whiteness features more and more often in the images of opulence, plenitude, luxury, comfort, empowerment, peace, light, brightness and visibility. Recounting veteran reunions, the narrator emphasizes the white finish of all attributes of festivity: "white tablecloth," "white flowers," "white cloth napkins," "a thick white linen tablecloth" and "sparkling crushed ice" also implicitly connoting whiteness (270). In line with the Western tradition of celebrating, whiteness is an almost indispensable hallmark of festivity, extending an air of honor and grandeur to the occasion. In a similar vein, for one of the veterans participating in the narrator's creative writing workshops, whiteness connotes domesticity, comfort and femininity. In his story about Johnny's coming home from war, he pictures Johnny's transition home among others in terms of color: "home from a hard green masculine world to one with the softness of beds and pillows and white wifely thighs welcome-home spread" (297). Another color featuring in his story is "red." Yet in this case red has nothing of its vibrancy or symbolism of life. Instead it stands for death when Johnny, suffering from the post-traumatic stress syndrome, looks at the Chickahominy River and imagines that it turns red, following the mentally visualized sound of cannon and musket fire (298). The homely whiteness of "white wifely thighs welcome-home spread" in Johnny's story is a transformation of whiteness appearing in the extratextual reality in which the narrator of the "Earth" section introduces Johnny to the reader. At the time when Johnny presents his story on coming home from war, he no longer wears "skull pants" which he used to wear when the narrator first met him (297). Whiteness as a marker of death evoked by "skull pants" is transformed into the marker of home warmth, domesticity, hospitality and femininity albeit rendered in somewhat sexist terms. It is also crucial to notice that the transformation that whiteness as a cultural category undergoes in the consecutive sections of *The Fifth Book of Peace* may be related to the changing perspective representing to a greater extent the viewpoint of the veterans many of whom are white westerners with a different sensibility than that displayed by the Asian American, Chinese American narrator.

As *The Fifth Book of Peace* progresses, whiteness appears more and more often as a positive element of magic, featuring across cultures and heralding peace. The mythical beliefs invoked by Kingston belong to the realm of Native American culture, Vietnamese Buddhism and Taoism. Whiteness in question is an example of archetypal valorization of whiteness across cultures which I mention in *The Fruit 'N Food* chapter. In particular, Kingston brings up those examples of mythical beliefs into which whiteness becomes interwoven as a herald of peace similar to the white dove on the peace flag discussed earlier. Relentless in her quest for peace, the narrator of the "Earth" section desperately tries to find harbingers of peace that would portend the end of seemingly never ending war. This is how she perceives the birth of a female white buffalo, which, according to Native Americans is to bring peace among nations (335). A Native American cited by the narrator compares this particular birth to the birth of Christ in Christian cultures, calling the "White Buffalo Woman" "'the Princess of Peace'" (335). The narrator portrays the buffalo in very feminine terms, drawing the reader's attention to her white curls and a pink nose. The birth of the White Buffalo Woman is predicted in an earlier section of "Earth" in juxtaposition with the birth of a white elephant coinciding with the birth of Buddha. Searching for the peaceful future of the United States and the world, the narrator looks to the cultural beliefs of the original inhabitants of America, confronting them with beliefs of other cultures. A similar connotation of whiteness is to be traced in a short story by a veteran participant of Kingston's writing workshops. In "Shopping Cart Soldiers," John Mulligan's protagonist, Finn the Albanach, witnesses the bestial and unnecessary shooting of the white bull, an act which apparently significantly compromises Finn's humanity and sensitivity represented by an Asian woman living inside him. In the synopsis of the short story cited by Kingston in the "Earth" section, the Asian woman decides to leave Finn after the mercy killing of his wounded friend. In a more complete version of "Shopping Cart Soldiers" included in Kingston edited collection of veteran writing, the Asian woman leaves Finn after "the Great White water buffalo, the bull, is murdered" (*Veterans of War, Veterans of Peace* 369). Whiteness recurs once again in the snippet of "Shopping Cart Soldiers"[5] cited in *The Fifth Book of Peace* in the figure of a "good ghost, white fox" contrasting with other ill-disposed ghosts haunting Finn (*The Fifth Book* 323).

While Kingston embraces the archetypal appraisal of whiteness mostly in the context of magic and peace, she rejects the archetypal denigration of blackness. Like the blackness of the narrator's pictures in *The Woman Warrior*, blackness, apart from representing death and destruction, also figures in *The Fifth Book of Peace* as the color of power and potential. In the "Fire" section the narrator proclaims: "A black wildcat, like a hot, growling, hissing furnace, lives in a dark forest and in a broken cage and inside of me. I am filled with power. Black Elk empowers me. Through dream, I access—know about and thereby have—deep life" (37). Blackness conjures up the associations of the dream and the night. The black night invites unequivocally positive connotations of peace, stillness and quiet in the Vietnamese context of meditation in the Plum Village (372), thereby transposing what Robert Bosnack terms as "Thanatos blackness," that is, archetypal or universal images of blackness associated with the night and the fears supposedly triggered by the night (Bosnack cited in Adams 22).

Whiteness also appears in *The Fifth Book of Peace* as an overt or covert attribute of the recurring tropes of this study: the white stone, paper, light and brightness. In Joy Kogawa's *Obasan*, the white stone is initially introduced as the biblical white stone of the epigraph, the white stone that in the novel carries the promise of salvation at a very high price. Representing initially a desensitized object, the white stone of the epigraph is transformed towards the end of the novel in the image of the moon, "pure white stone," that is animated by its shimmering reflection on the surface of water (Kogawa 296). The dance of water and the moon helps Naomi to experience a spiritual reconnection with her dead relatives. In *The Fifth Book of Peace*, the white stone also signifies sharing and reconnection of the links. Ted, one of the veterans taken by the narrator to the Vietnamese Plum Village, brings white limestone rocks for all veterans to share (Kingston 393). On the one hand, rock is a symbol of stability, but on the other, the fact that it is made of limestone undermines its sturdiness and desensitization, exposing its ability to crumble into smaller chunks.

White paper receives a similar signification in *The Fifth Book of Peace* to that of *The Woman Warrior* and *Obasan*. Like the immature narrator's white paintings in *The Woman Warrior*, the blank paper of *The Fifth Book* carries infinite possibilities of envisioning things which are not yet there. The narrator of the "Earth" section reflects on the open-endedness of "blank typing paper" that is to be filled with meaning: "In paper a poet is able to see a tree, and a cloud, and water, earth, and the sun" (266). As in

Obasan, white paper of *The Fifth Book* is a witness of history unfolding itself through individual stories of veterans attending the narrator's creative writing workshops. The narrator introduces paper to veterans as a cathartic device that will provide a release from traumatic memories "I hold up the paper and say, 'Write things out, and you won't need to carry memories in your body as pain. The paper will carry your stories'" (266). In a similar vein to *Obasan*, paper is also a link with the generations of the dead, carrying their stories and being a vessel for the names of the deceased veterans: "The veterans carry a long sheet of white paper covered with flowers and the names of the fallen" (304). Finally, paper lies at the very root of *The Fifth Book of Peace* itself since the conception of the book begins with Kingston's search for the three lost books of peace whose finding is to augur peace. In the act of writing her book, she metaphorically helps to recover the lost scrolls to which she devotes a separate chapter of her work entitled "Paper."

The last whiteness related trope recurring in *The Fifth Book of Peace* is light. As I argue in the subchapter devoted to the imagery of whiteness in *The Woman Warrior*, the white color has a very special relation to light, being the only color reflecting all wavelengths (Adams 33). The very etymology of the term white firmly establishes its connection to shining, brightness and light (Casson 227, Taylor 76).[6] Light indirectly connects to another whiteness related trope, that is, paper. According to one of the veterans cited by the narrator, "'Writing, you shine light'" (266). In *The Fifth Book of Peace*, light signifies visibility, brightness, human presence and the radiance of the human body. Visibility represented by light equals in this case spotlight, being seen by other people, being embraced by them, belonging to the community. Brightness often occurs in the context of radiance and internal glow emanating from a human being: "The camp was the bright color on this gray beach, as if a spotlight shone on this group, or came from them" (104).... "Illumination comes from faces. (Soldiers blacken their faces because human faces shine, even at night.)" (327). "White light" also figures in the narrative as a sign of solidarity, peace and empathy when Wittman "cast[s] a white light around" passing soldiers, wishing them to "be safe" and "come back without getting killed or killing anyone" (118).

Conclusion

The Woman Warrior and *China Men* estrange whiteness, placing it in the position of the "other," unraveling the mechanisms of its socio-historical construction and exposing its enmeshment in oppression largely in the domestic context of the United States. *The Fifth Book of Peace* sheds light on white embroilment in oppression too. Yet the oppression at stake here is mostly imperialism and colonization unfolding in the transnational context, but still affecting negatively citizens of the United States, including white people. Kingston identifies whites as colonizers of Hawaii. She also implicitly and explicitly names whiteness as responsible for armed conflicts in Vietnam and Iraq. Overall, however, rather than portray whites chiefly as "others," "ghosts," "demons" or "barbarians," *The Fifth Book of Peace* to a greater extent aims at integrating whiteness and transforming it, incorporating whiteness in the work on behalf of peace and struggle against various miens of oppression. The transformation and integration of whiteness takes place in *The Fifth Book of Peace* not only through the multiracial and multiethnic organizations featuring in the narrative, but also on the aesthetic level of the work, through the images including whiteness, most of them constituting the recurring tropes of this study.

Conclusion

Kingston, Chang and Kogawa offer their own specific visions of whiteness grounded in the particular socio-historical context of the plot and the socio-historical context of writing. Yet in all their particularity, these visions contribute to the defamiliarization of whiteness and to making it more visible. The critique of whiteness materializes within the story lines of the works analyzed here and in the imagery complementing and further elucidating the emerging visions of whiteness. Asian American authors of the visions of whiteness presented in this study change the power dynamics which traditionally placed racial and ethnic minorities as those subjected to the defining gaze of whites rather than subjects of vision formulating their own criticisms of whiteness. Undermining the normativity of whiteness and its power to define others, Kingston, Chang and Kogawa still acknowledge the power of whiteness to influence the lives of Asian Americans and other racialized subjects. In most of the narratives examined here, the vision of whiteness that was and has been is also accompanied by the vision of whiteness that can be—whiteness transformed and cooperating with non-whites. Still, the full drawing of this vision belongs to white people themselves.

Before closing, I would like to reflect briefly on the status of whiteness in American society at the moment of closing the book—the cusp of 2013 and 2014. Both of these years mark grand anniversaries in the history of racial relations in the United States—the country setting the stage for four of the narratives analyzed here. 2013 witnessed the fiftieth anniversary of the 1963 March on Washington, while 2014—the fiftieth anniversary of the Civil Rights Act. How does the dream of the multicultural equitable society fare today and how does whiteness come into the tapestry of the dream? In his 2013 keynote address at a whiteness studies conference, Mike Hill said that whiteness was no longer a norm.[1] On the surface it might seem that it no longer is. Yet its normativity still persists albeit in more nuanced ways.

Conclusion

The deconstruction of whiteness in the academic world will be successful only if it goes hand in hand with the deconstruction of the power of whiteness in the real world. Therefore I would like to wrap up by addressing the following question: Is the apparatus of power in the United States still white and how does it bear upon the lives of racial minorities? On Barack Obama's inauguration night on January 20, 2009, political commentators spoke of the changing complexion of power in the United States. His first term in office saw the appointment of four Asian American secretaries[2] in his administration, more than there have been in any previous American administration. Still, the current political scene in the United States shows that the advancement to the positions of power and privilege by individual members of minorities does not necessarily need to signify radical empowerment for broader strata of marginalized groups, especially these least privileged, for example the people hidden behind "invisible walls"[3] of American inner cities. The crucial question is to what extent people of color benefit from policies executed by the apparatus of power. Obama's legislative proposals, for example the Health Care Bill, to a great extent address the issues which may be of particular significance not only to underprivileged white Americans but also to disenfranchised members of minorities. Overall, however, Obama's presidential campaign and his political agenda, like those of his Democratic predecessor John Kerry, were primarily tuned in to the middle class. While a significant percentage of Asian Americans do belong to the middle class, the same cannot be stated of African Americans or Hispanics. The median income of Asian Americans in 2012 was $68,636; of white, non–Hispanics $57,009; of Hispanics $39,005; of black Americans $33,321 ("Real Median Household Income" 1). Poverty rates between 2007 and 2011 were as follows: slightly over 10 percent for whites and Asian Americans with a higher percentage of poverty among Vietnamese Americans (14.7 percent) and Korean Americans (15 percent) as well as a lower percentage for Filipino Americans (5.8 percent); around 27 percent for black or African Americans; around 28 percent for Native Americans or Alaska Natives; and around 22 percent for Hispanics with 16.2 percent for Cuban Americans and 26.3 percent for Dominican Americans (Macartney, Bishaw and Fontenot 1). According to 2010 Census data, the segregation index for African Americans is 59 points (Logan and Stults 5), for Hispanics 50 points (ibid 11) and for Asian Americans 43 points (ibid 17). In their analysis of the 2010 Census data, Logan and Stults note the continuing slow rate of black-white desegregation and an unchanged level of segregation among Hispanics and Asian Americans in comparison to the segregation level thirty years ago (1).

On the one hand, Asian Americans are perceived as model minority subjects, who "outwhite" whites, while on the other hand, an air of alienness still hangs over them, their perception by the rest of American society often being closely linked to the perception of Asian countries occupying the center of attention at a particular historical moment. This holds not only for Asian Americans who can trace their heritage back to these countries, but to Asian Americans across the board because white Americans rarely distinguish between Asian American ethnicities. The Asian country riveting the attention of the United States and the world is China. The country once perceived as a sleeping giant has roared into the second decade of the twenty-first century as the world's second largest economy. Financial analysts argue that it is only a matter of time before China claims the number one spot. Those Americans who will choose to look at Asian Americans through the prism of China may once again view them in terms of a threat and unfair competition.[4]

In the perception of many African Americans, whiteness remains a norm in legal terms. The Equal Justice Initiative estimates that the ratio of African American incarcerations to white incarcerations is six to one, while those of Hispanic to white almost two to one ("Sentencing Bias" 1). In recent years the most public example of the tragic consequences of the criminalization of blackness was the Trayvon Martin case. On February 26, 2012, Trayvon Martin, a high school unarmed student was walking in the neighborhood of Sanford, Florida while on a visit to his father living in the neighborhood only to be confronted by a self-appointed, armed neighborhood watchman, George Zimmerman of white and Hispanic parental background.[5] In the ensuing scuffle Martin was fatally shot by Zimmerman. On July 13, 2013, a jury found Zimmerman not guilty of second degree murder and manslaughter. Commenting on the case, analysts questioning the verdict noted that the jury chose to identify with an armed man who claimed that his life was threatened by an unarmed one rather than a black, underage individual who was pursued by an armed individual without any proof that he was indeed a prowler in the neighborhood. Some claimed that the verdict of the jury would have been different if the situation was equivalent and a black vigilante shot a white man. Another publicized case bearing the marks of the criminalization of blackness and racial profiling was the 2009 arrest of Henry Louis Gates, Harvard professor of African American literature and African American studies. The white policeman suspected Gates of breaking into the house which in fact belonged to him. The questioning of Gates's house ownership puts into broader perspective ever more frequent flaunting of black ownership and black empowerment in the electronic media.[6]

The most graphic acts of racial discrimination depicted in the fiction analyzed here on the whole belong to the past. Yet some of the harshest trespasses against migrant workers described by Kingston in *China Men* still find their parallels in the present day American reality. One of the most chilling accounts of the migrant reality can be traced in the narrator's reflection when she looks at the cane fields of Hawaii: "Yet the rows and fields, organized like conveyor belts, hide murdered and raped bodies; this is a dumping ground" (85). While there are no pervasive reports of killings among migrant labor in the agricultural industry of the United States, 2013 witnessed a spate of reported rapes among female migrant agricultural workers in the mainland United States. In most cases those reports were made anonymously for fear of retribution, deportation or loss of employment. There is a strong suspicion that for the aforementioned reasons many of these rapes went unreported.

It might seem that whiteness is no longer a norm in the cultural world of entertainment if one takes into account substantial presence of African Americans and Hispanics in the electronic and printed media. Asian Americans are still not nearly so present as their African American and Hispanic counterparts. The representation of minorities leaves a lot to be desired, often consisting in very selective representation or misrepresentation like for example exoticization of racial or ethnic "others." While so much lip service is paid to cultural diversity, some Americans still appear to cherish the cultural white norm, if not directly, then at least indirectly. The best evidence of that attachment came in the numerous voices of dissatisfaction following the 2014 Super Bowl night when Coca Cola aired its commercial featuring representatives of various races and ethnicities singing the Star Spangled Banner in diverse languages rather than exclusively in English.

Considering everything that has been said here in the spirit of critical multiculturalism, even if America still marches to the ideal of democracy in which whiteness is truly no longer a norm, the most optimistic sign is ever more frequent public self-reflection and willingness to admit that race and ethnicity remain the outstanding issues within American society.

Chapter Notes

Introduction

1. For other features of postmodern aesthetics recurring in the works discussed here, please see the introduction to *The Woman Warrior* chapter.
2. I explain how the white apparatus of power shaped the urban landscape in the body of Chapter 3. For further reflection on the term "white cartographer" and the "white apparatus of power" see also note 6 to Chapter 3.
3. Despite Kingston's overt identification as the narrator of at least some sections of *The Fifth Book*, in my discussion of the narrative in Chapter 5, I preserve a distinction between the narrator and the author, keeping in mind the constructedness of all narrative personas.
4. I use the term "ethnic" with caution because ethnicity is no less a characteristic of white people than it is of racial minorities of the United States and Canada. Still, the term "ethnic literature" is well established in literary studies and it is difficult to replace.
5. The whole double consciousness formula unfolds as follows:
After the Egyptian and Indian, the Greek and Roman, the Teuton and Mongolian, the Negro is a sort of seventh son, born with a veil, and gifted with second-sight in this American world,—a world which yields him no true self-consciousness, but only lets him see himself through the revelation of the other world. It is a peculiar sensation, this double-consciousness, this sense of always looking at one's self through the eyes of others, of measuring one's soul by the tape of the world that looks on in contempt and pity. One ever feels his twoness,—an American, a Negro, two souls, two thoughts, two unreconciled strivings in one dark body, whose dogged strength alone keeps it from being torn asunder [Du Bois 5].
6. Richard Wright speaks about the split consciousness of white people in the Introduction to *Black Metropolis*. Ever since Du Bois used the term "double consciousness" in reference to African Americans, it has been attributed to African Americans and other people of color. Wright, on the other hand, ascribes split consciousness to white people. White people's split consciousness is a clash between their self-assumed air of righteousness and their attitudes to African Americans: "when the Negro problem is raised, white men, for a reason which as yet they do not fully understand, feel guilt, panic, anxiety, tension; they feel the essential loneliness of their position which is built upon greed, exploitation, and a general denial of humanity; they feel the naked untenability of their *split consciousness*, their *two-faced* moral theories spun to justify their right to dominate" (xxv, emphasis added). It is crucial to emphasize that both states are different. If African Americans' double consciousness is underlain by separation from the world of privilege, white people's split consciousness is triggered by the fear that their privilege may be lost or significantly compromised.

Chapter 1

1. The term location specifies not only physical location, but also what theoreticians of space, Neil Smith and Cindi Katz, term as "social location," that is, a place of standing in a broader social sense (69).

2. The debate between Kingston and Chinese American cultural nationalists, primarily Frank Chin, has been the subject of numerous critical investigations. Therefore I devote limited space to the issue in the book. King-Kok Cheung offers probably the most exhaustive analysis of Kingston-Chin debate in her article "The Woman Warrior versus the Chinaman Pacific: Must a Chinese American Critic Choose between Feminism and Heroism?" The problem also recurs in Cynthia Sau-lin Wong's "Autobiography as a Guided Chinatown Tour?"

3. I refer to the narrator as the narrator rather than as the Woman Warrior because she also becomes the Woman Warrior in the very act of writing the narrative. The narrative registers her process of becoming the Woman Warrior. The name "the Woman Warrior" is the name to live up to. Françoise Lionnet associates autobiographic writing with "see[ing] beyond the constraints of the here and now to the idealized vision of a perfect future" (Lionnet cited in Sidonie Smith 438). Françoise Lionnet's statement corresponds to Paul Skenazy's findings on autobiographic writing. By creating a vision of the past, one is also able to "create a vision of the future, by creating a past to live on, move from" (Skenazy's 1989 interview with Kingston, "Coming Home" 110). The name of the Woman Warrior will fully belong to the narrator after the completion of her narrative enterprise and even more so after she allows the self-knowledge gained in the process of composition to branch out into her life.

4. In an interview with Arturo Islas and Marilyn Yalom, Kingston explains what she understands through "claiming America." She accentuates her Americanness and the rootedness of Chinese Americans in the United States by calling herself a "native American": "When I say I am a native American with all the rights of an American, I am saying, 'No, we're not outsiders; we Chinese belong here. This is our country, this is our history, we are part of America. If it weren't for us, America would be a different place.' When I write I also claim America in a literary way, in an artistic way. When people claim countries, it's usually thought of as conquering them in war. I'm claiming America in a pacifist way, in an artistic way" (25).

5. I derive the term "bounded" from Ruth Frankenberg, who traces the boundedness of non-white communities to the colonial discourse. Frankenberg cites Trinh T. Minh-ha's application of the term in reference to ostracized communities (Frankenberg, "Whiteness and Americanness" 64). The narrator of *The Woman Warrior* leaves Chinatown among other reasons in order to transcend the boundedness of her culture and the sense of being proscribed, of being outside the perimeter of the rest of society.

6. Kathleen Brogan interprets the No Name Woman's story as a "partially submerged narrative" (18). The submerged nature of the No Name Woman's narrative parallels her liminal state of ghosthood. Just as submerged narratives offer an alternative to other forms of storytelling, "the fluid, shape-shifting spectral body offers an alternative to the anchored, all too physically defined bodies of women trapped in the role of guardians of a changeless, patriarchal culture" (Brogan 26).

7. In *The Woman Warrior* Kingston draws on Chinese folktales, karate films, autobiographies, first-person narratives, memoirs, maturation novels and the gothic tradition. For Saemi Ludwig, the desert of the "White Tigers" chapter conjures up the associations of T.S. Eliot's *The Waste Land*. In other sections of *The Woman Warrior* Ludwig also finds the echoes of such works as William Carlos Williams's *In the American Grain* and Nathaniel Hawthorne's *The Scarlet Letter*.

8. I am indebted for the use of the term "eccentric" in reference to *The Woman Warrior* to Paula Rabinowitz's interview with Maxine Hong Kingston, "Eccentric Memories: A Conversation with Maxine Hong Kingston."

9. The term "poor white trash" is believed to have been coined by black slaves in the early 19th century (Newitz and Wray 170). The written record of the term reaches back to 1833, registering the use of "poor white trash" by black slaves in reference to white servants

(Newitz and Wray 184). Upper class whites appropriated the term by 1855 (Newitz and Wray 170). I would like to distance myself from stereotypical images of white trash as violent, incestuous and criminal. I concur with Newitz and Wray, who claim that the negative stereotyping of poor people helps to justify the economic marginalization of these people (171). Newitz and Wray also link the formation of white trash to the tensions arising from the encounters between white "natives" (already settled immigrants) and new white immigrants. "White trash" was just one of the many hateful names given to those who seemed to pose a threat to the existing economic and social order (Newitz and Wray 182).

10. I problematize various applications of the term mimicry in African American and Asian American literature in *Invisibility in African American and Asian American Literature: A Comparative Study*.

11. The exclusivity of whiteness and its exclusionary character were guaranteed in the 1790 statute (Act of March 23, 1790: 1 Stat. 103), which gave the right to naturalization only to white people (Gotanda 140). African Americans were found worthy of American citizenship only in 1870, when the Nationality Act extended naturalization rights to black people. It was 94 years after the founding of the American state and 251 years after the first slaves were brought to the American continent in 1619, when the first slave ship arrived at Jamestown, Virginia (*African American History* 1). Chinese Americans began traveling to the United States in large numbers in the early 1850s, Japanese Americans in the 1880s (Chan 25). They had to wait for their right to citizenship for around 150 years until 1952. The McCarran-Walter Act not only made it possible for Asian Americans to become citizens of the United States, but also eliminated the "white persons" caveat of the naturalization law (Gotanda 145).

Apart from the American naturalization law, the exclusive and exclusionary character of whiteness was also guaranteed through discriminatory laws like segregation laws, also known as Jim Crow laws, granting white people exclusive access to various facilities like educational facilities, health facilities, recreational grounds, etc. The 1896 ruling of the Supreme Court in *Plessy v. Ferguson* enunciated the "separate but equal" doctrine, legally sanctifying segregation in public places.

Property laws supported the exclusionary practices of white people as well. It is only in 1948 that Japanese Americans gained the right to own and lease land (Takaki 399). In 1913 California passed an alien land law barring Asian Americans from land purchase and land lease for a period longer than three years (Chan 195).The law was supposed to exclude Asian Americans from property ownership and prevent them from setting roots in the state. It was repealed only in 1956 (Chan 197).

The exclusive quality of whiteness is further illustrated by the study cited in Andrew Hacker's 1992 book *Two Nations*. A group of white students was asked to say how much money they would like to be paid for the change of their skin color from white to black. The majority asked for $50 million or $1 million for each year of being black (Hacker cited in Harris 1759).

12. Even if a particular group of Asian descent was in favor at a particular moment, it was still subjected to negative stereotyping because most white people could not distinguish between different Asian American ethnicities.

13. African American poet Sterling A. Brown (1901–1989) makes similar observations in his poem "Old Lem," already mentioned in the introduction in the context of thwarted visual exchanges. African Americans are scared of the overwhelming, multiplied power of whiteness:

> But they come by tens.
> They got the judges
> They got the lawyers
> They got the jury-rolls
> They got the law
> They don't come by ones
> [Brown's poem in Roediger's *Black on White* 332–333].

"They come by tens" is the refrain of the poem. Sterling A. Brown's representation of whiteness and white power in numerical terms corresponds to Frank London Brown's portrayal of whiteness. Perceiving whiteness as an overwhelming, crowding, mobbing, suffocating force, Frank London Brown represents whiteness as a bulk that weighs down on him: "The weight of everything white ... was what scared me: white bosses, white working buddies, white policemen, white housing authority, white people, white mobs" (Brown, in Roediger's *Black on White* 318).

14. The trope of immigrants' always planning on return to their native country recurs in other literatures featuring immigrants, for example in *The Emigrants* by Polish playwright Sławomir Mrożek.

15. The translation of the term "Kuei" is only one of the points that Asian American cultural nationalists criticize in Kingston's works. They also charged her with perpetuating stereotypes about Chinese Americans, pandering to white people and their tastes, with vilifying and emasculating Chinese American men. In their 1975 first anthology of Asian American literature *Aiiieeee* Jeffery Paul Chang, Frank Chin, Lawson Fusao Inada and Shawn Hsu Wong put stress on masculinity, American nativity and heterosexuality.

16. By lying in order to create a picture of a near perfect community, Chinese Americans of *The Woman Warrior* to a certain extent corroborate the model minority myth, which according to Robert Lee helped white people to promote white racial liberalism, in line with which individual effort should preponderate over any measures taken by the state (160). Model minority articles contrasted the black ghetto with the communities inhabited by Asian Americans: Chinatowns, Little Tokyos, Koreatowns etc. The authors of model minority articles contrasted among others Asian American self-reliance with African American dependence on welfare. In the previously cited passage Kingston debunks the myth of the Asian American lack of unemployment, linking it to Asian American fear of speaking the truth in order to avoid deportation.

17. While lynching was still very real for African Americans in the discussed period of the 1940s and 1950s, it was no longer a menace for Chinese Americans in the period. The threat of violence was very real for Chinese immigrants in the 19th century. Historian Sucheng Chan distinguishes three patterns of violence against Chinese Americans: attacks against individuals, outbursts of violence against Chinatown communities and, finally, organized attempts to oust the Chinese from certain towns (48). Some of those violent outbreaks against Chinatown communities took place in Los Angeles in 1871 and in Chico in 1877. Especially drastic acts of violence occurred in Rock Springs, Wyoming, in September 1885, and in Seattle, Washington, from October 1885 to February 1886.

18. The narrator of *The Woman Warrior* is not emphatic about the fact second generation Chinese Americans perceive the success of their children as emblematic of their own success in the United States. As Peter Kwong notes in *The New Chinatown*: "Others pin their hopes on their children. Some, despite expecting limited achievements for themselves, seek opportunities for their offspring. If the next generation can succeed by joining the American middle class and moving out of the ghetto, parents see their American dream fulfilled and all their hard work and self-sacrifice worthwhile" (70).

19. The association of ghosthood with indistinctness is also visible in the above cited nineteenth century research of ethnologist and philologist N.B. Dennys, who claims that ghosts are presented as figures without a chin. Addressing someone as "'You're no chin'" equals "'You're a Ghost'" (Dennys 72). The plain and superfluous nature of whiteness is also evoked by a "white pig." To give someone a white pig means to give them something plain and unnecessary (Dennys 148).

20. Writing from the perspective of the 1970s, the narrator notices the polished, morphed mien of racism. Yet the two encounters with white executives depicted by the narrator date back to the 1960s, the period witnessing not only the 1964 passage of the Civil Rights Act, affirmative action but also the acme of racial turmoil in the Southern United States: lynchings, the 1963 Alabama Birmingham bombing, the Selma "Bloody Sunday" of 1965, student demonstrations in Greensboro in 1960 and in Albany in 1961, to name just a few milestone events. Their echo is visible in the narrator's statement: "I marched to change the world" (Kingston, *The Woman Warrior* 57).

21. The narrator's struggle against being silenced and her searching for voice has been the subject of such studies as Paul John Eakin's "Maxine Hong Kingston: 'I Had to Tell My Mother,'" King-Kok Cheung's *Articulate Silences*, Linda Hunt's "I Could Not Figure Out What Was My Village," Steven V. Husnaker's "Nation, Family and Language," and Ruth Y. Jenkins' "Authorizing Female Voice and Experience."

22. The first articles extolling the success of Asian Americans began to appear in the American press in the second half of the 1960s. They are "Success Story, Japanese American Style" (*New York Times Magazine* Jan 9, 1966), "Success Story of One Minority in the United States" devoted to the purported success of Chinese Americans (*U.S. News and World Report*, Dec. 26, 1966), "Success Story: Outwhiting Whites" dedicated to the success of Japanese Americans (*Newsweek* June, 1971). Robert Lee traces the beginnings of the model minority discourse to the 1950s and the logic of the Cold War (145). The model minority myth went hand in hand with the rhetoric of assimilation and accommodation, which according to Lee was to assuage white fears of the red scare, black-white miscegenation and homosexuality. For an extensive study of other model minority articles that appeared in the American press see Keith Osajima's article "Asian Americans as the Model Minority: An Analysis of the Popular Press Image in the 1960s and 1980s."

23. She also claims to "squeak" while asking if the chosen restaurant is not the one boycotted by CORE and the NAACP.

24. Reflecting on her childhood in the 1950s, Chinese American author Amy Ling says: "Being 'yellow' was perhaps not as bad as being 'brown' or 'black,' but, without a doubt, it was not as good as being 'white'" ("Whose America Is It" 28). "Being yellow" certainly sheltered Asian Americans from stereotypes which seriously impeded the lives of black people.

25. In Schroeder's interview with Kingston, Kingston does not mention the fact that peaceful as it is, the second executive scene takes a violent turn in the narrator's imagination, although there is no bloodshed in the confrontation proper.

26. Karen Tei Yamashita gives a vivid example of such urban restructuring in her novel *Tropic of Orange*:

people saying they used to live here or there. Now here or there is a shopping mall, locate the old house somewhere between Mrs. Field's and the Footlocker. Or here or there is now the Dorothy Chandler Pavilion, or Union Station, or the Bank of America, Arco Towers, New Otani, or the freeway.... Move some houses over, appropriate streets, buy out the people in the way [81–82].

27. Originally, the Gold Mountain (Gam Saan) referred to California (Takaki 31).

28. Dennys also notes that the tiger is very popular in Chinese fables. The monkey often outsmarts the tiger. According to the French sinologue, Professor Julien, some of the tiger fables are of Indian origin (Dennys 148).

29. The term "memory" here does not necessarily refer to one's mental capacity to remember but to the attachment to one's heritage and reverence for tradition. According to Brave Orchid, white people do not show sufficient respect for their ancestors and their heritage. Similar sentiments were expressed by Chinese anthropologists visiting the United States. Fei Xiaotong perceives the United States as a "land without ghosts," that is "without strong traditions or bonds with the past" (Fei Xiaotong paraphrased in Arkush and Lee 11). According to Fei Xiaotong, Americans are constantly on the move, which is why they are permanently uprooted. That is also why they have no ghosts, according to Fei Xiaotong: "Always being on the move dilutes the ties between people and dissolves the ghosts" (Fei's article "A World Without Ghosts" in Arkush and Lee 179–180).

30. David Leiwei Li dates the ballad of Fa Mu Lan back to fifth century BC (Leiwei Li 505), while Kathryn Van Spanckeren dates the warrior song of Lady Mu to the Book of Songs completed in 600 BC, its earliest parts reaching back to 1122 BC (Van Spanckeren 44). Cynthia Sau-ling Wong claims that in her creation of Fa Mu Lan Kingston draws on martial arts novels/romances, and upon traditional fantasy lore, that is "Ballad of Mulan" and the tale of Yue Fei, the male hero who had his back tattooed by his mother with four characters calling upon him to preserve loyalty to his country (Wong, "Autobiography as Guided Chinatown Tour" 33). In "Cultural Misreadings by My Reviewers" Kingston herself maintains that she did not mean the "White Tigers" chapter to be read as a "Chinese myth but one transformed by America, a sort of kung fu movie parody" (57).

31. The narrator of Chang-rae Lee's *Native Speaker*, Henry Park, makes a parallel declaration: "This is your own history. We are your most perilous and dutiful brethren, the song of our hearts at once furious and sad. For only you could grant me these lyrical modes. I call them back to you. Here is the sole talent I ever dared to nurture. Here is all of my American education" (320).

Apart from being a burden, "fury" and "sadness" are also a well-spring for "lyrical modes." The passage is to a certain degree an accusation against the society which conditioned Henry Park to be a spy: "This is your history." As he makes it evident throughout the narrative, it is not so much a history of peaceful cooperation, but of mutual exploitation.

32. Reminiscing on Naomi's childhood, her activist Aunt Emily says: "What a serious baby—fed on milk and Momotaro" (Kogawa 68). Both Naomi and the narrator of *The Woman Warrior* struggle against silence, searching for and reasserting their voice among others through the composition of first person narratives. Having said that, I would like to stress that the socio-historical circumstances in which both find themselves are diametrically different.

33. I discuss the narration of the No Name Woman's story in "The Trope of the No Name Woman in American Fiction and Ethnography Featuring Asian Women." The other three no name women discussed in the article are Mrs. Tan of Margery Wolf's *Thrice Told Tale*, Po Po of Maxine Hong Kingston's *Tripmaster Monkey* and Ahjuhma of Chang-rae Lee's *Native Speaker*.

34. For an overview of various approaches to skin as a literary trope, see an introduction to Maureen Frances Curtin's dissertation "Skin Tropes in Twentieth Century Anglo-American Literature: Interfacing Biotechnical, Political and Visual Discourses of Identity." In her dissertation Curtin focuses in particular on four works: Virginia Woolf's *Mrs. Dalloway*, Ralph Ellison's *Invisible Man*, Thomas Pynchon's *Gravity's Rainbow*, and Kathy Acker's *Empire of the Senseless*.

35. The immature narrator's taste in black clothes matches the predilection for black clothing displayed by Wittman Ah Sing, the protagonist of Kingston's third work, *Tripmaster Monkey*.

36. The village crazy lady is yet another example of a no name woman in the narrative. Her only name by which she is referred to is that constructed by the community, which dubs her as the village crazy lady.

37. The publisher of *The Woman Warrior* assigned the book the status of non-fiction. This characterization was later undermined by critics, who treated it as fiction or as a hybrid of fiction and non-fiction.

38. Milk functions in a similar way in another work of American minority literature, in Toni Morrison's *Beloved*. Sethe's husband smears his face with buttermilk, having witnessed the exploitation of his wife—the suckling of her milk by the slave master's nephews. Covering his face with buttermilk, Sethe's husband manifests his sense of emasculation, his inability to protect his wife and intervene on her behalf. For Sethe, milk is a "natural" source of nutrition. The same milk marks the slave master's nephews as effeminate and cowardly. The signification of milk in reference to male characters cuts across cultures. The portrayal of Shakespeare's Macbeth as a man full of milk also undermines his manhood.

39. Significantly for this study, Aristotle also relates whiteness to sight, arguing that white may hurt the eyes of people with "weaker sight" (Aristotle cited in Taylor 394).

40. "*Hue*" is one of the three psychophysical dimensions of color. The other two are: *brightness* and *saturation*. *Hue* (prismatic color) is the "property of light determined by spectral position (measured in wavelengths)" (Casson 238). *Brightness* ranges from light to dark and is determined by the quantity of luminescence and the degree of reflectivity. *Saturation* is "determined by the amount of its admixture with white or black (Casson 238).

41. In Middle English the hue denotation of hwit gained primacy over its brightness denotation. Hwit came to signify mainly the hue of milk, flour, salt; alabaster, marble, pearl; ivory, (whale) bone; chalk; paper; clothing; swan, horse and mule; sheep's fleece, boar's tusk; hair and beard of old-aged people; skin and complexion; paleness stemming from illness or fear (Murray; Burnley cited in Casson 227).

The term "black" underwent an equivalent transition in Middle English. While in Old English it signified primarily a level of brightness, in Middle English the hue sense again gained primacy over the brightness denotation (Casson 227-228). Middle English "black" signified the darkness of night and clouds; the hue of soot, coal and pitch; pigment and ink; hair, beard, complexion; the pupil of the eye; the devil crow; raven's feather; sloe-berry; fur; cloth, clothing, mourning garb; species of animals and plants (Murray; Kurath and Kuhn; Burnley cited in Casson 227-228). It is worth noting that in his study of Old English and Middle English color terms Casson acknowledges his debt to Carol Biggam and Richard Diebold. Carol Biggam is the author of "A Lexical Semantic Study of Blue and Grey in Old English. A Pilot Study in Interdisciplinary Semantics" in two volumes, an unpublished Ph.D. dissertation, Strathclyde University and *Sociolinguistic Aspects of Old English Color Lexemes*.

42. Richard Dyer traces a similar process in the film industry, where some cinematographers display a varied level of multicultural sensitivity when dealing with black actors. What is primarily responsible for disparate lighting requirements with black and white actors is different reflectance of light for light skin and dark skin: 43 per cent for light skin and 29 per cent for dark skin (89). Dyer gives an example of Spike Lee's cinematographer, Ernest Dickerson, as a filmmaker who employs light technology differently when approaching black actors, for instance he uses "warmer" light and gold rather than silver reflectors (98).

43. Orange is a derived basic color closely connected to the landmark/primary basic colors yellow and red. Orange constitutes a link between both of them. Orange is a darker color than yellow, but lighter than red (Boynton 143).

44. The patriarchal in *The Woman Warrior*, closely interlinked with the carving of the words upon the narrator's back, is the topic of the following publications: Steven V. Husnaker's "Nation, Family, and Language in Victor Perera's *Rites* and Maxine Hong Kingston's *Woman Warrior*," Malini Schueller's "Questioning Race and Gender Definitions: Dialogic Subversions in *The Woman Warrior*," Shirley Geok-lin Lim's "The Tradition of Chinese American Women's Life Stories: Thematics of Race and Gender in Jade Snow Wong's *Fifth Chinese Daughter* and Maxine Hong Kingston's *The Woman Warrior*," Joan Lidoff's "Autobiography in a Different Voice: *The Woman Warrior* and the Question of Genre," Donald C. Goellnicht's "Father Land and/or Mother Tongue: The Divided Female Subject in Kogawa's *Obasan* and Hong Kingston's *The Woman Warrior*," Leslie W. Rabine's "No Lost Paradise: Social Gender and Symbolic Gender in the Writings of Maxine Hong Kingston."

45. The use of "wetbacks" and "stowaways" by immigrants is an example of reappropriation. In a similar way it is not uncommon to hear African Americans call each other "nigger," although both words have a different history and carry a different intensity. Helene A. Shugart sees the practice of appropriation as an act of resignification. In the process of appropriation "the original meaning ... is destroyed" (211). Shugart gives examples of appropriation practices among other oppressed groups, for example homosexuals referring to themselves as "dykes" or "faggots." She nonetheless warns that appropriation carries its own risks.

46. The timing of Moon Orchid's arrival is to be deduced most accurately by the information that Brave Orchid's son is aboard the United States ship during the Vietnam war. President Kennedy proposed an immigration reform that was enacted several years after his death—in 1965. In a letter to Lyndon B. Johnson, President of the Senate and John McCormack, Speaker of the House, Kennedy calls for the abolishing of the "national origin system of selecting immigrants," because "it discriminates among applicants for admission into the United States on the basis of accident of birth" (Kennedy 1). Kennedy put stress in the proposed legislation on the skills of prospective immigrants and their family ties to people already living in the United States. Proponents of the reform did not expect that it would lead to the large influx of Asian population (Hing 39). They anticipated more immigrants from southern and eastern Europe, from countries like Greece and Italy. In his letter, Kennedy draws our attention to the fact that Greek and Italian immigrants have to wait eighteen months or longer before their relatives can join them in the United States.

47. The examples of critical studies analyzing *The Woman Warrior* in the context of the autobiographical tradition are: Paul John Eakin's "Maxine Hong Kingston: 'I Had to Tell My Mother,'" Rocio G. Davis's "The Self in the Text versus the Self as Text: Asian American Autobiographical Strategies," Cynthia Sau-ling Wong's "Autobiography as Guided Chinatown Tour? Maxine Hong Kingston's *The Woman Warrior* and the Chinese American autobiographical Controversy," Shirley Geok-lin Lim's "Semiotics, Experience, and the Material Self: An Inquiry into the Subject of the Contemporary Asian Woman Writer," Patricia P. Chu's "*The Woman Warrior*: *Memoirs of a Girlhood among Ghosts* by Maxine Hong Kingston," Silvia Caporale Bizzini's "Sara Suleri's *Meatless Days* and Maxine Hong Kingston's *The Woman Warrior*: Writing History and the Self After Foucault," Katherine Hyunmie Lee's "The Poetics of Liminality and Misidentification. Winnifred Eaton's *Me* and Maxine Hong Kingston's *The Woman Warrior*," Sarah Gilead's "Emigrant Selves: Narrative Strategies in Three Women's Autobiographies."

48. An analogous metaphoric representation of the untenability of white identity can be traced in Herman Melville's *White Jacket*, in which the eponymous protagonist has to cut off his assiduously treasured white jacket in order to save his life after falling into the ocean.

49. Paul D. reaches for a similar epithet in Toni Morrison's *Beloved* to speak of Sethe's love for Beloved: "Your love is too thick" (164).

50. The passage conjures up distant echoes of John Keats' "Ode on a Grecian Urn": "Heard melodies are sweet, but those unheard/Are sweeter" (Keats 531).

51. It is also worth noting that while I do not identify the narrator with Kingston and Kingston herself is emphatic about the fact that she should not be identified with the narrator of *The Woman Warrior*, she still indicates that the childhood paintings incident took place in her own life (Kay Bonetti's "Interview with Maxine Hong Kingston" 33).

52. Theater features very prominently as a medium of striving for Chinese American visibility in Kingston's above cited third novel, *Tripmaster Monkey* (1989). The narrator of *Tripmaster Monkey* states: "Whenever Chinese Americans performed, they wanted to be seen"—literally and figuratively (13). Theatre reverses the condition of visibility and invisibility. Those who are usually invisible enter the stage to claim spotlight and their visibility.

53. The examples of the negative signification of blackness are as follows:
- The blackness accompanying the No Name Woman's lonely delivery. The No Name Woman is engulfed by blackness of the night, sky and space: "The black *well* of sky and stars went out and out forever.... Black space opened" (Kingston, *The Woman Warrior* 16, emphasis added). The "black well of sky and stars" foreshadows the No Name Woman's suicide death by drowning in a family well.
- The "black hole" opened by the No Name Woman's alleged trespassing, the hole which, according to the villagers, makes the "break" "in the 'roundness'" of the community (Kingston, *The Woman Warrior* 14). Paul John Eakin argues that the No Name Woman's death "plug[s]" the hole opened by the No Name Woman's act of self-individuation and insubordination (Eakin, *Fictions in Autobiography. Studies in the Art of Self-Invention* 258).
- The blackness of the night for example in the Sitting Ghost episode and during Brave Orchid's night medical calls.
- The darkness of the landscape before the narrator as Fa Mu Lan enters the "yellow, warm world" of her apprenticeship with the guru couple.

54. The performativity of racial categories comes to the foreground in Kingston's *Tripmaster Monkey*. The Chinese American protagonist of the novel, Wittman Ah Sing, performs his Chinese American ethnicity. In his play he also stages the performance of Chinese American ethnicity and stereotypes about Chinese Americans.

The protagonist of Karen Tei Yamashita's *Tropic of Orange*, Emi, makes an interesting reflection on the fiction of multiculturalism and performativity of racial identities. Emi claims that representatives of diverse racial and ethnic groups are invisible to each other and that white people who celebrate cultural diversity usually express very superficial interest in the people of a different racial or ethnic origin, seeing them through the prism of sushi bars, never reaching beneath the surface of cultural difference, but merely skimming it: "Cultural diversity is bullshit.... It's a white guy wearing a Nirvana T-shirt and dreds. That's cultural diversity.... We're all invisible. It's just tea, ginger, raw fish, and a credit card" (Yamashita 128). Emi also pokes fun at the white restaurant patron proclaiming her sincere embrace and appreciation of all aspects of multiculturalism to be traced in Los Angeles. Chopsticks in her hair are to be one of the manifestations of this multicultural bent. Emi asks the white lady if she would also consider wearing forks in her hair.

55. It needs to be emphasized that immediately after portraying Japanese American children as "noisy and tough" (193), the narrator mentions their release from concentration camps (193). Yet no further reflection follows why they are "noisy and tough" or if there may be any possibility of reverse power dynamics at play.

Chapter 2

1. To read more on how whiteness reaffirmed its status through legal practices, see Ian Haney López's *White by Law*.

2. Monica Chiu cites Arnold Genthe's etymological analysis of the term "coolie." According to Genthe, "coolie" is the Anglicized version of the Tamil term "hireling." In Mandarin "kuli" means "bitter strength" (Genthe cited in Chiu 194).

3. No direct description of a lynching is furnished in William Melvin Kelley's *A Different Drummer*, but a child's misinterpretation of the sounds of a lynching as those of a play may exert as powerful an impact on the reader as if the event was directly recounted.

4. Further discussion of compensatory wages of whiteness takes place in the last section of the chapter, "Toppling the Myth of White Exclusivity in Founding the Nation."

5. A similar portrayal of Japanese American children emerges from *Tripmaster Monkey*, in which the protagonist Wittman Ah Sing suspects his best friend Lance Kamiyama of being a bully at school.

6. Reflecting on modern day arrangements in particular on the Mexican border, Ali Behdad claims that the modern gaze of border supervision has become "unverifiab[le]" (158). There may be no "architectural figure of the Panopticon," but there are "little gadgets" like night-vision goggles that perform an equivalent role (156–157).

7. Kingston employs the metaphor of "simulated curtains" of Rilke's *The Notebooks of Malte Laurids Brigge* to figuratively render Wittman Ah Sing's invisibility. The metaphor of raising a curtain can also be traced in Wittman's striving for the visibility of Chinese Americans and his own visibility.

8. The narrator of *China Men* emphasizes a synesthetic approach to vision: "There is no word like *vision* for what one hears" (263, original emphasis). The statement suggests that the narrator can see in her mind's eye what she can hear. Another synesthetic juxtaposition of sight to hearing occurs when the narrator notes that ears "don't sleep like eyes" (87). Linda Chin Sledge notes the close link between the visual and the auditory in Kingston's construction of imagery: Kingston "challenge[s] the prospective literary historian to listen for the living word behind the narrow letter" (153). At one point *China Men* also emphasizes women's ability to see. Like Uncle Bun, the San Francisco aunt is very class conscious: "There are rich people who don't see poor people, but she never stopped seeing them" (210). Looking is also employed to render Sing Kay's (Friday's) endearment for his father at whom he "stared" as a sign of recognition.

9. I borrow the term "to mimic" from Homi Bhabha, who defines "mimicry" as a repetition with a difference (88), a very apt way to depict Chinese immigrants' near-replication of white oppression. Their imitation of white oppression is never fully complete, because ultimately they do not speak from the position of power. They may be above the people whom they exploit, but they themselves still have someone above them as well.

10. Bedhad defines nativism as a "defensive form of nationalism" viewing America as a "'threatened paradise' ... in need of a patriotic movement to save it from the 'alien invasion'" (118).

11. I first came across the sociological application of the term "triage" in James Kyung Lee's book *Urban Triage*, in which Lee appropriates the term in the context of the 1960s policies towards inner city communities.

12. A statement by Oliver corresponds to Bhabha's rumination on the relation of the other to the self: "the 'other' is never outside or beyond us; it emerges forcefully, within cultural discourse, when we *think* we speak most intimately and indigenously 'between ourselves'" (Bhabha cited in Frost X, emphasis original).

13. Brook Thomas draws a distinction between citizens and subjects, claiming that subjects are inferior to citizens: "All citizens might be subjects, but not all subjects are citizens" (702).

14. Kingston does not specify if the aforementioned federal courts repealed anti-Chinese legislation as a result of their own supervision of the state courts or on account of the Chinese appealing their decisions. Yet the following "immigrant acts" cited by Kingston suggest that the latter is the case.

15. In "*China Men*, United States v. Wong Kim Ark, and the Question of Citizenship," Brook Thomas delves into the details of the case, introducing the context in which the case appeared before the Supreme Court (695). Wong Kim Ark was born in 1873 in San Francisco in a Chinese immigrant family. Wong Kim Ark stayed in the United States, while his parents returned to China. After visiting his parents in 1890, Wong Kim Ark had no problems entering the United States, but no entry permission was granted on his return in 1895. When the case came before the Supreme Court in 1898, the Supreme Court Justices ruled 6 to 1 in Wong Kim Ark's favor.

16. For more on Yick Wo v. Hopkins case see also Gabriel J. Chin, "Unexplainable on Grounds of Race: Doubts About Yick Wo," and David E. Bernstein "Revisiting Yick Wo v. Hopkins."

17. As I mention earlier, this panoptic power of whiteness is undermined when the white police look in vain for the black man living in the narrator's Chinatown, whereas the narrator and her siblings can see him every day.

18. The same rule operates in the case of the narrator's uncle Mad Sao, who is awarded citizenship in recognition of his service in World War II.

19. I explain the concept of Asian American panethnicity in Chapter 1.

20. I discuss Asian American struggle against the black-white dyad dominating the debate on racial relations in the United States in the article "Beyond Black and White: Striving for Visibility in *Tripmaster Monkey* by Maxine Hong Kingston and *Native Speaker* by Chang-rae Lee" as well as chapters of my book *Invisibility in African American and Asian American Literature: A Comparative Study*.

21. In his book *Orientals. Asian Americans in Popular Culture*, Lee cites the analogies originating at the time of the Vietnam War, the analogies between the invisibility of the Viet Cong fighters and the alleged invisibility of Asian Americans as enemies within the country: "the ubiquitous and invisible enemy" (190).

22. Eng calls Kingston the matriarch and Chin the patriarch of Asian American literature (30).

Chapter 3

1. Only on one occasion in the narrative does white light exert a soothing effect on Tom (21). It is the light of "the soft white street lamps" (21). At that point the light and brightness are associated with the moon, not the sun. White light receives similar positive signification in juxtaposition with the moon in the next work analyzed here, Joy Kogawa's *Obasan*.

2. On March 18, 1991 Latasha Harlins, an African American teenager, was shot by a Korean American female grocer Soon Ja Du after punching her three times on the face, having refused to return a bottle of orange juice which she allegedly stole. The sentencing of Soon Ja Du came about six months later. The judge fined her $500, giving her a probationary sentence and declaring that she should perform 400 hours of community service (Park 60). The black community reacted to the incident and the sentencing with the boycotts of Korean American stores. For an incisive interpretation of the events see Kwang Chung Kim's *Koreans in the Hood* and Nancy Abelman's *Blue Dreams*.

3. The Rodney King riots in South Central Los Angeles was sparked by the acquittal of four white policemen on April 29, 1992, by a predominantly white jury in Simi Valley, California, with black population of only two percent (Baker 43). Everything began on March 3, 1991, when the four white policemen brutally beat twenty-five-year-old Rodney King, who initially was trying to evade police before eventually stopping the car. King and his two black companions were far outnumbered by police officers, of which there were twenty-one at the site. For a detailed analysis of the incident and the Los Angeles urban uprising that followed, see Robert Gooding-Williams's *Reading Rodney King: Reading Urban Uprising*, Haki R. Madhubuti's *Why L.A. Happened*, and *Los Angeles Struggles Towards a Multiethnic Community*, by Russell Leong and Edward T. Chang.

4. Leonard Chang is also the author of crime fiction: *Over the Shoulder* (2001), *Underkill* (2003), *Fade to Clear* (2004), a trilogy series following the footsteps of the Korean American investigator, Allen Choice. Korean American themes resurface more explicitly in his 2009 novel, *Crossings*, rendering the ordeal of human trafficking and illegal immigration. Chang's most recent work, *Triplines*, published in 2014, is an autobiographical novel. Chang received two literary awards: the Black Heron Press Award for Social Fiction for *The Fruit 'N Food* and the San Francisco Bay Guardian Goldie Award for Literature for *Dispatches from the Cold*. For an in-depth interview with Leonard Chang, see Charse Yun's "Crossing Borders."

5. Korean American immigrants were able to open their stores thanks to the help of "kye," a credit association, in which each member contributes a specified amount of money weekly or monthly. A pool goes each week or month to a different member of the association. Usually you can be a recipient only once (Heon Cheol Lee 128). "Ggeh" is a money club that operates under the system.

6. Speaking of the white cartographer, I have in mind the apparatus of legislative and executive power dominated by and catering mainly to the needs of white people. Consecutive Republican and Democratic administrations kept silent about residential segregation and the problems beleaguering the inner city. They failed to address racial discrimination in the real estate development. Nor did they address the restrictions on black ownership in white neighborhoods. The word "ghetto" remains unmentioned in the public debate as if urban ghettos no longer existed in American society. The media talk about the gentrification of Harlem is a good story rather than any substantial turn of events for people living there, let alone a trend in other ghettos.

7. In their 1998 essay "Grounding Metaphor: Towards a Spatialized Politics" Neil Smith and Cindi Katz speak of "the absent if omniscient cartographer" (70).

8. Gary Taylor cites medieval scholars who associate whiteness with people living in an inhospitable cold climate. The two scholars to whom Taylor devotes most of the attention are Albertus Magnus, German author of *De Natura Locorum* (written between 1248 and 1252), as well as Bartolomaeus Anglicus, English author of *De Proprietatibus Rerum*, written between 1230 and 1250. Like Aristotle, Anglicus claims that "cold is the mother of whiteness and of paleness" (Anglicus cited in Taylor 78).

9. Proponents of polygenesis maintained that white people were created in a different way than people of color. Monogenesis assumed common origin. Some of the pseudoscientific theories sought substantiation in the Bible. According to one of the Bible related theories, black people were descended from Ham, cursed by God and condemned to constant toil and servitude to Shem and Japheth. Pseudoscientific statements propagated in Arthur de Gobineau's *Essay on the Inequality of Races* (published between 1853 and 1855) kept surfacing for the next hundred years. De Gobineau distinguished between higher and lower races. According to de Gobineau, superior races composed higher cultures. The matches between higher and lower races led to the degradation of superior races (Omi and Winant 59). Proponents of eugenics argued that interracial relationships were a transgression against nature and lead to biological throwbacks. A legal ban on interracial relationships was held in some states until the 1980s of the 20th century. Mississippi was the last state to repeal the ban, in 1987 (Tennessee in 1978, Virginia 1967, Wyoming 1965, Nebraska 1963) (Sollors 410). Social Darwinism—especially popular at the end of the 19th and the beginning of the 20th century treated all racial and class inequalities as "natural." Social privilege was attributed to inherent qualities like industriousness, moderation, self-restraint, and frugality. Major representatives of social Darwinism in Britain were Herbert Spencer and Walter Bagehot, in the United States William Graham Sumner. The American law approached race as a biological concept. It was especially visible in the theory of hypodescent, the term coined by anthropologist Marvin Harris (Cheryl Harris 1738, 1739). The theory of hypodescent made a person with black and white ancestors automatically black legally. Hence people of biracial origin found themselves deprived of privileges reserved for white citizens. Even if a person was phenotypically white, they were classified as black. Very remote black ancestry sufficed to make someone black. The theory of hypodescent did not apply to Native Americans. The legal situation of people with Native American descent was and is precisely opposite to that of people with black ancestry. Very remote Native American ancestry is no longer enough to define oneself as a Native American before the law. Once again financial issues are at stake. Anyone who proves one-eighth of Native American descent is entitled to financial benefits from the state (Piper 427).

10. Color psychologist Faber Birren claims that "white is associated with normativity," "expressing the vanity of the Caucasian race" (Birren cited in Adams 35–36).

11. It needs to be emphasized that the traditional color theory identifies black and white as non-colors or as achromatic colors because what is of primary importance in the traditional color theory is light, the participation of light waves. While white reflects all wavelengths of light, black absorbs all wavelengths of light (Adams 33). Undermining the traditional color theory, Patricia Sloane shifts the focus from light to sight. Sloane argues that the definition of black and white as achromatic colors falls short of the "actual visual experience" (Adams 33). Sloane asserts that black is also a color and she defends it by claiming that "black is a color because we see it as a color" (Sloane cited in Adams 34).

12. At this point of the narrative, whiteness visiting Tom in his dreams bears some correspondence to clinical whiteness thrust on Ralph Ellison's Invisible Man during the lobotomy treatment when whiteness inundates him from all sides, posing a danger to his identity and pushing him towards colorlessness.

13. The accounts of skirmishes between African Americans and Korean Americans unfold against the background of the color-line imagery. The "divider" and the "chalk-line" separate both sides (189). An image of the "wall" recurs twice, first when Tom falls against the wall after black people attack him (190), the second time when a black man, Mr. Harris, leans against the wall after suffering an attack from four Asian men (213).

14. Tom's physical immobility to some extent parallels his hospital immobility after each day of grueling work at the Fruit 'n Food. On returning home, he is also largely immobile, unable to move, staring passively at one point.

Chapter 4

1. In all of Naomi's dreams sexual aggressors are white soldiers (Gottlieb 45) even though her white sexual aggressors were not soldiers. All incidents of sexual exploitation in *Obasan* occur just before and after the forced relocation and disintegration of Naomi's family. Separate as they are, racial discrimination and sexual abuse run parallel tracks in the narrative.

2. The transitional area is referred to in *Obasan* as the Pool area. Naomi's aunt, Emily, describes the appalling conditions of the center in her diary entry:

There are no partitions of any kind whatsoever and the people are treated worse than livestock, which at least had their own pens and special food when they were there. No plumbing of any kind. They can't take a bath. They don't even take their clothes off. Two weeks now. Lord! Can you imagine a better breeding ground for typhus? [Kogawa 107].

3. This is how "concerned missionaries" in *Obasan* describe the plight of Japanese Canadians:

Conditions were worse than evacuation. Repatriation and dispersal policies the cruelest cut of all. Expensive, inhuman, and absolutely unnecessary. Not even a semblance of democracy or common sense in this latest racial persecution. Segregation being rushed. Loyal people being squeezed out. Elderly parents separated from families. Work offered to the Japan-bound but none for those who stay [220].

4. The total distribution of Japanese Canadian relocation in numbers looks as follows: 12,000 Japanese Canadians settled in abandoned mining towns inside British Columbia, 4,000 undertook employment on farms in Alberta and Manitoba, over 2,000 were road construction laborers in British Columbia and almost 1,000 were imprisoned in a concentration camp at Angler, Ontario, for defying relocation orders (Goellnicht 289).

5. Remembering the life in Alberta, Naomi speaks of the dehumanization of Japanese Canadians, turning them into automatons who work, eat, sleep and barely talk (235). She also reflects on further fracturing of Japanese Canadian families: "Families already fractured and separated were permanently destroyed. The choice to go east of the Rockies or to Japan was presented without time for consultation with separated parents and children. Failure to choose was labeled non-cooperation. Throughout the country the pressure was on." (219)

6. Joy Kogawa was born in Vancouver in 1935. In addition to being the author of *Obasan* and such novels as *The Rain Ascends* (1995) and *Itsuka* (1992), a sequel to *Obasan*, dealing with the Japanese Canadian Redress Movement, Kogawa is also the author of children's literature: *Naomi's Road* (1986), *Naomi's Tree* (2009); collections of poetry: *The Splintered Moon* (1968), *A Choice of Dreams* (1974), *Jericho Road* (1977), *Six Poems* (1978), *Woman in the Woods* (1985), *A Song of Lilith* (2000), *A Garden of Anchors: Selected Poems* (2003); and individual poems and essays. *Obasan* won Kogawa four different literary awards: Books in Canada, First Novel Award; Canadian Authors Association, Book of the Year Award; Periodical Distributors of Canada, Best Paperback Fiction Award; Before Columbus Foundation, The American Book Award. In recognition for her work, Kogawa was made a Member of the Order of Canada in 1986 and a Member of the Order of British Columbia in 2006. In 2010, she was also awarded with the Order of the Rising Sun by the Japanese government, which thus acknowledged her input into the preservation and better perception of Japanese History.

Joy Kogawa attended the University of Alberta, the University of Toronto, the Anglican Women's Training College and the University of Saskatchewan. Aside from being a writer, she also taught at an elementary school, was a staff writer in the Prime Minister's Office from 1974 to 1976 and a writer in residence in 1978.

As noted in the chapter, during World War II, Kogawa and her family were forced by the Canadian government to relocate to the mining town of Slocan in the interior of British Columbia. Since the Canadian government deprived her family of their Vancouver possessions and since they were unable to return to British Columbia, they were forced to move once again after World War II, to a beet farm in the town of Coaldale, Alberta. Through all these relocations Kogawa's family managed to stay together (Lo 100 and "Joy Kogawa" 1).

7. Kittagawa's writing was an inspiration particularly for chapter fourteen of the novel (Lo 102).

8. Aunt Emily overtly reflects on the power of print as one of the tools employed by the Canadian government in its battle against Japanese Canadians:

"The power of print," Aunt Emily interrupted. "The power of government, Nomi. Power. See how palpable it is? They took away the land, the stores, the businesses, the boats, the houses—everything. Broke up our families, told us who we could see, where we could live, what we could do, what time we could leave our houses, censored our letters, exiled us for no crime. They took our livelihood" [44].

9. Aunt Emily observes tersely: "With language like that you can disguise any crime" (41). Several times in the narrative Aunt Emily reflects on the fact that language has the power to conceal oppression.

10. For more on the subject of Christian missionaries and their relations with people of Asian origin see Chapter 1 of Dominika Ferens' book *Edith and Winnifred Eaton: Chinatown Missions and Japanese Romances*.

11. Silence features prominently in *Obasan*. It has also been the subject of numerous critical investigations, such as King-Kok Cheung's *Articulate Silences*, Gayle K. Fujita's "'To Attend the Sound of Stone': The Sensibility of Silence in *Obasan*," Laurie Kruk's "The Voices of Stone," Gurleen Grewal's "Memory and the Matrix of History," and Chinmoy Banerjee's "Polyphonic Form and Effective Aesthetic in *Obasan*."

12. Naomi mirrors her aunt's sentiments in her private rendition of the Canadian anthem, in which she strongly proclaims a sense of belonging to the Canadian nation but at the same time expresses bitter disenchantment at the way Canada dealt with its own people: "We come from the country that plucks its people out like weeds and flings them into the roadside" (271). This disillusionment continues into the lines when Naomi claims that Japanese Canadians thrive on invisibility and on silence, which provide them with a protective shield from the outside world. Once invisible and dispersed as a community, they are not perceived as a threat by the dominant society: "We grow where we are not seen, we flourish where we are not heard" (271). In further lines of the passage Naomi expresses skepticism at "dan[cing] to the multicultural piper's tune" questioning Canada's ostensible embrace of multiculturalism (271). Despite asserting her belonging to the Canadian nation, she still feels far from secure in her own country. Comparing herself and many other Japanese Canadians with her activist Aunt Emily, Naomi concludes: "We seek the safety of our invisibility" (38).

Naomi's narrative is an attempt at capturing part of that activist spirit and chipping away at the invisibility of her people. In her 1984 interview Kogawa herself made similar comments on Japanese Canadian compulsion to invisibility in post–World War II years: "Many Nisei, like myself, who suffered the drawn out trauma of racial prejudice during our formative and young adult years have a deep timidity burned into our psyches with the injunction that we must never again *risk the visibility of community*. Perhaps as a result, no Japan town exists anywhere in Canada today" (Kogawa cited in Grewal 147). Kogawa's own activism and her writing, on the one hand, are informed by this invisibility, while on the other, they transcend it.

13. Certain fragments of the memorandum seem to exonerate the actual World War II internment and the policy of dispersal: "The necessity of removing persons of Japanese origin from the coastal regions during the war, was referable to the emergency.... There is therefore no need for fear of concentration on the Pacific coast as in the past" (Kogawa 298-299). The revocation of internment orders took place only in 1949.

14. The whiteness of the atomic bombing of Nagasaki is also accentuated in Steven Spielberg's film *Empire of the Sun*. The young protagonist does not realize at first that what he witnesses is a nuclear explosion: "I saw white light in the sky as if God was making a photograph. I thought it was Mrs. Victor's soul going up to heaven." In the eyes of the young white protagonist released from Japanese internment, whiteness acquires celestial attributes. Only later does he realize that whiteness which he saw is a hallmark of death and unutterable destruction.

15. For the textualization of the stream see Gottlieb, Grewal and Banerjee.

16. The death of yellow chickens is a recurring trope in the novel. The event must leave an indelible imprint on Naomi's memory because she returns to the event several times in the narrative.

17. Olivia, the female Japanese American protagonist of Cynthia Kadohata'a novel *The Floating World* derives the same sense of security from her family: "We were stable, traveling through an unstable world" (3). The action of *The Floating World* unfolds in the post–World War II years, still tumultuous for Japanese Americans. Olivia's working class parents migrate from one place to another, searching for employment. Unlike Naomi, Olivia barely mentions World War II and unlike Naomi Nakane's family, Olivia Fujitano's immediate family remains largely whole.

18. Chinmoy Banerjee calls the epigraph to *Obasan* a "metalinguistic poem" (103).

19. In "The Riddle of Concentric Worlds in *Obasan*" Erika Gottlieb argues that "silence speaks many tongues" (37).

20. The compulsion to disappear was inculcated into Japanese Canadians by already discussed consecutive relocations, internment orders, the enforced separation of families, and the breaking up of communities: "Everything was done, Aunt Emily said, officially, at all levels, and *the message to disappear* worked its way deep into the Nisei heart and into the bone marrow" (Kogawa 219, emphasis added).

21. Remembering her dead mother's "breath, wordless word," Naomi is wondering how she will "attend that speech," implying that she needs to learn to read the silence (289).

22. In one of her interviews Kogawa herself champions transformational identity politics, claiming that a particular kind of oppression often foreshadows for the oppressed other types of victimization. She also seems to locate the oppressor not only outside but also within:

[I]n North America one of the problems we have is the competing voices of the victims; whether we're women or whoever we are of the various minority groups, we become competitors for center stage. That tends to nullify a lot of the change we could bring about if we could identify with and assist one another. If we fail to do this we could find ourselves in the role of victimizer [Kogawa cited in Goldman 366].

Chapter 5

1. Although Kingston explicitly identifies herself as the narrator of the autobiographic sections of *The Fifth Book of Peace* and as mentioned earlier, she also reflects on the blurring of the lines between fact and fiction in *The Fifth Book of Peace*, I am hesitant to address the narrator of the autobiographic sections as Kingston, keeping in mind the constructedness of all literary personas.

2. It is true that the BBC is the first to reach out to the narrator and offer the sponsorship of the trip. Yet the trip that in the end materializes is totally different to that proposed by the BBC. Originally, the BBC wants to make the narrator a part of their documentary about writers travelling across borders back to their ancestral villages, in the narrator's case back to China. Rather than acquiesce to the BBC's original design, the narrator suggests an alternative one in line with which the narrator travels together with Vietnam veterans to the Vietnamese Buddhist sangha community, Plum Village.

3. "Ethnicity" is the term featuring at this point in Whittaker's study although race would seem more appropriate since she speaks of "Caucasians" usually identified as a racial group including diverse ethnicities manifesting some common features.

4. Elvi Whittaker identifies "aina" as "homeland" (116).

5. John Mulligan (1950–2005) is also the author of the novel under the same title *Shopping Cart Soldiers*, winner of a PEN Award for excellence in literature.

6. For the etymology of the term "white" see the "Imagery of Whiteness" section of Chapter 1, in particular the portion devoted to the representation of light.

Conclusion

1. The statement comes from Mike Hill's opening keynote lecture entitled "Whiteness during Wartime: Dispatches from an Aerial Empire" delivered on October 18, 2013, at the conference "Travelling Whiteness: Interchanges in the Study of Whiteness" hosted by the University of Turku, Finland.

2. Asian American secretaries in Barack Obama's administration were Secretary of Commerce Gary Locke, Secretary of Energy Steven Chu, Secretary of Veterans Affairs Eric

K. Shinseki, and Cabinet Secretary Chris Lu, the last one holding considerable clout in the administration, but resigning at the beginning of the president's second term. The only remaining Asian American secretary during Obama's second term in office was Secretary of Veterans Affairs Eric K. Shinseki, who resigned in May of 2014 in the midst of several VA scandals. Asian American lawmakers complained to Obama about the lack of Asian Americans in top positions in the Obama administration. In her letter to Obama, Representative Judy Chu, Democrat from California, the chair of the Congressional Asian Pacific American Caucus, expressed concern over the lack of Asian American undersecretaries or deputy secretaries in the Obama administration. Although Asian Americans compose 6 percent of the population, they are the fastest growing minority in the United States (Nakamura 1).

3. I borrow the term "invisible walls of the ghetto" from sociologist Kenneth Clark, whose full statement on the invisibility of the walls of the ghetto is as follows: "The dark ghetto's invisible walls have been erected by the white society" (11).

4. The belief persists that China has an unfair advantage in its dealings with the United States. Such an appraisal of the situation was conspicuous during Chinese President Hu Jintao's visit to the United States on January 19, 2011, a visit accompanied by pomp and ceremony, including a gun salute. Apart from an uproar among American congressmen censuring China for its human rights record, the visit unfolded to the accompaniment which went along these lines: "China gets more out of the visit through the signed deals than the United States does." The *New York Post* editorial on January 20 made a terse reference to the state dinner, stating that "China President toasts us with one hand, while the other rips us off" (Hurt and Sanderson 1). One day after Hu Jintao's visit, the news broke that the Chinese government allows the Chinese to trade outside China in yuans. Earlier they could trade exclusively in dollars. The move instantly triggered speculations that the red bag wants to catch up with the green bag. A recurring charge against China is that it steals American jobs because a significant percentage of U.S. production was shifted abroad. It is difficult to give a precise number because as experts on the issue point out, statistics are scarce. Burke, Epstein and Choi claim that "The share of foreign-sourced goods in total manufactured inputs almost doubled—from 12.4 percent to 22.1 percent—in U.S. manufacturing between 1987 and 2002" (2). The authors of the research trace a close link between job losses in U.S. manufacturing and outsourcing of production.

5. Zimmerman's mother is Hispanic and his father is white.

6. An example of this flaunting comes in commercials shining a spotlight on the black middle and upper class. Usually these commercials show black people engaging in conspicuous consumption. If in the past African Americans were often represented in terms of lack and privation through the noun "underclass," today they are often represented in terms of excess rendered by the term "overclass." In 2010 and 2011 CNBC devoted a one hour special to so-called New BOs, that is, New Black Overclass, represented in the program mostly by young African American males, who brag about their expeditiously amassed wealth. Such a portrayal creates an illusion of even distribution of resources and equal access to the American dream.

In his 1992 article "Two nations ... both black" published in the collection of essays *Reading Rodney King. Reading Urban Uprising*, Henry Louis Gates declares: "We [meaning the black middle class] are isolated from the black underclass and yet still vulnerable to racism, in the form of random police harassment, individual racial insults from waitresses and attendants in stores, the unwillingness of taxi drivers to pick us up, systematic discrimination by banks and bank loan officers, in the corporate world" (252). Gates's 2009 incident shows that even if the lapse of twenty years significantly decreased African Americans' vulnerability to such injustices, they are not totally immune to them.

Bibliography

Abelman, Nancy, and John Lie. *Blue Dreams: Korean Americans and the Los Angeles Riots.* Cambridge: Harvard University Press, 1995.
Adams, Michael Vannoy. *The Multicultural Imagination: "Race," Color, and the Unconscious.* New York: Routledge, 1996.
African American History. 6 Dec. 2003. afr_am_history.htm.
Anderson, Benedict. *Imagined Communities: Reflections on the Origin and Spread of Nationalism.* New York: Verso, 1995.
Arkush, David R., and Leo O. Lee, eds. *Land Without Ghosts: Chinese Impressions of America from the Mid-Nineteenth Century to the Present.* Berkeley: University of California, 1989.
Babb, Valerie. *Whiteness Visible: The Meaning of Whiteness in American Literature and Culture.* New York: New York University Press, 1998.
Baker, Houston. "Scene...Not Heard." *Reading Rodney King: Reading Urban Uprising.* New York: Routledge, 1993. 38–50.
Bal, Mieke. "Figuration." *PMLA* 119.5 (Oct. 2004): 1289–1292.
Baldwin, James. *Notes of a Native Son* [1955]. New York: Bantam Books, 1972.
———. *The Fire Next Time.* New York: Dell, A Laurel Edition, 1977.
Banerjee, Chinmoy. "Polyphonic Form and Effective Aesthetic in *Obasan*." *Canadian Literature* 160 (1999): 101–119.
Bedhad, Ali. *A Forgetful Nation. On Immigration and Cultural Identity in the United States.* Durham, NC: Duke University Press, 2005.
Beedham, Matthew. "*Obasan* and Hybridity: Necessary Cultural Strategies." *The Immigrant Experience in North American Literature. Carving Out a Niche.* Ed. Katherine B. Payant and Toby Rose. Westport, CT: Greenwood, 1999.
Begum, Khani. "Conforming the Place of 'The Other': Gender and Ethnic Identity in Maxine Hong Kingston's *The Woman Warrior*." *New Perspectives on Women and Comedy.* Ed. Regina Barreca. Philadelphia: Gordon and Breach, 1992. 143–156.
Bennett, Juda. *The Passing Figure: Racial Confusion in Modern American Literature.* New York: Lang, 1996.
Bernstein, David. "Revisiting Yick Wo v. Hopkins." *Social Science Research Network* Sept. 4 2008. 3 July 2013. papers.ssrn.com/sol3/papers. 1–12.
Bizzini, Silvia Caporale. "Sara Suleri's *Meatless Days* and Maxine Hong Kingston's *The Woman Warrior*: Writing History and the Self After Foucault." *Women: A Cultural Review* 7.1 (1996): 55–65.
Blinde, Patricia Lin. "The Icicle in the Desert: Perspectives and Form in the Works of Two Chinese American Women Writers." *MELUS* 6.3, *The Ethnic Perspective* (Autumn 1979): 51–71.
Bondi, Liz. "Locating Identity Politics." *Place and the Politics of Identity.* Ed. Michael Keith and Steve Pile. New York: Routledge, 1993. 84–102.
Bonetti, Kay. "Interview with Maxine Hong Kingston." *Conversations with Maxine Hong*

Kingston. Ed. Paul Skenazy and Tera Martin. Jackson: University Press of Mississippi, 1998. 33-46.

Boynton, Robert M. "Insights Gained from Naming the OSA [Optical Society of America] Colors." *Color Categories in Thought and Language*. Ed. C. L. Hardin and Luisa Maffi. New York: Cambridge University Press, 1997. 135-150.

Brogan, Kathleen. *Cultural Haunting: Ghost and Ethnicity in Recent American Literature*. Charlotesville: University Press of Virginia, 1998.

Brown, Sterling A. "Old Lem." *Black on White: Black Writers on What It Means to Be White*. Ed. David R Roediger. New York: Schocken, 1998. 332-334.

Burke, James, Gerald Epstein, and Minsik Choi. "Rising Foreign Outsourcing and Employment Losses in United States Manufacturing, 1987-2002." *Working Papers Series* 89. Political Economy Research Institute, University of Massachusetts, Amherst. 29 April 2011. www.peri.umass.edu/fileadmin/pdf/working papers. 1-18 .

Burnley, J.L. "Middle English Color Terminology and Lexical Structure." *Linguistische Berichte* 41(1976): 39-49.

Butler, Judith, Ernesto Laclau, and Slavoj Žižek. *Contingency, Hegemony, Universalism: Contemporary Dialogues on the Left*. New York: Verso, 2000.

Casson, Ronald W. "Color Shift: Evolution of English Color Terms from Brightness to Hue." *Color Categories in Thought and Language*. New York: Cambridge University Press, 1997. 224-239.

Chambers, Ross. "The Unexamined." *Whiteness: A Critical Reader*. Ed. Mike Hill. New York: New York University Press, 1997. 187-203.

Chan, Sucheng. *Asian Americans: An Interpretive History*. Boston: Twayne, 1990.

Chang, Leonard. *The Fruit 'N Food*. Seattle: Black Heron Press, 1996.

Chesnutt, Charles Waddell. "What Is a White Man." *Stories, Novels and Essays*. New York: Library Classics of the United States, 2002. 837-844.

Cheung, King-Kok. *Articulate Silences. Hisaye Yamamoto, Maxine Hong Kingston, Joy Kogawa*. Ithaca: Cornell University Press, 1993.

_____. "The Woman Warrior Versus the Chinaman Pacific: Must a Chinese American Critic Choose Between Feminism and Heroism?" *Other Sisterhoods: Literary Theory and United States Women of Color*. Ed. Sandra Kumamoto. Chicago: University of Illinois Press, 1998. 173-199.

Chin, Frank. Afterword to *MELUS* 3.2 (1976): 13-17.

_____. *Donald Duk*. Minneapolis: Coffee House Press, 1991.

_____, and Jeffrey Paul Chan, Lawson Fusao Inada, and Shawn Hsu Wong, eds. *Aiiieeee! An Anthology of Asian American Writers*. Washington: Howard University Press, 1974.

Chin, Gabriel J. "Unexplainable on Grounds of Race: Doubts About Yick Wo." *Arizona Legal Studies* Working Paper No. 30-07 (2007): 1358-1457. http://ssrn.com/ abstract=1075563.

Chiu, Monica. "Being Human in the Wor(l)d: Chinese Men and Reworking of *Robinson Crusoe. Journal of American Studies* 34.2 (2000):187-206.

Chu, Patricia P. "*The Woman Warrior: Memoirs of a Girlhood Among Ghosts* by Maxine Hong Kingston." *A Resource Guide to Asian American Literature*. Ed. Cynthia Sau-ling Wong and Stephen H. Sumida. New York: The Modern Language Association of America, 2001. 86-96.

Chua, Cheng Lok. "Mythopoesis East and West in *The Woman Warrior*." *Approaches to Teaching the Woman Warrior*. Ed. Shirley Geok-lin Lim. New York: MLA, 1991. 146-150.

Clark, Kenneth. *Dark Ghetto*. New York: Harper and Row, 1965.

Crenshaw, Kimberlè. "Demarginalizing the Intersection of Race and Sex: A Black Feminist Critique of Antidiscrimination Doctrine, Feminist Theory and Antiracist Politics." *University of Chicago Legal Forum* 1989. 4 Feb. 2014. philpapers.org/archive.CREDIT.pdf. 139-167.

Cross, Ira B. *A History of the Labor Movement in California*. Berkeley: University of California Press, 1974.

Curtin, Maureen Frances. "Introduction." "Skin Tropes in Twentieth Century Anglo-

American Literature: Interfacing Biotechnical, Political and Visual Discourses of Identity." Dissertation. The University of Tulsa, 1999. 1–16.
Davis, Rocio G. "The Self in the Text versus the Self as Text: Asian American Autobiographical Strategies." *Asian American Literary Studies*. Ed. Guiyou Huang. Edinburgh: Edinburgh University Press, 2005.
De Bary Nee, Victor, and Brett De Bary Nee. *Longtime Californ': A Documentary Study of an American Chinatown*. New York: Pantheon, 1973.
DeLillo, Don. *White Noise*. New York: Viking, 1985.
Dennys, Nicholas B. *The Folklore of China and Its Affinities with That of the Aryan and Semitic Races*. 1876. Amsterdam: Oriental Press, 1968.
"DREAM Act." 10 July 2013. en.wikipedia.org/wiki/DREAM_Act. 1–6.
Du Bois, W.E.B. *Black Reconstruction* [1935]. New York: Atheneum, 1962.
_____. *The Souls of Black Folk*. New York: Penguin, 1989.
_____. "The Souls of White Folk." In *Writings*. Ed. Nathan Huggins. New York: Library of America, 1986. 923–938.
_____. "The White World." In *Writings*. Ed. Nathan Huggins. New York: Library of America, 1986. 652–680.
Dyer, Richard. *White*. New York: Routledge, 1997.
Eagleton, Terry S. *Literary Theory: An Introduction*. Hoboken, NJ: Wiley Blackwell, 1996.
Eakin, Paul John. "Maxine Kong Kingston: 'I Had to Tell My Mother.'" *Fictions in Autobiography: Studies in the Art of Self-Invention*. Princeton, N.J.: Princeton University Press, 1985. 256–277.
Ellison, Ralph. *Invisible Man* [1952]. New York: Vintage, 1972.
_____. *Shadow and Act* [1964]. New York: Signet, 1966.
Eng, David. *Racial Castration: Managing Masculinity in Asian America*. Durham, NC: Duke University Press, 2001.
Espiritu, Yen Le. *Asian American Panethnicity: Bridging Institutions and Identities*. Philadelphia: Temple University Press, 1992.
Fei, Xiaotong. "Some Judgments About America." [1943–1944]. *Land Without Ghosts: Chinese Impressions of America from the Mid-Nineteenth Century to the Present*. Ed. R. David Arkush and Leo O. Lee. Berkeley: University of California Press, 1989. 175–181.
Ferens, Dominika. *Edith and Winnifred Eaton: Chinatown Missions and Japanese Romances*. Urbana: University of Illinois Press, 2002.
Foucault, Michel. "Body/Power." *Power/Knowledge. Selected Interviews and Other Writings*. Ed. Colin Gordon. Brighton: Harvester, 1980. 55–62.
_____. "The Eye of Power." *Power/Knowledge. Selected Interviews and Other Writings*. Ed. Colin Gordon. Brighton: Harvester, 1980. 146–165.
_____. "Panopticism." *New Historicism and Cultural Materialism*. Ed. Kiernan Ryan. London: Hodder Education Publishers, 1996. 11–16.
_____. *Power*. Ed. James D. Faubion. New York: The New Press, 2000.
Frankenberg, Ruth. "Introduction: Local Whiteness, Localizing Whiteness." *Displacing Whiteness: Essays in Social Criticism*. Durham, NC: Duke University Press, 1997. 1–31.
_____. "Whiteness and Americanness: Examining Constructions of Race, Culture, and Nation in White Women's Life Narratives." *Race*. Eds. Steven Gregory and Roger Sanjek. New Brunswick: Rutgers University Press, 1994. 62–77.
Frost, Linda. *Never One Nation: Freaks, Savages and Whiteness in U.S. Popular Culture*. Minneapolis: University of Minnesota Press, 2005.
Fujita, Gayle K. "'To Attend the Sound of Stone': The Sensibility of Silence in *Obasan*." *MELUS* 12.3 *Ethnic Women Writers* IV (1985): 33–42.
Gates, Henry Louis. "Two Nations...Both Black." *Reading Rodney King: Reading Urban Uprising*. Ed. Robert-Gooding Williams. New York: Routledge, 1993. 249–254.
Gilead, Sarah. "Emigrant Selves: Narrative Strategies in Three Women's Autobiographies." *Criticism* 30.1 (1988): 43–62.
Goellnicht, Donald C. "Minority History as Metafiction: Joy Kogawa's *Obasan*." *Tulsa Studies in Women's Literature* 8.2 (Autumn 1989): 287–306.

_____. "Father Land and/or Mother Tongue: The Divided Female Subject in Kogawa's *Obasan* and Hong Kingston's *The Woman Warrior*." *Redefining Autobiography in Twentieth Century Women's Fiction*. Ed. Janice Morgan and Colette T. Hall. New York: Garland, 1991. 119–134.
Goldman, Marlene. "A Dangerous Circuit: Loss and Boundaries of Racialized Subjectivity in Joy Kogawa's *Obasan* and Kerri Sakamoto's *The Electrical Field*." *Modern Fiction Studies* 48.2 (2002): 362–368.
Gooding-Williams, Robert, ed. *Reading Rodney King/Reading Urban Uprising*. New York: Routledge, 1993.
Gordon, Avery. *Ghostly Matters: Haunting and the Sociological Imagination*. [1997] Minneapolis: University of Minnesota Press, 2004.
Gordon, Colin. Introduction. *Power* by Michel Foucault. Ed. James D. Faubion. New York: The New Press, 2000. XI–XLI.
Gotanda, Neil. "Exclusion and Inclusion. Immigration and American Orientalism." *Across the Pacific: Asian Americans and Globalization*. Ed. Evelyn Hu De Hart. Philadelphia: Temple University Press, 1999. 129–147.
Gottlieb, Erika. "The Riddle of Concentric Worlds in *Obasan*." *Canadian Literature* 109 (1986): 34–56.
Grewal, Gurleen. "Memory and the Matrix of History: The Poetics of Loss and Recovery in Joy Kogawa's *Obasan* and Toni Morrison's *Beloved*." *Memory and Cultural Politics: New Approaches to American Ethnic Literature*. Ed. Amritjit Singh, Joseph T. Skerrett, Jr., and Robert E. Hogan. Boston: Northwestern University Press, 1996. 140–174.
Gsoels-Lorensen, Jutta. "Impossibilized Subjects in Maxine Hong Kingston's *China Men*: Thoughts on Migrancy and the State of Exception." *Mosaic* (Winnipeg) 43.3 (Sept. 2010): 1–8. Literature Resources from Gale. 16 Aug. 2010. http://go.galegroup.com/ps.
Hardin, C.L. *Color for Philosophers. Unweaving the Rainbow*. Indianapolis: Hackett, 1988.
Harris, Cheryl. "Whiteness as Property." *The Harvard Law Review* 106.8 (1993): 1709–1791.
Harris, Trudier. "White Men as Performers in the Lynching Ritual." *Black on White: Black Writers on What It Means to Be White*. Ed. David R Roediger. New York: Schocken, 1998. 299–304.
Hawaiian Dictionaries. 13 Sep. 2013. wehewehe.org/gsdl2.85/cgi-bin.1–1.
Hill, Mike. "Can Whiteness Speak?" *White Trash: Race and Class in America*. Matt Wray and Annalee Newitz. New York: Routledge, 1997. 155–170.
_____. "Whiteness During Wartime: Dispatches from an Aerial Empire." Lecture delivered at the conference "Travelling Whiteness: Interchanges in the Study of Whiteness," University of Turku, Finland, October 18, 2013.
Hing, Bill Ong. *Making and Remaking Asian America Through Immigration*. Stanford: Stanford University Press, 1993.
hooks, bell. *Black Looks: Race and Representation*. Boston: South End Press, 1992.
Hooper, Barbara, and Edward Soja. "The Spaces That Difference Makes: Some Notes on the Geographical Margins of the New Cultural Politics." *Place and the Politics of Identity*. Ed. Keith and Pile. New York: Routledge, 1993. 183–206.
Hunt, Linda. "'I Could Not Figure Out What Was My Village': Gender vs. Ethnicity in Maxine Hong Kingston's *The Woman Warrior*." *MELUS* 12.3, *Ethnic Women Writers* IV (Autumn 1985): 5–12.
Hurt, Charles, and Bill Sanderson. "China President Toasts Us with One Hand, While the Other Rips Us Off." *New York Post* 20 Jan, 2011: 1.
Husnaker, Steven V. "Nation, Family, and Language in Victor Perera's *Rites* and Maxine Hong Kingston's *Woman Warrior*." *Autobiography and National Identity*. Charlottesville: University Press of Virginia, 1999. 83–107.
Ichigashi, Yamato. "Emigration from Japan and Thence Their Immigration Into the State of California." Diss. Harvard University, 1913.
Islas, Arturo, and Marilyn Yalom. "Interview with Maxine Hong Kingston." *Conversations with Maxine Hong Kingston*. Ed. Paul Skenazy and Tera Martin. Jackson: University Press of Mississippi, 1998. 21–32.

Jenkins, Ruth Y. "Authorizing Female Voice and Experience." *MELUS* 19.3, *Intertextualities*. (Autumn 1994): 61–73.
"Joy Kogawa." *The Writers' Union of Canada*. Sept. 2013. http://www.writersunion.ca/member/joy-kogawa. 1–2.
Juan, E. San, Jr. "Dialectics of Aesthetics and Politics in Maxine Hong Kingston's *The Fifth Book of Peace*." *Criticism* 51.2 (2009): 181+. *Literature Resources from Gale*. 18 Aug. 2011. http://go.galegroup.com/ps. 1–15.
Juan, Karin Aguilar-San. "Book Review of *Reading Asian American Literature: From Necessity to Extravagance* by Cynthia Sau-ling Wong." *The Woman's Review of Books* 11.7 (Apr. 1994): 17.
Kadohata, Cynthia. *The Floating World*. New York: The Viking, 1989.
Kalogeras, Yiorgos. "Producing History and Telling Stories: Maxine Hong Kingston's *China Men* and Zeese Papanikolas's *Buried Unsung*." *Memory and Cultural Politics*. Ed. Amritjit Singh, Joseph T. Skerrett, Jr., and Robert E. Hogan. Boston: Northeastern University Press, 1996. 227–244.
Kaplan, E. Ann. "The 'Look' Returned: Knowledge Production and Construction of Whiteness in Humanities Scholarship and Independent Film." *Whiteness. A Critical Reader*. Ed. Mike Hill. New York: New York University Press, 1997. 317–325.
Keating, Analouise. "(De)Centering the Margins? Identity Politics and Tactical (Re)Naming." *Other Sisterhoods*. Ed. Sandra Kumamoto. Chicago: University of Illinois Press, 1998. 23–43.
_____. "Interrogating 'Whiteness,' (De)Constructing 'Race.'" *College English* 57.8 (1995): 901–918.
Keats, John. "Ode on a Grecian Urn." *The Norton Anthology of English Literature*. Volume 2. Ed. M.H. Abrams. New York: W.W. Norton, 1981.
Kennedy, John F. "Letter on Revision of the Immigration Laws." *Presidential Papers Historical Series*. 18 Feb. 2005. http://www.ilw.com/lawyers/articles/2004,0301-kennedy.shtm.
Kim, Kwang Chung. *Koreans in the Hood: Conflict with African Americans*. Baltimore: The Johns Hopkins University Press, 1999.
_____, and Shin Kim. "The Multiracial Nature of Los Angeles Unrest in 1992." *Koreans in the Hood*. Ed. Kwang Chung Kim. Baltimore: Johns Hopkins University Press, 1999. 17–38.
Kingston, Maxine Hong Kingston. *China Men* [1980]. New York: Ballantine Books, 1986.
_____. "Cultural Misreadings by American Reviewers." *Asian and Western Writers in Dialogue*. Ed. Guy Amirthanayagam. Hong Kong: Macmillan, 1982: 55–65.
_____. *I Love a Broad Margin to My Life*. New York: Vintage, 2011.
_____. *The Fifth Book of Peace* [2003]. New York: Vintage, 2004.
_____. "The Novel's Next Step." *Mother Jones* 14.10 (1989): 37–41.
_____. *The Woman Warrior: Memoirs of a Girlhood Among Ghosts* [1976]. New York: Vintage, 1977.
_____. *Tripmaster Monkey: His Fake Book*. New York: Vintage, 1989.
_____. *Veterans of War, Veterans of Peace*. Kihei, Hawaii: Koa Books, 2006.
Kogawa, Joy. *Obasan* [1981]. New York: Doubleday, 1994.
Kristeva, Julia. *The Powers of Horror*. New York: Columbia University Press, 1982.
Kruk, Laurie. "Voices of Stone: The Power of Poetry in Joy Kogawa's *Obasan*." *ARIEL: A Review of International Literature* 30.4 (1999): 75–94.
Kurath, H., and S.M. Kuhn, ed. *Middle English Dictionary*. Ann Arbor: University of Michigan, 1954.
Kwong, Peter. *The New Chinatown*. New York: Hill and Wang, 1987.
Lee, Chang-rae. *Native Speaker*.1995. New York: Riverhead, 1996.
Lee, Heon Cheol. "Conflict Between Korean Merchants and Black Customers: A Structural Analysis." *Koreans in the Hood: Conflict with African Americans*. Baltimore: The Johns Hopkins University Press, 1999. 113–130.
Lee, James Kyung-Jin. *Urban Triage*. Minneapolis: University of Minnesota Press, 2003.
Lee, Katherine Hyunmie. "The Poetics of Liminality and Misidentification. Winnifred

Eaton's *Me* and Maxine Hong Kingston's *The Woman Warrior*." *Transnational Asian America*. Philadelphia: Temple University Press, 2006. 181-196.

Lee, Rachel. "Claiming Land, Claiming Voice, Claiming Canon: Institutionalized Challenges in Kingston's *China Men* and *The Woman Warrior*." *Re-Viewing Asian America: Locating Diversity*. Ed. Wendy L. Ng and Gary Okihiro. Pullman: Washington State University Press, 1995. 147-159.

Lee, Robert G. *Orientals. Asian Americans in Popular Culture*. Philadelphia: Temple University Press, 1999.

Leong, Russell. Foreword. *On a Bed of Rice: An Asian American Erotic Feast*. Ed. Geraldine Kudaka. New York: Doubleday, 1995. XI-XXX.

_____, and Edward T. Chang. *Los Angeles Struggles Toward Multiethnic Community*. Seattle: University of Washington Press, 1994.

Li, David Leiwei. "China Men: Maxine Hong Kingston and the American Canon." *American Literary History* 2.3 (Autumn 1990): 482-502.

_____. "The Naming of a Chinese American 'I': Cross-Cultural Sign/ifications in *The Woman Warrior*." *Criticism* XXX.4 (Fall 1988): 497-515.

Lidoff, Joan. "Autobiography in a Different Voice: *The Woman Warrior* and the Question of Genre." *Approaches to Teaching the Woman Warrior*. Ed. Shirley Geok-lin Lim. New York: MLA, 1991. 116-120.

Lim, Shirley Geok-lin. "Reading Back, Looking Forward: A Retrospective Interview with Maxine Hong Kingston (University of California, Santa Barbara)." *MELUS* 33.1 (Spring 2008): 157-170.

_____. "Semiotics, Experience, and the Material Self: An Inquiry into the Subject of the Contemporary Asian Woman Writer." *Women, Autobiography, Theory: A Reader*. Ed. Sidonie Smith and Julia Watson. Madison: University of Wisconsin Press, 1998. 441-452.

_____. "The Tradition of Chinese American Women's Life Stories: Thematics of Race and Gender in Jade Snow Wong's *Fifth Chinese Daughter* and Maxine Hong Kingston's *The Woman Warrior*." *American Women's Autobiography: Fea(s)ts of Memory*. Ed. Margo Culley. Madison: University of Wisconsin Press, 1992. 252-267.

Ling, Amy. "Whose America Is It?" *Weber Studies* 12.1 (1995): 27-35.

Linton, Patricia. "'What Stories the Wind Would Tell': Representation and Appropriation in Maxine Hong Kingston's *China Men*." *MELUS* 19.4 (Winter 1994): 37-47.

Lipsitz, George. *The Possessive Investment in Whiteness: How White People Profit from Identity Politics*. Philadelphia: Temple University Press, 1998.

Liu, Toming Jun. "The Problematics of Kingston's 'Cultural Translation': A Chinese Diasporic View of *The Woman Warrior*." *Journal of American Studies of Turkey* 4 (1996): 15-30.

Lo, Marie. "*Obasan* by Joy Kogawa." *A Resource Guide to Asian American Literature*. Ed. Cynthia Sau-ling Wong and Stephen H. Sumida. New York: The Modern Language Association of America, 2001.

Logan, John R., and Brian J. Stults. "The Persistence of Segregation in the Metropolis: New Findings from the 2010 Census." 24 March 2011. 12 March 2014. www.s4.brown.edu/us2010/Data/Report/report2.pdf. 1-25.

López, Ian Haney. *White by Law*. New York: New York University Press, 2006.

Lowe, Lisa. *Immigrant Acts*. Durham, NC: Duke University Press, 1996.

Ludwig, Saemi. "Celebrating Ourselves in the Other, or: Who Controls the Conceptual Allusions in Kingston?" *Asian American Literature in the International Context: Readings on Fiction, Poetry and Performance*. Hamburg: LIT Verlag, 2002. 37-55.

Macartney, Suzanne, Alemayehu Bishaw, and Kayla Fontenot. "Poverty Rates for Selected and Detailed Race and Hispanic Groups by State and Place: 2007-2011." 11 March 2014. www.census.gov/prod/2013pubs/acsbr11-17.pdf. 1-20.

Madhubuti, Haki R. *Why L.A. Happened: Implications of the '92 Los Angeles Rebellion*. Chicago: Third World Press, 1993.

Madsen, Deborah. "(Dis)figuration: The Body as Icon in the Writings of Maxine Hong Kingston." *Yearbook of English Studies* 24 (1994): 237-250.

Maher, Frances, and Mary Kay Thompson Tetrault. "They Got the Paradigm and Painted It White." *White Reign: Deploying Whiteness in America.* Ed. Joe L. Kincheloe, Shirley R. Steinberg and Nelson M. Rodriguez. New York: St. Martin's Press, 1998. 139–154.
Marable, Manning. *Beyond Black and White.* New York: Verso, 1996.
Massey, Douglas, and Nancy Denton. *American Apartheid.* Cambridge: Harvard University Press, 1992.
Melville, Herman. *Moby-Dick; or, The Whale* [1851]. Evanston and Chicago: Northwestern University Press and The Newberry Library, 1988.
_____. *White-Jacket; or, the World in a Man-of-War.* New York: Literary Classics of the United States, 1983.
Min, Pyong Gap, and Andrew Kolodny. "The Middleman Minority Characteristics of Korean Immigrants in the United States." *Koreans in the Hood: Conflict with African Americans.* Ed. Kwang Chung Kim. Baltimore: Johns Hopkins University Press, 1999. 131–157.
Montrose, Louis A. "Professing the Renaissance: The Poetics and Politics of Culture." *The New Historicism.* Ed. H. Aram Veeser. London: Routledge, 1989. 15–36.
Morrison, Toni. *Beloved.* New York: Signet, 1991.
_____. *Playing in the Dark: Whiteness and Literary Imagination.* Cambridge: Harvard University Press, 1992.
Mosley, Walter. *Devil in a Blue Dress.* New York: Pocket Books, 1997.
Moy, James. "Asian American Visibility: Touring Fierce Racial Geographies." *Staging Difference.* Ed. Marc Maufort. New York: Peter Lang, 1995. 16–28.
_____. *Marginal Sights: Staging the Chinese in America.* Iowa City: University of Iowa Press, 1993.
Mrożek, Sławomir. *Emigranci.* Warszawa: Oficyna Literacka Noir sur Blanc, 2003.
Murray, J.A.H., ed. *The Oxford English Dictionary.* 13 Volumes. London: Oxford University Press, 1993.
Nakamura, David. "Asian American Lawmakers to Press Obama on Diversity in Administration." *The Washington Post* 23 July 2013. www.washingtonpost.com/blogs/post-politics/wp/2013/07/23/asian-american-lawmakers-to-press-obama-on-diversity-in-administration.1–2.
Newitz, Annalee, and Matt Wray. "What Is 'White Trash'? Stereotypes and Economic Conditions of Poor Whites in the United States." *Whiteness: A Critical Reader.* Ed. Mike Hill. New York: New York University Press, 1997. 168–184.
Ngai, Mae M. "Brokering Inclusion: Education, Language, and the Immigrant Middle Class." *Citizenship, Borders, and Human Needs.* Ed. Rogers M. Smith. Philadelphia: University of Pennsylvania, 2011. 135–156.
Nguyen, Viet Thanh. "Model Minorities and Bad Subjects." *Race and Resistance: Literature and Politics in Asian America.* Oxford: Oxford University Press, 2002. 143–154.
Nishime, Lei Lani. "Engendering Genre: Gender and Nationalism in *China Men* and *The Woman Warrior*." *MELUS* 20.1 (Spring 1995): 67–82.
Okihiro, Gary Y. *Margins and Mainstreams: Asians in American History and Culture.* Seattle: University of Washington Press, 1994.
Oliver, Kelly. *The Portable Kristeva.* Ed. Kelly Oliver. New York: Columbia University Press, 2002.
Omi, Michael, and Howard Winant. *Racial Formation (from the 1960s to the 1980s).* New York: Routledge, 1986.
Osajima, Keith. "Asian Americans as the Model Minority: An Analysis of the Popular Press Image in the 1960s and 1980s." *Reflections on Shattered Windows.* Eds. Shirley Hune and Gary Okihiro. Pullman: Washington State University Press, 1988. 165–174.
Palumbo-Liu, David. Introduction. *The Ethnic Canon.* Minneapolis: University of Minnesota Press, 1995: 1–19.
_____. "The Politics of Memory: Remembering History in Alice Walker and Joy Kogawa." *Memory and Cultural Politics: New Approaches to American Ethnic Literature.* Ed. Amritjit Singh, Joseph T. Skerrett, Jr., and Robert E. Hogan. Boston: Northwestern University Press, 1996. 211–226.

Park, Kyeyoung. "Use and Abuse of Race and Culture: Black-Korean Tension in America." *Koreans in the Hood. Conflict with African Americans*. Baltimore: The Johns Hopkins University Press, 1999. 60–74.

Perry, Donna. "Maxine Hong Kingston." *Conversations with Maxine Hong Kingston*. Ed. Paul Skenazy and Tera Martin. Jackson: University Press of Mississippi, 1998. 168–188.

Piper, Adrian. "Passing for White, Passing for Black." *Critical Whiteness Studies: Looking Behind the Mirror*. Eds. Richard Delgado and Jean Stefancic. Philadelphia: Temple University Press, 1997. 425–431.

Portes, Alejandro. "Introduction: The Debates and Significance of Immigrant Transnationalism." *Global Networks* 1.3 (2001): 181–193.

Prashad, Vijay. *Afro-Asian Connections and the Myth of Cultural Purity*. Boston: Beacon, 2001.

Rabine, Leslie W. "No Lost Paradise: Social Gender and Symbolic Gender in the Writings of Maxine Hong Kingston." *Signs* 12 (1987): 471–492.

Rabinowitz, Paula. "Eccentric Memories: A Conversation with Maxine Hong Kingston." *Conversations with Maxine Hong Kingston*. Ed. Paul Skenazy and Tera Martin. Jackson: University Press of Mississippi, 1998. 67–76.

"Real Median Household Income by Race and Hispanic Origin: 1967 to 2012." www.businessinsider.com/heres-median-income-in-the-us-by-race-2013-9.

Roediger, David R., ed. *Black on White: Black Writers on What It Means to Be White*. New York: Schocken, 1998.

_____. *The Wages of Whiteness: Race and the Making of the American Working Class*. London, Verso, 1991.

Said, Edward. *Orientalism*. London: Penguin, 1978.

Sato, Gayle K. Fujita. "*The Woman Warrior* as a Search for Ghosts." *Approaches to Teaching The Woman Warrior*. Ed. Shirley Geok-lin Lim. New York: Modern Language Association, 1991. 139–145.

Saxton, Alexander. *The Indispensable Enemy: Labor and the Anti-Chinese Movement in California*. Los Angeles: University of California Press, 1971.

Schroeder, Eric J. "As Truthful as Possible: An Interview with Maxine Hong Kingston." *Conversations with Maxine Hong Kingston*. Ed. Paul Skenazy and Tera Martin. Jackson: University Press of Mississippi, 1998. 215–228.

Schueller, Malini. "Questioning Race and Gender Definitions: Dialogic Subversions in *The Woman Warrior*." *Criticism* Fall XXXI.4 (1989): 421–437.

Schultermandl, Silvia. "Writing Against the Grain: The Cross-Over Genres of Maxine Hong Kingston's *The Woman Warrior, China Men*, and *The Fifth Book of Peace*." *Interactions: Aegean Journal of English and American Studies* 16.2 (Fall 2007): 111–122.

"Sentencing Bias." *Equal Justice Initiative*. 15 March 2014. www.eji.org/raceandpoverty/sentencingbias

Seshachari, Neila C. "Reinventing Peace: Conversations with Tripmaster Maxine Hong Kingston." *Conversations with Maxine Hong Kingston*. Ed. Paul Skenazy and Tera Martin. Jackson: University Press of Mississippi, 1998. 192–214.

Shimakawa, Karen. *National Abjection: Asian American Body Onstage*. Durham, NC: Duke University Press, 2002.

Shounan, Hsu. "Writing, Event, and Peace: the Art of Peace in Maxine Hong Kingston's *The Fifth Book of Peace*" *College Literature* 37.2 (Spring 2010): 103+. *Literature Resources from Gale*. 23 Aug. 2011. http://go.galegroup.com/ps. 1–11.

Shugart, Helene A. "Counterhegemonic Acts: Appropriation as a Feminist Rhetorical Strategy." *Quarterly Journal of Speech* 83 (1997): 210–229.

Sin Far, Sui. *Leaves from the Mental Portfolio of an Eurasian: The Heath Anthology of American Literature*. Ed. Paul Lauter. Lexington, MA: Heath, 1994. 884–895.

Skenazy, Paul. "Coming Home." *Conversations with Maxine Hong Kingston*. Ed. Paul Skenazy and Tera Martin. Jackson: University Press of Mississippi, 1998. 104–117.

Sledge, Linda Ching. "Oral Tradition in Kingston's *China Men*." *Redefining American Literary*

History. Ed. A. La Vonne Brown Ruoff and Jerry W. Ward, Jr. New York: Modern Language Association of America, 1990. 142-154.
Sloane, Patricia. *The Visual Nature of Color*. New York: Design Press, 1989.
Smith, Neil, and Cindi Katz. "Grounding Metaphor: Towards a Spatialized Politics." *Place and the Politics of Identity*. Ed. Michael Keith and Steve Pile. New York: Routledge, 1993: 67-84.
Smith, Sidonie. "Autobiographical Manifestos." *Women, Autobiography, Theory: A Reader*. Ed. Sidonie Smith and Julia Watson. Madison: University of Wisconsin Press, 1998. 433-440.
Sollors, Werner. *Neither Black Nor White Yet Both*. Cambridge: Harvard University Press, 1997.
Spielberg, Steven. "Empire of the Sun." Amblin Entertainment, 1987.
"Success Story, Japanese American Style." *New York Times Magazine* 9 Jan. 1966: 20-22.
"Success Story: Outwhiting the Whites." *Newsweek* 21 June 1971: 26-27.
"Success Story of One Minority Group." *U.S. News and World Report* 26 Dec. 1966: 6-9.
Sumida, Stephen. "Centres Without Margins: Responses to Centrism in Asian American Literature." *American Literature* 66.4 (1994): 803-815.
Szmańko, Klara. "Beyond Black and White: Striving for Visibility in *Tripmaster Monkey* by Maxine Hong Kingston and *Native Speaker* by Chang-rae Lee." *Close Encounters of an Other Kind: New Perspectives on Race, Ethnicity and American Studies*. Eds. Roy Goldblatt, Jopi Nyman and John A. Stotesbury. Joensuu: Faculty of Humanities, Joensuu, 2005.
―――. *Invisibility in African American and Asian American Literature: A Comparative Study*. Jefferson, NC: McFarland, 2008.
―――. "The Trope of No Name Woman in American Fiction and Ethnography Featuring Asian Women." *Brno Studies in English* 10 (2004) Ed. Pavel Drabek. 189-204.
Takaki, Ronald. *Strangers from a Different Shore*. Boston: Little, Brown, 1989.
Taylor, Gary. *Buying Whiteness: Race, Culture and Identity from Columbus to Hip-Hop*. New York: Palgrave Macmillan, 2005.
Thomas, Brook. "China Men, United States v. Wong Kim Ark, and the Question of Citizenship." *American Quarterly* 50.4 (Dec 1998): 689-717.
Tsai, Shi-Shau Henry. *The Chinese Experience in America*. Bloomington: Indiana University Press, 1986.
Van Spanckeren, Kathryn. "The Asian Literary Background of *The Woman Warrior*." *Approaches to Teaching the Woman Warrior*. Ed. Shirley Geok-lin Lim. New York: MLA, 1991. 44-51.
Whittaker, Elvi. *The Mainland Haole*. New York: Columbia University Press, 1986.
Wiegman, Robyn. "Whiteness Studies and the Paradox of Particularity." *boundary 2* 26:3, (1999): 115-150.
Wong, Cynthia Sau-ling. "Autobiography as Guided Chinatown Tour? Maxine Hong Kingston's *The Woman Warrior* and the Chinese American Autobiographical Controversy." *Maxine Hong Kingston's* The Woman Warrior. *A Casebook*. New York: Oxford University Press, 1998. 29-53.
Wooten, Bill, and David L. Miller. "The Psychophysics of Color." *Color Categories in Thought and Language*. Ed. C. L. Hardin and Luisa Maffi. New York: Cambridge University Press, 1997. 59-87.
Wright, Richard. Introduction. *Black Metropolis*. By St. Clair Drake and Horace R. Cayton. New York: Harcourt, Brace, 1945. XVII-XXXIV.
―――. "The Man Who Lived Underground." *Eight Men*. New York: Pyramid Books, 1976.
Yamashita, Karen Tei. *Tropic of Orange*. Minneapolis: Coffee House, 1997.
Yang, Caroline. "Indispensable Labor: The Worker as a Category of Critique in *China Men*." *Modern Fiction Studies* 56.1 (Spring 2010): 63-89.
"Yick Wo v. Hopkins—Case Brief Summary." *Lawnix*. July 2, 2013. www.lawnix.com/cases/yick-wo-hopkins.html.
Yu, Ning. "A Strategy Against Marginalization: the 'High' and 'Low' Cultures in Kingston's

China Men. (Maxine Hong Kingston) ([De] Colonizing Reading/[Dis]Covering the Other)." *College Literature* 23.3 (Oct. 1996): 73–81. *Literature Resources from Gale.* August 29, 2011. http://go.galegroup.com.1–8.

Yun, Charse. "Crossing Borders." *KoreAm Journal* (September 2014): 1–7. September 27, 2014. https://dl.dropboxusercontent.com/u/52992565/KoreAm2014.pdf.

Zackodnik, Teresa. Photography and the Status of Truth in Maxine Hong Kingston's *China Men.*" *MELUS* 22.3 (Fall 1997). *Literature Resources from Gale.* http://go.galegroup.com. 1–8.

Zhang, Yanjun. "The American Dream in Selected Works by Three Chinese American Women Writers: From Dreams to Nightmares." Diss. Indiana University of Pennsylvania, 2010.

Index

Abelman, Nancy 181
abjection 38, 90, 100, 101, 194
Acker, Kathy 176
Adams, Michael Vannoy 3, 44, 50, 61, 125, 130, 163, 164, 182
African Americans 3, 4, 7, 8, 9, 27, 32, 33, 37, 47, 63, 64, 73, 76, 84, 85, 86, 87, 88, 90, 102, 106, 115, 116, 119, 122, 123, 124, 125, 127, 128, 131, 132, 133, 134, 135, 136, 137, 158, 159, 167, 168, 169, 171, 173, 174, 177, 180, 181, 182, 186
Almaguer, Tòmas 104
Althusser, Louis 109
Anderson, Benedict 154
Anglicus, Bartolomaeus 181
anti-miscegenation laws 182
apparatus of power 4, 5, 98, 103, 111, 167, 171, 181
Aristotle 49, 129, 176, 181
Arkush, David R. 40, 175
Asian American literary aesthetics 9–10, 19, 43–45, 159
Asian American nationalists 14, 25, 31, 56, 117, 172, 174
Asian American political participation 167, 185–186
assimilation 28, 101, 144, 145, 175
Atilla 75
autobiography, first person-narrative 14, 18, 42, 43, 56, 66, 76, 172, 175, 176, 177, 178, 189, 190, 192, 195

Babb, Valerie 2, 75, 98, 99, 103
Bagehot, Walter 182
Baker, Houston 181
Bal, Mieke 45, 159
Baldwin, James 11, 76, 134
Banerjee, Chinmoy 142, 184, 185
Baraka, Amiri 11
Bedhad, Ali 99, 100, 101, 104, 179, 180
Beedham, Matthew 145
Begum, Khani 18
Berkeley, George 77
Bennett, Juda 102

Bernstein, David E. 180
Bhabha, Homi 179, 180
Bible 98, 181
Biggam, Carol 177
Birren, Faber 44, 182
Bishaw, Alemayehu 167
Bizzini, Silvia Caporale 178
black nationalism 11, 72
Blinde, Patricia Lin 18, 51, 123, 133
Boas, Franz 131
bones 19, 44, 47–48, 50, 54, 57–58, 75, 94, 138, 141–142, 177, 185
Bonetti, Kay 43, 49, 62, 178
Bosnack, Robert 130, 163
Boynton, Robert M. 152, 177
Bradstreet, Anne 161
Brogan, Kathleen 18, 172
Brown, Frank London 174
Brown, Sterling A. 8, 173
Buntline, Ned 74
Burke, James 186
Burnley, J.L. 177
Bush, George Herbert Walker 96
Butler, Judith 6

Carmichael, Stokely 11
Casson, Ronald W. 51, 164, 176, 177
Chambers, Ross 14, 64
Chan, Jeffrey Paul 31, 69, 117
Chan, Sucheng 76, 104, 174
Chang, Edward T. 181
Chang, Leonard 181; *The Fruit 'N Food* 2, 4–5, 7, 14, 19, 23, 36, 51, 92, 121–137, 152, 162, 180–182, 188
chauvinism /gender oppression 6–7, 14–16, 19, 40, 42–43, 117
Chesnutt, Charles Waddell 11
Cheung, King-Kok 172, 175, 184
Chicago School of Sociology 9
Chin, Frank 14, 31, 82, 116–117, 172, 174
Chin, Gabriel J. 180
Chinatown 14, 16, 21, 28, 31–32, 35–36, 40–42, 50, 53, 57, 74, 76, 82–83, 88, 90–91, 151, 172, 174, 178, 180, 184, 189

197

Index

Chiu, Monica 73, 179
Choi, Minsik 186
Chu, Judy 186
Chu, Patricia P. 178
Chu, Steven 185
Chua, Cheng Lok 39
Civil Rights Act 166, 174
Clark, Kenneth 186
class sensibility 6–7, 15–16, 22, 36, 42, 69, 71, 75, 82, 86, 91, 100, 106, 112, 119–120, 127, 131, 158, 167, 173–174, 179, 182, 184, 186, 188, 190, 193–194
Cleaver, Eldridge 11
Clement, Catherine 10
Clinton, Bill 96
color-blind rhetoric 2, 126
color theory 3, 50–52, 61, 131, 152, 176, 182
compensatory wages of whiteness 82, 112, 119, 120, 179
conflict between Korean Americans and African Americans 4, 7, 122, 125–128
Conrad, Joseph 55
cooliesm 73, 119, 179
CORE 32, 175
Crenshaw, Kimberlè 6
Crèvecoeur, John Hector St. John 99
critical multicultural aesthetics 51, 177
critical multiculturalism 10, 169, 149–165
Curtin, Maureen Frances 56, 176

Darwin, Charles 131, 182
Davis, Rocio G. 6, 178
De Bary Nee, Brett 35–36, 54
De Bary Nee, Victor 35–36, 54
De Certeau, Michel 18
De Gobineau, Arthur 130, 181–182
Delilo, Don 134
Dennys, N.B. 9, 26, 39, 52, 55, 174–175
Denton, Nancy 35, 156
Diebold, Richard 177
double consciousness formula 8, 41, 171
DREAM Act 110, 189
dreams 4, 16, 30, 34, 51, 54, 58, 81, 122–125, 128–132, 134–135, 142–143, 157, 181–183, 187, 196
Du Bois, W.E.B. 8–9, 11, 41, 63, 119–120, 124, 171
Duncan, Patti 108
Dyer, Richard 68, 177

Eakin, Paul John 56, 175, 178
Eaton, Winnifred 178, 184
Eliot, T.S. 172
Ellison, Ralph 10, 11, 51, 56, 76, 89, 91, 150, 176, 182
Eng, David 116
Epstein, Gerald 186
Espiritu, Yen Le 32
Exclusion Acts 20, 92, 102–104, 107–108

Fa Mu Lan 15, 17, 39–42, 51, 54, 59, 65, 93, 175, 178
Far, Sui Sin (Eaton, Edith) 8
Fei, Xiaotong 9, 175
Ferens, Dominika 184
Fontenot, Kayla 167
Foucault, Michel 10, 67–68, 73–74, 77, 87, 98, 178
Fourteenth Amendment 106
Frankenberg, Ruth 2, 15, 22, 29, 58, 60, 64, 68, 172
Freud, Sigmund 125
frontier 101, 118
Frost, Linda 2, 74, 104, 180
Fujita, Gayle K. 184

Galton, Francis 131
Gates, Henry Louis 168, 186
Geertz, Clifford 45
generic hybridity 18–19, 48, 176
Genthe, Arnold 74, 179
Gilead, Sarah 18, 178
Goellnicht, Donald C. 36, 97, 139–140, 177, 183
Gold Mountain 20, 39, 40, 81, 87, 93, 175
Golden Enterprise 96
Golding, Sue 56
Goldman, Marlene 144, 185
Gooding-Williams, Robert 181
Gordon, Avery F. 9–10, 128
Gordon, Colin 10
Gotanda, Neil 20, 55, 111, 173
Gottlieb, Erika 182
Greenblatt, Stephen 9
Greenlee, Sam 11
Grewal, Gurleen 140, 146, 184
Gsoels-Lorensen, Jutta 110–111

Hacker, Andrew 173
Ham 181
Hamilton, Alexander 99
Hardin, C.L. 131, 152
Harris, Cheryl 2, 34, 102, 120, 133, 173, 182
Harris, Marvin 182
Harris, Trudier 27
Hawaii 82–86, 115–117, 153, 155–159, 190
Hawthorne, Nathaniel 172
Health Care Bill 167
Hemingway, Ernest 59
Hill, Mike 3, 166, 185
Hillman, James 130
Hing, Bill Ong 55, 92, 107–108
Hispanics 167, 169
Hom, Marlon Kau 40
hooks, bell 8, 119
Hooper, Barbara 119
Hooper, William 73
Hunt, Linda 18, 175
Hurt, Charles 186

Husnaker, Steven V. 175, 177
hypodescent 102, 182

Ichigashi, Yamato 102
immigrants 4, 13, 20–21, 27–28, 30, 37, 43, 54–56, 67–69, 71–76, 78, 82–83, 89, 91–92, 96–97, 99–104, 106, 108, 110–111, 115, 117, 119, 121, 126, 132, 150, 173–174, 177–179, 181, 193
imperialism 149, 155–157, 165
Inada, Lawson Fusao 117, 174
Indians 92, 99, 105
inner city 4–5, 7, 122, 124–128, 131, 133–136, 174, 180, 181, 186, 188
interracial connections 33, 82–90, 92, 105–106, 125–128
intersectionality 6, 149
invisibility 184
Irwin, Will 74–75
Islas, Arturo 46, 172

Jackson, George 11
Jamestown, Virginia 68, 173
Japanese Canadians 5, 7, 36, 137–148, 183–184
Japheth 181
Jenkins, Ruth Y. 175
Jim Crow laws 173
Jintao, Hu 186
Johnson, Lyndon Baines 76, 155, 177
Juan, E. San, Jr. 44–45, 160
Juan, Karin Aguilar-San 44–45
Jung, Carl 125

Kadohata, Cynthia 184
Kallen, Horace Meyer 131
Kalogeras, Yiorgos 97
Kang, Younghill 24
Katz, Cindi 124, 172, 181
Keats, John 178
Keh 127, 181
Kelley, William Melvin 76, 179
Kennedy, John F. 92, 177–178
Kerry, John 167
Khan, Genghis 75
Kim, Kwang Chung 126, 181
Kim, Shin 126
Kingston, Maxine Hong 16–17, 33, 35, 43–44, 62, 67, 150, 151, 153, 161; *China Men* 2, 4, 7, 15, 19, 26, 36, 52, 54–55, 58, 60, 67–121, 123, 137, 150–151, 155–156, 158–160, 164, 169, 179–180; *The Fifth Book of Peace* 2, 5, 7, 16–17, 19, 33–34, 52, 66, 84, 137, 149–165, 185; *I Love a Broad Margin to My Life* 118; *Tripmaster Monkey* 15, 17, 60, 87, 94, 150–151, 153, 176, 178–180; *Veterans of War, Veterans of Peace* 162; *The Woman Warrior* 2–7, 13–66, 67–72, 76–79, 81, 83, 85, 88–94, 96, 117–118, 121, 137, 149–150, 154, 156–157, 159–160, 163–164, 171–179, 174, 176–178
Kittagawa, Muriel 140, 183
Koch, Edward 36
Kogawa, Joy 183; *Obasan* 2, 4–5, 7, 11, 14, 19, 36, 42, 51–53, 57–59, 137–148, 149, 157, 159, 163, 166, 176–177, 180, 183–185
Kolodny, Andrew 126
Korean Americans 4, 7, 37, 121–137, 167, 182, 187
Kristeva, Julia 100
Kruk, Laurie 184
Kuhn, S.M. 177
Kurath, H. 177
Kwong, Peter 36, 174

labor relations 69, 119–120
La Capra, Dominick 9
Latasha Harlins incident of 1991 4, 125, 181
Lee, Chang-rae 176, 180
Lee, Heon Cheol 181
Lee, James Kyung 180
Lee, Katherine Hyunmie 178
Lee, Leo O. 40, 175
Lee, Rachel 110, 118, 158
Lee, Robert G. 21, 112
Leong, Russell 181
Li, David Leiwei 25, 27, 97, 118, 175
Lidoff, Joan 18, 177
Lim, Shirley Geok-lin 177–178
Ling, Amy 95, 175
Lionnet, Françoise 172
Lipsitz, George 2, 34–35
Li Sao 114
Liu, Toming Jun 46
Lo, Marie 36, 138–140, 183
location 13, 16–17, 19, 32, 34, 97, 124, 127–128, 148, 151, 172
Locke, Gary 185
Logan, John R. 167
López, Ian Haney 179
Lowe, Lisa 20, 106
Lu, Chris 186
Ludwig, Saemi 172
lynching 28, 76, 89, 90, 159, 174, 179

Macartney, Suzanne 167
Madhubuti, Haki R. 181
Madsen, Deborah 97
Magnus, Albertus 181
Magnuson Act 20, 92
Maher, Frances 2
Malcolm X 11
Manifest Destiny 118, 158
March on Washington 166
marginality 19, 83, 114, 119
Martin, Trayvon 168
massacres of Asian Americans 75–76, 174
Massey, Douglas 35, 156
McCarran-Walter Act 20, 106, 173

Melville, Herman 122, 178
middle man minority 128
Miller, David L. 152–153
mimicry 173, 179
Min, Pyong Gap 126
Minh-ha, Trinh T. 172
model minority rhetoric 31, 100, 128, 132, 168, 174–175, 193
Momotaro 42, 145, 176
monogenesis 181
Montrose, Louis 9
Morrison, Toni: *Beloved* 176, 178; *Playing in the Dark* 1, 9, 45, 47, 59, 60, 62, 72, 80
Mosley, Walter 27
Moy, James 74–75
Mrożek, Sławomir 174
Mulligan, John 162, 185
Murray, J.A.H. 177

NAACP 32, 175
Nagasaki 7, 141, 143, 147, 184
Nakamura, David 186
narration 13–14, 18–20, 44–46, 70–72, 97–98, 111, 150–151, 172, 176, 178, 185
nation 5–6, 153–155, 172
Native Americans 99, 102, 106, 123, 162, 167, 182
nativism 99, 180
Naturalization Act 98, 173
New Historicism 9, 189, 193
Newitz, Annalee 2, 172–173
Ng, Fae Myenne 57, 96
Ngai, Mae M. 107
Nguyen, Viet Thanh 31
Nishime, Lei Lani 97, 118

Obama, Barack 167, 185–186
Okihiro, Gary 73
Oliver, Kelly 100, 180
Omi, Michael 126, 182
Orientalist discourse 74–75
Osajima, Keith 175

panethnicity 110, 180, 189–190
Panopticon 67, 77, 88, 109, 179–180, 189
paper sons 54, 56
Park, Kyeyoung 127, 181
Park, Robert E. 9, 131
particularism 10, 59, 68, 96–97, 130, 166, 195
pastiche 19
performance of ethnicity and racial categories 27, 33, 39, 63, 111, 178
Perry, Donna 56, 98
Piper, Adrian 102, 182
Plessy vs. Ferguson 173
polyphony 18–19, 147, 184, 187
poor white trash 22, 172–173, 190, 193
Portes, Alejandro 154
Position 1, 4, 8–9, 11, 14, 19, 22, 25, 30, 33– 34, 49, 60, 66, 68–71, 80, 84, 86, 89–90, 92, 96–97, 101, 104, 106, 120, 124, 131, 133–135, 137, 161, 164, 167, 171, 176, 180, 186
Postmodernism 3, 19, 44, 49, 134, 147, 154, 171
Powderly, Terence 100
Prashad, Vijay 70
Probyn, Elspeth 56
Pynchon, Thomas 176

Rabine, Leslie W. 177
Rabinowitz, Paula 43, 62, 172
Reagan, Ronald 126
recentering 113, 117, 120–121
Reed, Alfred C. 100
replicating oppression 113, 117–118, 159
reverse power dynamics 1, 48, 158, 179
Rilke, Rainer Maria 179
Rodney King rebellion of 1992 4, 125, 181, 186, 187, 190
Roediger, David 2, 82, 105, 120, 173–174
Roosevelt, Theodore 105

Said, Edward 79
Sanderson, Bill 186
Sato, Gayle K. Fujita 26, 56, 69
Schroeder, Eric J. 34, 175
Schueller, Malini 177
Schultermandl, Silvia 44
Seshachari, Neila C. 62, 151
Shakespeare, William 176
Shem 181
Shimakawa, Karen 101
Shinseki, Eric K. 186
shounan, Hsu 160
Shugart, Helene A. 177
sign 23, 25–26, 29, 31, 32, 39, 44–46, 48, 49, 51–52, 58, 63, 68, 69, 71, 72, 82, 86–87, 112, 114, 149, 152, 159–160, 163–164, 176–177, 177, 178, 179, 180
silence 25, 27, 47–48, 53, 61–62, 74–75, 78, 140–141, 145, 147, 175–176, 184–185, 188, 189
Skenazy, Paul 35, 97, 151, 172
skin 23, 32–33, 47, 50, 56, 63, 80, 99, 129, 153, 158, 173, 176–177
Sledge, Linda Ching 97, 179
Sloane, Patricia 9, 61, 182
Smith, Neil 124, 172, 181
Smith, Sidonie 172
social Darwinism 182
Soja, Edward 119
Sollors, Werner 182
Songs from Gold Mountain 40
Soon Ja Du's case 181
Spencer, Herbert 182
Spielberg, Steven 184
Stuart, Ken 139
Stults, Brian J. 167
Sumner, William Graham 182

synesthesia 129, 143
Szmańko, Klara 3, 176

Takaki, Ronald 73, 104, 173, 175
Taylor, Gary 2, 23, 49, 51, 99, 129, 134, 164, 176, 181
Theatre 40, 74, 178
Thomas, Brook 97–98, 110–111, 118, 176, 180
Thompson, Mary Kay 2
Todorov, Tzvetan 61, 130
Tong, Ben 14, 25, 31, 69, 117
Toomer, Jean 85
Transcontinental Railroad 69–70, 73, 86, 93, 115–116
Transformational identity politics 6, 10, 15, 65, 82, 110, 133, 148–149, 155, 185
Tsai, Shih-Shau Henry 73
Turner, Victor 130
Twain, Mark 59

urban restructuring 4, 25, 29, 34–36, 38, 43, 70, 83, 126–127, 175

Van Spanckeren, Kathryn 175
Veeser, H. Aram 9
Viewpoint 37, 70, 72, 162
Vision: critical gaze 1; cultural nature of vision 9, 95; second sight 8–9, 30, 40–41, 77, 91–96, 123–125, 129, 134, 171; veil 8, 41, 63, 107, 124–125, 171; visual dynamics 1, 2, 8, 11, 21–22, 30, 32–33, 81, 91, 93–94, 173; visual objectification of racial "others" 1, 8, 11, 67, 91, 93, 109; visual objectification of whites 1, 8, 11, 21–22, 67, 68, 93; visual perception of color 9, 61, 182; visuality of the text 43–45, 49, 62, 147; white blindness 30, 41, 81, 91–96

Wang, Alfred S. 73
white working class 119–120, 184, 194
whiteness: and Americanness 15, 20, 30, 38, 98–103, 112, 189; archetypal 130, 162–163; association with artificiality, mechanization and syntheticity 23, 81; association with coldness 14, 19, 44, 49–50, 58, 65, 123, 129, 131, 157; association with light 5, 17, 19, 44, 46, 50–52, 61, 118, 129–130, 137–138, 143, 146–148, 149, 159, 161, 163–164, 176, 177, 180, 182, 184, 185; blinding quality 4, 123, 129; and bones 48, 57–58, 141; compensatory wages 82, 112, 119–120, 179; defamiliarization 1, 3, 4, 10, 19–29, 44, 65–66, 69–82, 156–157, 159, 166, 195; double consciousness 6, 171; essentialization 14, 46, 78–82; familiar 82–83; gender specificity 70, 107–108; imagery, aesthetics 5, 9–10, 33, 43–66, 137–150, 152, 159–164; implication of in the oppression and exploitation of racial minorities 4, 5, 11, 29–43, 72–78, 85, 137, 143–146, 156, 157,

160; indistinctness 46–49; intrusive 3, 19, 23, 45–46, 65; invisibility of 2–3, 4, 10, 11, 96, 128, 131, 135; invisibility of racial minorities because of their marking by white people 3, 10, 33, 91, 147, 167, 178, 179, 180, 184, 186, 189; legal construction 4, 96–113; making visible 1–3, 29, 70, 124, 128, 135, 166, 187; minoritizing 24, 155; normativity 2, 10, 11, 13, 15, 20, 22, 44, 58, 67, 96, 113, 121, 138, 139, 166, 182; objectification of racial "others" 1, 8, 11, 34, 67, 69, 86, 93, 112; oxymoronic 58–59, 67–69, 96–98, 112–113, 121, 123, 131; and paper 52–57, 139–142, 163; particularization and universalization 4, 68, 117; performativity 33; power dynamics 1, 9, 14, 48, 67, 87, 93, 98, 158, 166, 179; proliferating 23, 25, 173; and property 34, 103–104, 139, 156; representation as colorless 3, 33, 51, 78, 79, 81, 143, 157, 182; representation through the metaphor of demons and devils 25–26, 67, 68, 69–82, 156; representation through the metaphor of ghosthood 25–27, 29, 37, 47, 50, 156; socio-historical construction 2, 4, 23, 44, 58, 60, 65, 67, 68, 69, 96, 108, 113, 122; synecdochic 78, 79; tandemic 44, 59–65; terrorizing 72–78, 79, 122–136; transformation 5–6, 65, 89, 137, 148, 149, 151, 155, 159, 161, 162, 165; in transnational context 5, 82, 85, 149, 153, 154, 165, 192, 194
Whitney, Thomas 99–100
Whittaker, Elvi 156–157, 185
Wiegman, Robyn 2, 24, 59, 155, 157
Williams, William Carlos 172
Winant, Howard 126, 182
Wong, Cynthia Sau-ling 25–26, 42, 69, 172, 175, 178
Wong, Shawn Hsu 174
Wong Kim Ark 106, 180
Woolf, Virginia 176
Wooten, Bill 152–153
Wray, Matt 172–173
Wright, Richard 11, 93–94, 171
writerly/scriptible text 49, 151

Xenophobia 99

Yalom, Marilyn 46, 172
Yamashita, Karen Tei 128, 175, 179
Yang, Caroline 84–85
Yellow Peril 23, 32, 46, 100, 144
Yellow Power 32
Yu, Ning 75

Zack, Naomi 3
Zackodnik, Teresa 115
Zhang, Yanjun 108
Zimmerman, George 168, 186
Žižek, Slavoj 70

www.ingramcontent.com/pod-product-compliance
Lightning Source LLC
Chambersburg PA
CBHW032058300426
44116CB00007B/800